PREVENTING ALCOHOL AND TOBACCO PROBLEMS VOLUME 2

Preventing Alcohol and Tobacco Problems Volume 2

Manipulating Consumption: information, law and voluntary controls

Edited by

CHRISTINE GODFREY
Research Fellow, University of York

and

DAVID ROBINSON
Professor of Health Studies, University of Hull

E|S|R|C

Avebury

Aldershot · Brookfield USA · Hong Kong · Singapore · Sydney

Published by

Avebury

Gower Publishing Company Limited
Gower House
Croft Road
Aldershot
Hants GU11 3HR
England

Gower Publishing Company,
Old Post Road,
Brookfield,
Vermont 05036,
U.S.A.

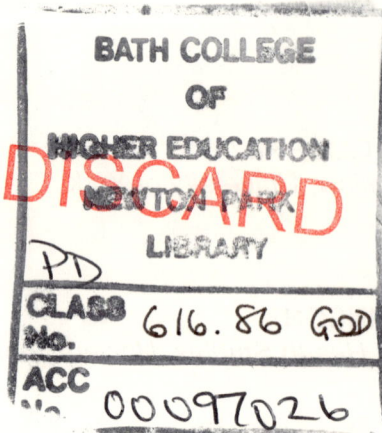

ISBN 0 566 05702 6

Printed and bound in Great Britain by
Athenaeum Press Limited, Newcastle-upon-Tyne

Laserset by Computype, 241 Hull Road, York YO1 3LA

Contents

List of tables

List of contributors

Rob Baggott*	Lecturer in Politics, Leicester Polytechnic
	Research Fellow, University of Hull (1983-85)
Christine Godfrey*	Research Fellow, University of York (1983-88)
Larry Harrison*	Research Fellow, University of York (1983-88)
Wendy Leedham*	Research Fellow, University of Hull (1986-88)
Alan Maynard	Professor of Economics, University of York
David Robinson	Professor of Health Studies, University of Hull
Philip Tether*	Senior Research Fellow, University of Hull (1984- 88)

* The asterisk indicates those Addiction Research Centre Staff who were financed by the Economic and Social Research Council.

Foreword

Preventing Alcohol and Tobacco Problems

Volume 1. The Addiction Market: consumption, production and
policy development

Volume 2. Manipulating Consumption: information, law and
voluntary controls

The two volumes on *Preventing Alcohol and Tobacco Problems* (each
published separately) are the products of the Economic and Social Research
Council-funded programme of work of the Addiction Research Centre at the
Universities of Hull and York during the period 1983–1988. In addition to
these volumes the staff of the Centre have published another five books and
over 80 articles on various social science aspects of addiction.

The Addiction Research Centre

Addiction research presents a wide range of stimulating challenges for
biomedical, clinical and social scientists. The Addiction Research Centre
(ARC) in Hull-York is primarily concerned with socio-economic, policy and
service issues and has focused its work particularly on the analysis of the
obstacles to the creation of prevention policies which identify both their costs

and benefits. The majority of projects which make up the ARC's activities are concerned with alcohol and tobacco. However, researchers in the group are also working on social science aspects of drugs, both licit (pharmaceuticals) and illicit.

Funding for the staff of economists, political scientists, health and social policy analysts and others employed in the Centre, comes from a variety of public and private sources. Most funding is short-term from Research Councils, government departments such as the Department of Health and the Home Office and other bodies such as the Institute for Alcohol Studies, the Health Promotion Research Trust and the Health Education (Council) Authority. The major grant, so far, has been from the Economic and Social Research Council (ESRC) for the five year programme of work concerned with national prevention policy which is reported on in these two volumes.

In addition to the ESRC programme, the researchers in the ARC have conducted projects concerned with problem drinkers and the statutory services; volunteer alcoholism counselling; the prevention of alcohol problems at the local level; the identification of high alcohol using patients in a District Hospital and the evaluation (cost-effectiveness) of intervention policies; the quantification of the prices, quality and volume of illicit drugs traded in the UK and the cost-effectiveness of police and Customs and Excise control policies; the analysis of European integration on the markets for alcohol and tobacco; and several aspects of the social costs of alcohol and tobacco use.

The external working relations of ARC staff are extensive and include close contact with funders and with the national bodies and professional associations concerned with addiction problems. Advice has been given by staff members to, among others, the Royal Colleges, House of Lords Select Committees, the European Economic Community and World Health Organisation. In 1986 the Hull-York group, together with the Department of Health Education at Leeds Polytechnic, was designated as a *WHO Collaborating Centre for Research and Training in the Psychosocial and Economic Aspects of Health* in recognition of our work on addictions and other health issues.

The ESRC programme

The ESRC Programme in Addiction Research was established in 1983 following the report on Research Priorities in Addiction by the Council's Exploratory Panel on Addiction. The authors of the Report believed that addiction problems are not trivial, that they are the legitimate concern of the social sciences, and that a multidisciplinary approach could reasonably be expected not only to be of interest to the social sciences but also to produce guides to policy alternatives and national strategy. After competitive tendering, the Hull-York Centre was chosen as the site for a programme concerned with 'the identification and minimisation of impediments to co-ordinated approaches to the prevention of alcohol and tobacco-related problems'. Stage I of the programme, from 1983–1986, was made up of three closely-related projects which focused on current prevention policy, the policy formation process, and industrial structures and activity.

During Stage II of the programme, 1986–1988, the insights and analyses of Stage I were used to illuminate policy choices and identify the barriers to co-ordinated national prevention policy and the factors which might mitigate them. In particular, attention was paid to the role of price regulation; the role of information, public opinion and education; and the role of legal and voluntary controls, with liquor licensing, drinking and driving, advertising and sports sponsorship as some of the specific cases in point. In addition to the policy specific work, the programme was designed to demonstrate the value of different social science disciplines being brought together to address common issues of intellectual interest and national concern.

This process has been challenging: to enable the overall multidisciplinary aim of the programme to be carried forward, while at the same time allowing the specific disciplinary skills of the staff to be brought to bear in the particular projects for which they had prime responsibilities, is not an easy task. If this has worked at all successfully it is because continuous and vigorous efforts were made to maintain a well-structured system of internal communication. In practice, this meant meeting together regularly formally and informally, exploiting each other's knowledge and skills to develop arguments and revise analyses; developing a common data base; and working closely with those on other addiction research projects and with our associates in Hull and York. The development of a research agenda and work practices across two institutions which are thirty-five miles apart has stimulated all the Hull-York researchers to ensure that communications are efficient.

Throughout the ESRC programme there have been monthly ARC meetings, alternating between Hull and York, at which the overall progress of each project has been discussed and the Centre's administrative and housekeeping issues managed. All project staff also meet together monthly and there was a full programme of seminars attended by all staff. Some of these seminars were 'closed' because the speakers reported 'off the record' to the ARC researchers about their personal involvement in core policy issues. Just as it has been vital to meet together regularly to discuss ARC organisation and project progress, it was also important for the establishment of the Centre's coherence and liveliness for all members to produce regular working papers for their colleagues' information and comments, as well as external publications (see the ARC Bibliography at the end of this volume.)

The data which were accumulated in connection with the wide range of Hull-York addiction research are stored in the ARC Data Bank. The main runs deal with alcohol and tobacco use since 1960 and related issues such as price, taxation, production, employment, distribution, advertising, offences, mortality, morbidity, public opinion and accidents. These and other data have already formed the basis of sixteen of the regular series of Data Notes published in the *British Journal of Addiction* (1986–1988).

The rationale of the overall programme of work was that it would have clear implications for policy and the prevention of problems associated with the consumption of addictive substances and clear implications also for the social sciences. The pay-offs for policy and prevention will be in terms of a better understanding of *de facto* national prevention policy, the policy formation process, relevant industrial structures and activities and the construction of strategies for the prevention of alcohol and tobacco-related problems. The pay-offs for the social sciences will be in terms of the range of detailed case studies in the politics, administration and economics of prevention, health, organizations, policy and industry. Both the policy insight and the methodological challenges form a stimulating and extensive agenda for future social science work on addictive substances.

David Robinson, Institute for Health Studies, University of Hull

Alan Maynard, Centre for Health Economics, University of York

Co-Directors ESRC Addiction Research Centre (1983–1988)

January 1989

Acknowledgements

We would like to express our thanks to the very many people who have made it possible for us to complete what many felt, at the beginning, was a very ambitious programme. That it has been completed at all satisfactorily is due to:

the ESRC programme staff,
Rob Baggott (1983–1986)
Roy Boakes (1983–1984)
Mark Booth (1985–1987)
Christine Godfrey (1983–1988)
Geoffrey Hardman (1984–1988) part-time
Larry Harrison (1983–1988)
Wendy Leedham (1986–1988) part-time
Melanie Powell (1987–1988) part-time
Philip Tether (1985–1988)

the Associates of the ARC who gave us so much sound advice,
Andy Alaszewski
Keith Hartley
Edward Page
Gilbert Smith
Albert Weale
Ron Weir

our ESRC Advisors who were always so helpful and encouraging,
Nicholas Deakin
Griffith Edwards
Julian Le Grand
Gerry Stimson

and the support staff in Hull and York who provided so much more than just secretarial expertise
Sarah Boocock (1987–1988)
Sally Cuthbert (1986–1988)
Valerie Hurst (1983–1987)
Judith Landers (1983–1986)

Special thanks are also due to Lorna Foster for copy-editing the volumes, to Vanessa Windass for preparing the manuscripts, and to the far-too-many-to-mention individual members of government departments, trade associations, service organisations, and others, who so generously gave us their time and interest in our attempts to understand the policy process in relation to the prevention of alcohol and tobacco problems.

Editors' introduction

CHRISTINE GODFREY AND DAVID ROBINSON

Many of those concerned with how to prevent the wide variety of health, social and legal problems associated with alcohol and tobacco seek to manipulate consumption through additional government regulation—in particular, legislation. Legislation or the reform of existing laws is, however, only one form of regulation which is available. Voluntary agreements and self-regulatory codes of practice are a much-used, and much-criticised, alternative. During the 1980s there has also been an expansion in the Government's use of the mass media for prevention-related information campaigns. So whether by regulation, voluntary controls or information measures, a wide range of policies is available to governments wishing to manipulate the consumption of alcohol and tobacco.

In this book, which complements *The Addiction Market: consumption, production and policy development* (Maynard and Tether, 1989), the current mix of regulation strategies is examined, together with some alternative prevention policies and the barriers to their implementation. In order to understand current regulation policy and to evaluate alternatives, it is necessary to draw material from a number of sources and academic disciplines. In the following chapters there is discussion of the broad political and organisational factors which determine the choice of policy instrument, along with more detailed analyses of specific policies in relation to advertising, liquor licensing and drinking and driving.

In contrasting legislation with voluntary controls or information measures, the advantages and disadvantages of alternative policies are not always clear cut. Legislation may seem to be the most obvious means of achieving a given objective, in that framing a new law does not formally need the cooperation of the potential offenders against it and has its own symbolic value in changing attitudes within society. But, during the long parliamentary process through which new legislation has to pass there can be substantial 'watering down' of original proposals. And even when laws, such as those concerned with the banning of the sale of alcohol and cigarettes to children, reach the statute books, there is no guarantee that they will be implemented. Legislation, therefore, may be seen by government as a long process with an uncertain outcome.

Voluntary agreements and self-regulated codes of practice, in contrast, may appear to involve fewer costs. Such agreements and codes form the basis of much current UK alcohol and tobacco control policy. Critics of this strategy suggest that these arrangements are ineffective and have too high a cost in that they foster 'cosy' relationships of dependency between the government and the industries concerned. In the real policy world, however, legislation and voluntary agreements are not stark alternatives. The threat of legislation can be a bargaining tool for governments to use in order to increase the likelihood of trade agreement on 'self-regulating' control, while some codes of conduct have semi-legal status.

A degree of consensus is necessary, whatever the choice of policy instrument. Government information policy has a role in shaping the climate of opinion and enhancing the acceptability of specific prevention policies. Public opinion is also subject to the influence of industry advertising and the media portrayal of alcohol and tobacco consumption. Mass media campaigns on health issues have been popular with governments in recent years, for example, against drug misuse and the spread of HIV. More focused campaigns have also been a part of drink-driving policy for a number of years. The issue of the effectiveness of such campaigns is not explored in depth in this volume. Emphasis is given instead to other aspects of information policy. In particular, the attempt by governments to control information through advertising policies is examined and the more general role of information and public opinion in determining the policy agenda and the effectiveness of other prevention measures is assessed.

Some general aspects of the costs and benefits of legislation and voluntary controls and their relationship to information policies are considered by Larry Harrison, Philip Tether, and Rob Baggott in Chapter 1. Within this broad framework, more detailed analyses of particular policies concerned with alcohol and tobacco advertising, liquor licensing and drinking and driving are examined in later chapters.

In *The Addiction Market: consumption, production and policy development* (Maynard and Tether, 1989), the companion volume to this book, many sets of self-interested agents are identified. The alcohol and

2

tobacco industries are characterised by large multinational organisations with common interests in opposing any measure which may effect their profitability. In contrast, the prevention lobbies are more diverse and less well co-ordinated. Responsibilities for alcohol and tobacco policies are spread between many different government departments. While some groups and organisations are common to all policy debates there is also considerable divergence between specific policy networks. Understanding the interaction within these networks and the links between them, provides the context for beginning to understand the development of current alcohol and tobacco policy and how policies are implemented.

Some policy networks are small and the participants have strong common interests. So, for example, as Larry Harrison and Philip Tether describe in Chapter 2, which deals with information policy, the Advertising Association plays a pivotal role in both the alcohol and tobacco advertising networks. There are many contrasts between this and the more diverse network centred around the Health Education Authority. The two regulatory networks related to liquor licensing and drinking and driving, outlined by Philip Tether, Wendy Leedham and Larry Harrison in Chapter 5, are different from each other, although more similar than either is to the information networks.

The Home Office plays an important role in any area that involves legislation. Other departments and interest groups may press for changes, but the Home Office considers that its officers have all the necessary expertise to evaluate proposed changes to the law. It is not surprising, with this organisation in the policy network, that the emphasis in liquor licensing policy debate has centred on law and public order problems, rather than on the possible public health consequences of changes in legislation. Both the Home Office and the Department of Transport have an interest in drink-driving legislation. The Department of Transport is the focus of the policy debate and research is based at the Transport and Road Research Laboratory within the Department at the Transport. The Home Office is primarily concerned with the enforcement of drink-driving legislation and provides the channel for police views. Enforcement issues and the relationship between the police and the public have played an important part in the drink-driving debate.

To provide illustrations of the importance of these information and legislation policy networks and of the general principles of policy choice explored in Chapter 1, four specific policy areas were chosen for more in-depth analyses. In Chapter 3, the self-regulated codes of practice which have been developed to control alcohol advertising are described by Larry Harrison and Christine Godfrey. As new technology has expanded the forms of broadcasting, new codes of practice have become necessary. The European Community is also attempting to resolve issues arising from

3

satellite television and the increased facility to broadcast across frontiers. Difficulties have arisen in agreeing common advertising polices across the Community. The UK government has already defended strongly the existing self-regulatory system against the legislative-based approach favoured by the European Commission.

There is little evidence to suggest that the present self-regulatory system has prevented misleading information or the development of alcohol-related problems. The most canvassed alternative to current alcohol advertising policy is a complete or partial ban. Empirical evidence reviewed in Chapter 3 suggests that any decreases in advertising expenditure resulting from such a strategy would at best result in only small decreases in consumption.

Advertising and associated sports sponsorship has been the subject of a series of voluntary agreements between the Government and the tobacco industry, as well as codes of practice similar to those for alcohol. The development of these agreements is examined by Philip Tether and Christine Godfrey in Chapter 4. The advertising of cigarettes on TV was banned in the UK in 1965 and this provides an illustration of one of the many non-legislative forms of regulation open to governments.

There is considerable public support for further legislation to control tobacco advertising, although the evidence on the effectiveness of these policies to reduce consumption is mixed. Impediments to further controls on tobacco advertising are, however, similar to those in relation to alcohol advertising outlined in Chapter 3. Again, changing technology may make specific new control strategies difficult to implement.

In contrast to advertising which has been regulated by voluntary controls, liquor licensing and the regulation of drinking and driving are examples of policy areas where legislation has been used. Liquor licensing is examined by Philip Tether and Christine Godfrey in Chapter 6. The history of licensing laws reflects the changing balance between concern for public order and trade interests. The resulting legislation has influenced the structure of the industry and the competition within it. Once the arguments about future reforms to the licensing law are disentangled, however, it becomes clear that the situation is much more complex than a straightforward conflict between health and trade concerns. Some regulation brings specific benefits to those who are regulated and hence attitudes by different sections of the alcohol industry to any relaxation or tightening of controls vary between proposals. So, for example, many sections of the on-licence trade united in the campaign for a relaxing of restrictions on the opening hours for on-licence premises. They would be expected, however, to oppose proposals which would result in a significant increase either in the number of licensees or in off-licence sales.

A constant for any programme of research on addiction policy is the paucity of adequate data, the rarity of evaluation studies and the difficulties encountered in attempting to forecast the effects of changes in policy on the consumption of addictive substances and on the pattern and range of related problems. The relationships are complex and few studies attempt to control for intervening factors. Unlike the self-regulated advertising area, there has been some official concern about the effect of changes in legislation on alcohol consumption and related problems. Tether and Godfrey indicate that the Home Office wanted to be convinced, by their own evaluation of changes in Scottish legislation, that the relaxation of licensing hours regulations in England and Wales would not increase problems before they would lend support to the considerable pressure for these changes from other government departments.

The development of legislation concerned with drinking and driving is described by Philip Tether and Christine Godfrey in Chapter 7. One objective of that legislation is to deter offenders. The Department of Transport has also used mass media campaigns in an attempt to change both individual behaviour and more recently the attitude of society both to the problem and to offenders. Inevitably there are complexities, as this mix of policy has developed incrementally with different foci of concern at different times. Tether and Godfrey set out the costs and benefits of alternative policies and provide insights into the often muddled policy debate.

A further factor explored in Chapters 6 and 7 is the interrelationship between tax, legislation, information and other policies. Alcohol and tobacco consumption are influenced by a number of factors and the effects of any one policy can be mitigated by other changes. Although manipulating consumption is a complex problem, many policies are available. In Chapter 8, Alan Maynard and David Robinson place much of the debate within a broader context of the current concern for the development of healthy public policy, indicate the shift from treatment to control, emphasise the need to disaggregate both the problem and the response, and conclude that—fortunately—there are many opportunities to exploit existing policy.

Although the levels of alcohol and tobacco consumption fluctuate, they will remain an important part of consumer spending and so will be associated with many problems for the foreseeable future. Discussion of prevention policies whose objective is to alter consumption and prevent specific problems, will continue to be of considerable public interest.

The analysis of alternative prevention polices suggests that much public debate is sterile and ill-informed. It is necessary to understand the formation of policy, current practice and the costs and benefits of different policy options in order to begin to be able to assess which policy alternatives are politically feasible and which can be predicted to accrue net benefits to society as a whole. The work in this volume is a contribution to that process and is designed to encourage more systematic analysis of preventive policies in order to determine which mix provides the most efficient means of manipulating consumption.

1 Regulation

LARRY HARRISON, PHILIP TETHER AND ROB BAGGOTT

Concern over the level of alcohol and tobacco-related problems is often translated into demands for legislative reform: tighter drink-driving laws, clearer licensing laws, the prohibition of smoking in public places, and so on. However, the equating of regulatory policies with legislation is misleading, since there is a spectrum of regulation available to government, ranging from primary and delegated legislation through non-statutory departmental circulars and guidelines to voluntary agreements and codes of practice (Baggott, 1986). At the legislative end of this spectrum, policies are carried out under powers granted by Acts of Parliament, either directly or indirectly, by statutory instrument. At the other end are codes of practice and voluntary agreements which can be the vehicle for major government policies. Voluntary agreement was, for instance, the cornerstone of the Labour government's economic policy in the 1970s with 'the social contract' and subsequent voluntary incomes policy.

Voluntary agreements and legislation are different forms of regulation and both these instruments are vehicles for alcohol and tobacco control policies. Self-regulatory codes of practice govern the advertising of both alcohol and tobacco products, shaping and controlling the information conveyed in both the broadcast and non-broadcast media. In contrast, legislation is the chosen policy instrument where issues such as liquor licensing and drink-driving are concerned.

It is commonly supposed that voluntary agreements are a 'soft option' which serve the interests of the regulated. This chapter takes a broader view and examines the strengths and limitations of regulation *per se*. The aim is

7

to provide an overview of regulatory issues as an introduction to the discussion, in later chapters, of both self-regulation and legislation as policy instruments.

THE SPECTRUM OF REGULATION

Primary Legislation. Policy is frequently identified with the process of formal authorisation, that is to say with the specific Acts of Parliament or the statutory instruments which, under delegated legislation, permit or require actions to be taken. Thus, government's alcohol policy can be seen as consisting of successive liquor licensing acts, road traffic acts and measures to deal with drunken offenders. However, legislation can be an uncertain instrument of policy because of the nature of the implementation process. There are many points during the passage and subsequent enforcement of a law when the original intention of the legislation can be distorted. For example, a government bill can be modified or rejected by Parliament. Members of Parliament do not usually influence the drafting of government legislation but they can force a shift in government policy when a bill is brought before the House for debate and approval. Since the Conservative Government of 1970-74, government backbench MPs have shown a readiness to vote against unpopular measures which would have been unthinkable in the immediate post-war years. Cross-voting resulted in the Conservative Government of 1970-74 being defeated on six occasions and the Labour Government of 1974-79 being defeated twenty-three times (Norton, 1987, p.53). Since 1979, Governments have modified or withdrawn measures whenever it looked as though a backbench revolt would result in defeat, and the threat of defeat is greater on cross-party issues like alcohol and tobacco, where party discipline in Parliament is weak (Baggott, 1989).

Legislation can be also be altered after it has reached the statute book. A government may choose to implement only certain sections of an Act, thereby altering its emphasis, as the incoming government did with the 1969 Children and Young Persons Act in 1970. Or the courts may interpret the law in a way that frustrates the original intention of the legislature. This happened with the 1967 Road Traffic Act, when many prosecutions failed because of a lack of precision in the wording of the law. Laws often contain areas of ambiguity as a result of the bargaining and compromise necessary to ensure their passage through Parliament, and these provide opportunities for the exercise of discretion by the agencies charged with implementation. Again, in a number of regulatory areas, the police choose priorities for enforcement. As a result certain laws, such as those prohibiting the sale of alcohol to minors, tend to be under-enforced.

There are particular problems associated with using legislation as part of a national prevention strategy. The legal system is different in Scotland, Northern Ireland, England and Wales, and even where similar legislation is in force, as with drinking and driving, there are considerable local variations in enforcement and sentencing patterns. Where the law grants Justices discretionary powers, as it does in relation to liquor licensing, the result may be a patchwork of different prescriptions and practices, accompanied by confusion over what is really required. Yet the costs associated with changing primary legislation are such that the system possesses a considerable degree of inertia. Incoming governments retain nearly all of the legislation passed by their predecessors, even legislation they had opposed while in opposition (Tether and Ingle, 1981).

The freedom of UK governments to introduce legislation is also constrained by membership of the European Community (EC). Under the European Communities Act 1972, EC law takes precedence over conflicting domestic legislation. Moreover, under the Treaties of Rome and Paris, the EC has responsibility for policy making in areas such as agriculture, trade and consumer protection. Transferring policy making competence to the EC in these spheres reduces the scope for national governments to introduce prevention policies (Harrison, 1989).

Nevertheless, legislation has a number of distinct advantages over other modes of control. In passing laws, governments are not restricted by the need to operate with the cooperation of industry. Legislation enables government to achieve a greater degree of regulation than is customary with voluntary agreements, and this can be important in areas where the need to protect the public is paramount. For example, no-one would expect governments to rely exclusively on voluntary agreements to maintain road, rail, aviation and marine safety standards. In these areas, where the social costs of non-compliance are likely to be high, it is recognised that legislation is necessary to provide effective sanction.

Legislation also has a symbolic value, in that it defines unacceptable conduct and standards, and signifies the government's commitment to achieving change. Conversely, the absence of legislation is often interpreted by the public as tacit approval of particular practices, like cigarette advertising and sponsorship by tobacco companies. A significant proportion of the British public believe that cigarette smoking cannot really be harmful, because the government permits cigarette advertising (Marsh and Matheson, 1983). Prohibiting cigarette advertising would convey an important message, therefore, about the gravity with which government regards the health risks associated with smoking, irrespective of the direct impact of such a ban on consumption. This symbolic value of legislation may be a powerful argument for its use in areas where it is difficult to influence individual behaviour.

9

Secondary legislation and circulars. Legislation has been increasingly used by successive British governments committed to interventionist social policies. This has been facilitated by the growing use of statutory instruments, and there has been much debate over the way governments use delegated legislation to evade parliamentary scrutiny (Walkland, 1968). However, where public health policies are concerned, the capacity of the executive to bypass Parliament through the use of delegated legislation represents an opportunity rather than an impediment. It may be one of the only ways to implement prevention policies in the face of opposition from the large number of MPs with alcohol and tobacco interests (Baggott, 1989). Thus it is unlikely that the Labour Government would have been able to ban cigarette advertising on television in 1965 if it had had to steer a bill through the House of Commons. The ban was achieved through the use of existing powers, conferred on the Postmaster General under the 1964 Television Act.

Departmental circulars have also been used to promote important policies, like the introduction of competitive tendering for National Health Service (NHS) ancillary services. The then Department of Health and Social Security used circulars to encourage health authorities to forbid smoking on NHS premises, while the Cabinet Office distributed guidelines to other government departments encouraging them to introduce alcohol and work policies. One stage down from legislation, circulars can be an exhortatory tool, reflecting governments' increased interest in the policy area, which stops short of a commitment to regulation (Griffith, 1966).

Voluntary agreements. The instrument which received little academic attention until recently is the voluntary agreement (Baggott, 1986; Goodwin, 1986). Voluntary agreements depend upon cooperation and consensus and are the outcome of a bargaining process, in which both government and other parties to the agreement may threaten sanctions, such as legislation or the withdrawal of cooperation, in order to reach agreement. For example, the Labour Government threatened to introduce legislation inhibiting pay rises in 1975, in order to secure an agreement on incomes policy, while the tobacco companies only agreed to print health warnings on cigarette packets in 1971 after the Government threatened to support a Private Members Bill that would restrict cigarette advertising (see Chapter 5).

Voluntary agreements form the basis for the UK's approach to the control of alcohol and tobacco advertising (see Chapters 3 and 4). Apart from provisions in the Trade Descriptions Act 1968 dealing with the false description of products, there is no general prohibition against misleading advertising in British law of the kind found in Sweden, France and West Germany. The British Government has resisted EC pressure to adopt such legislation, believing that it is preferable to encourage voluntary restraint

10

amongst the industries concerned (House of Lords, 1978).

One form of voluntary agreement is the use of self-regulated codes of practice. Advertising codes of practice have proliferated in recent years. Sales promotion is governed by the British Code of Sales Promotion Practice, whilst advertisements directed at the medical profession are controlled both by a law, the Medicines Act 1968, and by a Code of Practice administered by the Association of the British Pharmaceutical Industry. Other codes cover new media, for example, cable television and viewdata, and specialised fields such as investment advertising. In their general provisions, the codes are similar, most being specialised versions of the two principal codes, the British Code of Advertising Practice (BCAP), which covers advertising in most non-broadcast media, and the Independent Broadcasting Authority's (IBA) Code of Advertising Standards and Practice which applies to independent radio as well as independent television. In 1988, the Government announced that it intends to create a new authority to supervise independent radio with a 'light regulatory touch', which may lead to the relaxation of advertising regulations and the formulation of a new code of practice (Home Office, 1988). The IBA and the Cable Authority are to be replaced by a new body, the Independent Television Commission.

Some codes of practice have an ambiguous, quasi-legal status because the relevant authorities have a legal duty to enforce advertising standards (Baggott and Harrison, 1986). The IBA is a state broadcasting authority, required by successive Television Acts to draw up and enforce a code of advertising practice, and to consult with the Home Secretary over any major alterations to the code. The Cable Authority has a similar statutory responsibility in relation to advertising on cable television, under section 2 of the 1984 Cable and Broadcasting Act, while investment advertising is controlled by a code of conduct drawn up by the Securities Investments Board, under the 1986 Financial Services Act.

Because these codes have a statutory basis it is often argued that they are not part of the self-regulatory system. But it is difficult to make any kind of hard and fast distinction between State regulation and self-government since the British Government participates in many forms of self-regulation through the Office of Fair Trading (OFT). The OFT aims to improve trading standards by non-legislative means. Under section 124(3) of the Fair Trading Act 1973, the Director General of Fair Trading has a duty to encourage trade associations to introduce codes of practice aimed at safeguarding consumer interests. However, once an industry has adopted a code there are ways in which the law can be used to enforce its provisions. For example, the Director General of Fair Trading has the power to apply for an injunction restraining the publication of any advertisement in breach of the BCAP.

While there is minimal government involvement with some codes of practice, those adopted in the field of consumer protection and trading standards lie towards the formal end of the continuum (Baggott and Harrison, 1986). They are often introduced or strengthened only after the Government has threatened legislation. The codes are either formulated with the help of government departments, or they are submitted for the approval of government ministers or the OFT in draft form.

Legislation versus voluntary agreements. Why do policy makers find voluntary agreements preferable in some circumstances to legislation? First of all, there are a number of practical arguments which favour the use of voluntary agreements. The implementation of an agreement is generally a quicker and more flexible process than drawing up new legislation. Voluntary agreements also open up a considerable opportunity to shifting the costs of regulation onto industry. Finally, it could be argued, voluntary agreements are potentially more effective as they embody a spirit of cooperation which cannot always be guaranteed by legislation (Tether, 1989).

In addition to these practical arguments, voluntary agreements may also be preferable on political grounds. They are particularly suited where there is a high degree of cooperation between government and the regulated interests. In addition, voluntary agreements fit in well with the dominant style of British post-war government, which has placed a premium on compromise and the accommodation of interests (Richardson and Jordan, 1979). This may of course be less true today with the ending of the post-war consensus and the rise of conviction politics. Despite the Conservative Party's traditional suspicion of law, recent Conservative Governments have been quite prepared to introduce legislation against the trade unions while defending self-regulation for their allies in the City of London. The Labour Party, on the other hand, supports legislation where the Stock Market is concerned but favours self-regulation for trade unions. Ideological factors clearly influence the selection of policy instruments. Since voluntary agreements are a cheaper form of regulation, and as they tend to reduce the degree of bureaucratic intervention, the use of such instruments fits in rather well with the government's programme of deregulation. In short, there are political and practical arguments which underpin the choice of voluntary agreements. But the most critical factors appear to be the power and influence of the interests involved. Perhaps this is why voluntary agreements and self-regulation generally feature in policy areas dominated by powerful interests.

REGULATION AND SOCIAL WELFARE

Regulation will only result in a net gain in social welfare if it operates in the public interest, rather than in the interests of one section of the community. The greatest danger is that producer groups will benefit from regulation at the public's expense and this criticism applies to legislation as much as to self-regulation. There is some evidence that all forms of regulation can operate in the interest of regulated industries. According to Bernstein (1955) regulatory agencies often begin by operating in the public interest, but are subsequently captured or drawn into an accommodation with the regulated industry. This is because agencies come to rely on producer groups, both for information and material assistance, and for political support in the face of public and political indifference.

Even companies that resist industrial regulation initially may become its supporters if they find that regulation has the effect of restricting competition. Thus Jordan (1970) showed that after the founding of the American Civil Aviation Board (ACAB) in 1938 there were virtually no new entrants to the American airline industry, while air fares which were regulated by the ACAB were 24 per cent higher than those which were not. Keeler (1972) found consistently higher air fares on regulated routes, overcharging sometimes being as high as 80 per cent. A similar use of government regulation to restrict competition has been shown in fields as diverse as banking (Peltzman, 1965), road haulage (Volotta, 1967; Sloss, 1970; Stigler, 1971), and the professions (Holen, 1965; Pfeffer, 1974a). In most cases, regulation either had the effect of converting a competitive or oligopolistic industry into a cartel, whereby previously independent companies agreed to act together to restrict competition, or of protecting an existing cartel or monopoly from rival firms (Pfeffer, 1974b).

The formation of a cartel is particularly likely to occur in industries which have sought self-regulatory agreements, like the advertising industry. The British advertising industry first established a regulatory code in 1924, when there were no external demands for control. At the time this was seen as a move towards greater professionalism. But like the professions, the established companies sought to restrict competition from 'unethical' competitors, thereby ensuring a market for their expertise (Baggott and Harrison, 1986). Once established, advertising controls persisted long after the conditions which precipitated them. Although the maintenance of self-regulation imposes costs on advertising agencies, advertisers and media owners, especially as the system involves a self-imposed tax or levy to finance the regulatory agency, firms continue to support some form of regulation because it continues to provide net benefits.

There are various ways in which regulation can benefit the regulated, which include the restriction of competition over price and market entry, the reduction of uncertainty through control of the regulatory process, the legitimisation of the industry and access to government policy makers in the face of external pressures for State intervention. Even where firms have opposed any form of regulation, they may agree on a voluntary agreement as a compromise. The tobacco industry resisted regulation in the 1960s, but eventually agreed to voluntary agreements over product modification, the display of health warnings and advertising restrictions, as the lesser of two evils (see Chapter 4). There is no reason to doubt that the tobacco companies believe consumers would be better served by an unregulated market, but voluntary agreements are preferred to external control, and may, as critics allege, come to operate in the interests of the industry. For example, filter tips cut costs by reducing the tobacco content of cigarettes, while the move towards low tar cigarettes enables companies to recycle parts of the tobacco plant that were previously wasted. In the following sections we discuss the ways in which the alcohol and tobacco industries can benefit from regulation.

Competition

The regulation of trading and product standards is often a form of protectionism, which benefits national industries by restricting overseas competition. An example is the recently repealed West German *Reinheitsgebot* or beer purity law, which dated from 1516. The *Reinheitsgebot* established high standards for German beer, which could only be produced from water, barley or wheat, yeast and hops. The law had to be abandoned under the terms of EC competition rules because it effectively denied other European brewers access to German markets. British brewers, in particular, use large quantities of brewing sugar and chemical additives in the production of beer.

One of the main ways in which regulation restricts competition is by raising the cost of market entry. British brewers could only compete under the *Reinheitsgebot* laws if they brewed to German standards, and this would involve considerable costs. Restrictions on advertising and licensing laws also make it difficult for new companies to enter the market. The effects of regulation on competition are illustrated below with reference to advertising. Competition in the alcohol industry and the liquor licensing law are discussed in Chapter 6.

It is virtually impossible to introduce a new whisky or cigarette brand without a major advertising campaign capable of challenging existing brand loyalties. Yet advertising codes and other restrictions make it difficult for new brands to be promoted in a vigorous way. This may explain why some sections of the alcoholic drinks industry, notably the distillers, have supported advertising regulation. When commercial television was introduced in 1955, British distillers agreed to a voluntary moratorium on television advertising, as a 'money-saving device' (Advertising Association, 1981, p.20). In effect, the distillers formed a cartel, agreeing to limit competition through advertising.

A similar agreement to restrict advertising to the non-broadcast media existed between Australian distillers until 1982, when market pressures forced its abandonment. Cartels tend to be unstable during periods of economic uncertainty, some members defecting in the face of market pressures. Faced with the collapse of a cartel, firms may seek statutory regulation or the establishment of some kind of joint Standards Authority or Marketing Board as a means of maintaining group discipline during a short-term conflict of interests (Williamson, 1965). They may even seek the support of other industries. In Britain the distillers' agreement has been reinforced, in recent years, not by government but by the independent television companies, which have announced a policy of not accepting advertisements for 'hard liquor' (Henry, 1980).

This policy of excluding advertisements for spirits might seem surprising, in the light of the views on alcohol advertising expressed by the Independent Television Association, the trade association for the television programme companies. The Independent Television Association, formerly known as ITCA, commissioned research on alcohol advertising, and accepted findings suggesting that advertising has no effect on per capita consumption (Henry, 1980). Representatives of the Association have argued consistently that there is no case for banning tobacco or alcohol advertising. This suggests that whatever reasons the various interests might have had for introducing an advertising ban on spirits, it was not done on public health grounds.

The television programme companies agreed to the ban on spirits at a meeting with the distillers. Why the television companies should forego advertising revenues is not clear, but most distilleries are owned by companies that also have wine and brewing interests, which together account for seven per cent of all television advertising (see Chapter 3). Companies like Guinness-DCL may be able to use their market power to persuade the commercial television companies that advertising should be concentrated on beer, wine and cider.

British distillers have probably supported the television ban on spirits advertising in order to make it more difficult for competitors, particularly overseas competitors like the French spirits producers, to enter the British market. The French used to operate a selective ban on television advertising, permitting the advertising of French cognac and rum but banning whisky, gin, and pastis, until the European Court ruled in 1980 that this was discriminatory. It is clear that at least some EC members believe television advertising bans are being used to protect domestic markets from import penetration, in contravention of EC policy.

Although the tobacco industry fought against the prohibition of cigarette advertising on radio and television, the major companies have benefited from the way that the ban has affected competition. British American Tobacco (now BAT Industries) blamed advertising regulations when it abandoned its attempt to enter the UK market, claiming that it had been 'unable to promote its brands in a meaningful way' (*Campaign,* 1984).

Some economists believe that high levels of advertising expenditure represent a barrier to market entry, but it is possible that restrictions over advertising which stop short of a total ban could have a similar effect. The limited advertising permitted in the non-broadcast media favours established brand names, which need less exposure than new products, enabling the tobacco companies to stabilise existing market shares while avoiding competition over price. It is true that the industry has become vulnerable to competition from lower priced imports recently, but most of these cigarettes are marketed as 'own brands' and do not require mass advertising campaigns. The only firms to have entered the cigarette market in recent years have been those that were not dependent on advertising because they could promote the product through their own retail outlets.

The situation is rather different for the brewing, cider and wine sectors. Unlike the distillers, the brewers have not sought a ban on television advertising. It is possible that the tied-house system, under which brewers supply a large proportion of their output through premises which they own, is more of a barrier to market entry than any aspect of advertising. The tied-house system has been investigated by the Monopolies and Mergers Commission several times, as have the brewers' prices and profit levels. The brewing industry tends towards non-price competition, especially competition through advertising. Expenditure on beer advertising has increased substantially over the last few years, as beer sales have declined. Total advertising expenditure on alcohol increased from £20.6 million in 1955, when commercial television was introduced, to £119.9 million in 1987, at constant 1980 prices, while the proportion of all alcohol advertising revenues devoted to beer rose from 37 per cent to 54 per cent over the same period (Media Expenditure Analysis Limited, 1988).

At first glance, it appears as though foreign alcohol producers have made major inroads into the British market in recent years, with American and Australian brands gaining a substantial share of the market for lager. Following a vigorous advertising campaign in 1986 on British television, Fosters had 4.5 per cent of the draught lager market, with Castlemaine XXXX close behind at 3.1 per cent (*Morning Advertiser*, 1986). Because beer is expensive to import, however, most lager is produced in the United Kingdom under licence. Grand Metropolitan pays substantial royalties to the American giant Anheuser Busch for the right to brew Budweiser, while the licence to brew Fosters, which used to belong exclusively to Grand Metropolitan, is now shared with Courage. This unusual arrangement, with rival companies collaborating over the production and marketing of the same product, was introduced following the acquisition of Courage by the parent company, Elders IXL of Australia, in 1986.

Whether advertising controls have made it more difficult for these companies to enter the British market is not clear. Market entry rates can change in response to many variables apart from advertising regulation. In order to establish the effect of regulation on market entry, it would be necessary to isolate its effect from that of other changes in the economic characteristics of the alcohol industry, such as production costs.

Uncertainty

There has been increasing emphasis in organisation theory on the concept of environmental uncertainty (Cyert and March, 1963; Thompson, 1967). According to Pfeffer (1978), uncertainty is the result of complexity, or the number of elements decision makers have to take into account, and variability, the rate at which these elements change over time. This has implications for organisational decision making and has been used to explain variations in organisational structure. Thus Burns and Stalker (1961) held that 'organic', non-bureaucratic structures enabled firms in the electronics industry to perform more efficiently in conditions of market uncertainty, while hierarchical, 'mechanistic' structures were more suitable in stable conditions. Others have also argued that organisational structures are contingent on environmental factors (Gouldner, 1955; Duncan, 1972).

More recent approaches have stressed the way in which organisations seek to establish control over unpredictable aspects of their environment, so that the environment is just as likely to be shaped by organisations as they are to be designed to fit the environment. It is argued that, because modern organisations face increasingly turbulent environments, the reduction of uncertainty has become a major organisational task. This has been achieved through such diverse routes as the adoption of information technology, which provides better forecasting capabilities, diversification, and the pursuit of acquisitions and mergers aimed at eliminating dependence on external suppliers for components and raw materials. The tobacco industry, in particular, has achieved a high degree of vertical integration, with large transnational corporations controlling virtually every aspect of the production and distribution of tobacco products. The brewing industry has also established a degree of integration through the tied-house system.

One source of uncertainty for the alcohol and tobacco industries is the threat of future legislation over advertising, which would have implications for organisational autonomy. Statutory regulation allows external organisations—courts, tribunals or Ombudsmen—to make decisions which control the conduct of business and may affect profitability. It is, therefore, in the interest of companies to devise a form of self-regulation which will allow them to retain substantive control over the regulatory process, and which will forestall external interference. Since the aim is to reduce uncertainty and create stability and predictability, the industry will be inclined to introduce controls even when the threat of government regulation is a fairly remote one.

The alcohol appendix to the British Code of Advertising Practice appears to have been introduced in 1975 in the absence of a strong demand for regulation, because of concern about the fate of the tobacco industry, and because the alcohol trade anticipated future government regulation. Government was able to rule by 'anticipated reaction'; little pressure was needed because the alcohol and advertising industries were attempting to reduce uncertainty by predicting and forestalling future developments. The advertising industry has used similar tactics on other occasions. In 1986, the Advertising Association established a 'public inquiry' into advertising controls with the express purpose of 'pre-empting future Government intervention in the existing control system' (Advertising Association, 1987, p.7).

Legitimacy

Legitimacy, defined as the 'perceived congruence between social values and an organisation's products and actions' has been identified as a valued resource for modern organisations (Pfeffer, 1978, p.159). Firms that allow their products to become the centre of controversy may encounter sales resistance, and industries facing criticism over the social and health problems associated with their products, like the alcohol and tobacco industries, have to expend resources in order to maintain the products' legitimacy. They have to defend the social acceptability of drinking and smoking; activities that have, in other times and places, been considered deviant and even subjected to prohibition. The advertising industry too depends on legitimacy for the credibility of its product (Baggott and Harrison, 1986).

These industries are engaged in what amounts to a long-term public relations exercise, attempting to project an image of social approval and respectability, both for the product and for the corporation. But their claim to legitimacy depends on the interpretation of social values and can be

18

challenged, both by pressure groups and by other industries seeking to use legitimacy as a competitive weapon. The social acceptability of both the alcohol and tobacco industries has been contested, at different times, by public health campaigners, the temperance movement and others—though currently alcohol enjoys more acceptance than tobacco. In turn, the alcohol and tobacco industries are able to use legitimacy as an asset in their competition with illicit drugs.

Control over information is central to the struggle for legitimacy because of the importance of the capacity to define the nature, range and extent of alcohol or tobacco-related problems. It is through the interpretation of information about the consequences of the alcohol and tobacco industries' activities that their deviant or legitimate status becomes established. The media and advertising industries, the health-related professions, universities, and other organisations involved in producing and disseminating information, have a key role in establishing legitimacy, because they determine which information is available and how it is interpreted.

The media probably has the pre-eminent role in this process. Pfeffer (1974c) has shown that American firms facing critical problems of legitimisation are more likely to co-opt representatives of the media onto their boards of directors. Industries that face critical legitimisation issues are obliged to take defensive action, by forming organisational alliances or action groups, or co-opting those who have the power to confer legitimacy. In the UK, one of the largest publishers, IPC Magazines Limited, has been persuaded to join groups established to combat further restrictions over alcohol and tobacco advertising; so have television companies like HTV, the Independent Television Association, national newspapers like the *Daily Mail*, and London Transport Advertising. All of these organisations joined committees set up by the Advertising Association to co-ordinate the campaign to defend alcohol and tobacco advertising (Advertising Association, 1987). National newspapers, magazines and television companies are in a powerful position to organise support for the alcohol and tobacco industries, thereby protecting an important source of advertising revenues.

Continual criticism of alcohol and tobacco advertising detracts from its usefulness as a means of establishing legitimacy, and is something to be avoided; hence the importance of codes of conduct as a way of deflecting criticism and showing that business is being conducted ethically. It is not enough to avert the threat of an advertising ban, the codes of conduct must be able to legitimise advertising itself, demonstrating that whatever has been claimed is 'legal, decent, honest and true'.

The legitimacy of government policy also needs to be considered. Laws may appear to be the most effective instrument to deal with the problem in hand. But in practice, as was noted earlier, legislation may be under-enforced. Worst of all, as with prohibition in the United States, laws may fall into disrepute, provoking behaviour which defeats the original intentions of policy makers. Not only does over-stringent legislation undermine public confidence in the specific law in question, it also opens up a challenge to legislation in general, and this makes it more difficult to use the law, even in areas of behaviour where it is appropriate. In short, legislation which is out of step with public opinion undermines the legitimacy of legal controls.

Voluntary agreements may have greater legitimacy than the law, particularly where powerful vested interests are concerned. Voluntary agreements tend to have more legitimacy in the eyes of the regulated because they give them a key role in the formation and the implementation of policy. However, as Goodwin (1986) has noted, voluntary agreements can be used by governments to compel those with vested interests to modify their behaviour. Indeed, this can occur precisely because of the legitimacy of such policy instruments.

Access to policy makers

Any form of regulation gives the regulated industry closer contact with government. The introduction of legislation frequently involves government in widespread consultations with the interests that are likely to be affected. Views are sought by means of publication of a Green Paper or discussion document, circulation of draft proposals and informal meetings between representatives of industry and their sponsoring departments in Whitehall. Even a statutory instrument can be subjected to lengthy discussions; the Ministry of Agriculture's draft regulations on displaying the alcoholic content of drinks were circulated for comment to 150 organisations in 1988. Indeed, regulation can have the effect of incorporating industry into the policy making process, a tendency that can be seen most clearly in the negotiations that attend the establishment of self-regulatory agreements (Baggott and Harrison, 1986).

Both the alcohol and the tobacco industry have enjoyed closer links with government policy makers as a result of their cooperation over advertising controls. The alcohol industry already has access to government through the Alcoholic Drinks Division of the Ministry of Agriculture, Fisheries and Food (MAFF), while the tobacco industry has similar links with the Department of Trade and Industry (DTI). MAFF and the DTI are the departments responsible for identifying these industries' interests and representing them within government. However, voluntary cooperation over advertising controls extends both industries' contacts within government to the health departments. While access does not ensure influence, it does ensure that the

20

industries' views are taken into account at an early stage of decision making, and it reduces uncertainty by giving the industries advance warning of government intentions.

Incorporation into the policy making process can unite producer groups and facilitate the emergence of an industry-wide view, because responsibility for negotiating the content of voluntary agreements strengthens the role of trade associations like the Tobacco Advisory Council. Both government and industry prefer to use the trade associations as intermediaries, because it reduces the high transaction costs associated with complicated and protracted negotiations. The producers need strong, well-informed and authoritative trade associations to defend their interests in these negotiations, and they also need to develop a unanimous view on the problems confronting the industry, in order to strengthen the trade association's bargaining position. These pressures can lead to greater cohesiveness within the industry, and the emergence of strong, influential trade associations which can bargain effectively with government departments, though not all companies benefit equally from these developments. Smaller companies in particular may find their interests neglected in the drive for consensus, with larger, transnational corporations dominating discussions and influencing the direction of future policy.

CONCLUSION

Although public health campaigners tend to see non-legislative intervention as a 'soft option' for government policy makers, both legislation and self-regulation have advantages and disadvantages as vehicles for prevention policy. In some circumstances, legislation can provide more effective sanction than self-regulated codes of conduct, particularly when industries lack representative trade associations capable of securing agreement over trading standards. In other cases, the enforcement of a law can be difficult without industrial cooperation. The law can be ineffective where detailed technical matters have to be resolved and, in these cases, self-regulation can provide greater protection to consumers. Introducing primary legislation can be a slow process, the costs of law enforcement are high and the law may not be administered in the way that was originally envisaged. In contrast, voluntary agreements can be broader in scope, more flexible and cheaper than legislative intervention, because the industries concerned bear most of the costs of regulation.

Regulation, whether of the product's price, availability, or composition, or of the information conveyed in advertisements and packaging, can have unintended consequences, irrespective of the choice of regulatory instrument. Any form of regulation can operate in the interests of the industry, at the expense of the public. Regulation can benefit producer groups, either because they are able to influence government when the law or code of conduct is being drafted, or because they are able to 'capture' the regulatory authority at a later stage. The regulatory authorities may be drawn into a collusive relationship with the industries they are supposed to control because they are dependent on them for cooperation, for scarce resources like information and for political support in their negotiations with other government agencies over such things as the size of their budget. The regulated industries, in turn, benefit from the restriction of competition, the reduction of uncertainty and improved access to policy makers. Self-regulation may have the additional advantage of providing industries with a means of legitimating their activities. As a result, the industries' position is strengthened. These possibilities have to be taken into account when regulatory policies are being considered, so that regulations can be drafted and implementation structures designed that will minimise the risk of prevention policies being subverted.

The degree of government regulation and the choice of regulatory instrument are political issues. Any change to existing control practices will come as the result of pressure from organised groups. There are different configurations of party interest, trade associations, professional organisations, pressure groups and government agencies active in different policy areas and, depending on the nature of the issue, governments have more room for manoeuvre in some areas than others. These political constraints have to be taken into account when considering the options for policy change.

References

Advertising Association, (1981), *Alcohol Advertising in the Context of Consumption and Abuse*, Advertising Association, London.

Advertising Association, (1987), *The Advertising Association 1986/87*, Advertising Association, London.

Baggott, R., (1986), 'By voluntary agreement: the politics of instrument selection', *Public Administration*, 64, (1), 51-67.

Baggott, R., (1989), 'Alcohol and tobacco: the politics of prevention', in Maynard, A. and Tether, P. (eds.), *The Addiction Market: consumption, production and policy development*, Avebury/Gower, Aldershot.

Baggott, R. and Harrison, L., (1986), 'The politics of self-regulation: the case of advertising control', *Policy and Politics*, 14, (2), 143-159.

Bernstein, M., (1955), *Regulating Business by Independent Commission*, Princeton University Press, Princeton.

Burns, T. and Stalker, G., (1961), *The Management of Innovation*, Tavistock, London.

Campaign, (1984), 'Why BAT's loss is not in vain,' 10 February, 6.

Cyert, R. and March, J., (1963), *A Behavioural Theory of the Firm*, Prentice Hall, Englewood Cliffs, New Jersey.

Duncan, R., (1972), 'Characteristics of organisational environments and perceived environmental uncertainty', *Administrative Science Quarterly*, 2, 409-43.

Goodwin, R., (1986), 'The principle of voluntary agreement', *Public Administration*, 64, (4), 435-444.

Gouldner, A., (1955), *Patterns of Industrial Bureaucracy*, Routledge and Kegan Paul, London.

Griffith, J., (1966), *Central Departments and Local Authorities*, Allen and Unwin, London.

Harrison, L., (1989), 'The information component', in Robinson, D., Maynard, A. and Chester, R. (eds.), *Controlling Legal Addictions*, Macmillan, London.

Henry, H., (1980), 'Advertising alcohol—an ITV view', *British Journal of Alcohol and Alcoholism*, 15,(3),129-135.

Holen, A., (1965), 'Effects of professional licensing arrangements on inter-state labor mobility and resource allocation', *Journal of Political Economy*, 73, 492-98.

Home Office, (1988), *Broadcasting in the 1990s: Competition, Choice and Quality*, Cm. 517, HMSO, London.

House of Lords Select Committee on the European Communities, (1978), *Misleading Advertising*, 38th Report, Session 1977-78, 3, 31, HMSO, London.

Jordan, W., (1970), *Airline Regulation in America: Effects and Imperfections*, John Hopkins University, Baltimore.

Keeler, T., (1972), 'Airline regulation and market performance', *Bell Journal of Economics and Management Science*, 3, 399-424.

Norton, P., (1987), 'Parliament and policy in Britain: the House of Commons as a policy influencer', in Robins, L. (ed.), *Topics in British Politics 2*, Political Education Press, London.

Marsh, A. and Matheson, J., (1983), *Smoking Attitudes and Behaviour*, HMSO, London.

Media Expenditure Analysis Limited, (1988), *Quarterly Digest of Advertising Expenditure*, Media Expenditure Analysis Limited.

Morning Advertiser, (1986), April 8, 3.

Peltzman, S., (1965), 'Entry in commercial banking', *Journal of Law and Economics*, 8, 11-50.

Pfeffer, J., (1974a), 'Some evidence on occupational licensing and occupational incomes', *Social Forces*, 53, 102-11.

Pfeffer, J., (1974b), 'Administrative regulation and licensing: social problem or solution?', *Social Problems*, 21, 468-79.

Pfeffer, J., (1974c), 'Cooptation and the composition of electric utility boards of directors', *Pacific Sociological Review*, 17, 333- 63.

Pfeffer, J., (1978), *Organisational Design*, AHM Publishing, Arlington Heights.

Richardson, J. and Jordan, A., (1979), *Governing under Pressure*, Blackwell, Oxford.

Sloss, J., (1970), 'Regulation of motor freight transportation: a quantitative evaluation of policy', *Bell Journal of Economics and Management Science*, 1, 327-66.

Stigler, G., (1971), 'The theory of economic regulation', *Bell Journal of Economics and Management Science*, 2, 3-21.

Tether, P. and Ingle, S., (1981), *Parliament and Health Policy*, Gower, Farnborough.

Tether, P., (1989), 'Legal controls and voluntary agreements', in Robinson, D., Maynard, A. and Chester, R. (eds.), *Controlling Legal Addictions*, Macmillan, London.

Thompson, J., (1967), *Organisations in Action*, McGraw Hill, New York.

Volotta, A., (1967), *The Impact of Federal Entry Controls on Motor Carrier Operations*, Pennsylvania State University, State College, Pennsylvania.

Walkland, S., (1968), *The Legislative Process in Great Britain*, Allen and Unwin, London.

Williamson, O., (1965), 'A dynamic theory of interfirm behavior', *Quarterly Journal of Economics*, 79, 579-607.

2 Information and voluntary agreements: the policy networks

LARRY HARRISON AND PHILIP TETHER

As Chapter 1 shows, governments choose between a mixture of primary and secondary legislation, departmental circulars and guidelines, voluntary agreements and codes of conduct. Nevertheless, in each policy field there is usually one form of regulation that predominates. Advertising policy, for example, is largely characterised by self-regulation. The self-regulation of alcohol and tobacco advertising is discussed in detail in Chapters 3 and 4, together with an analysis of the costs and benefits of alternative policies. This chapter sets the scene for subsequent discussions by mapping the relations between government, commercial and professional organisations with an interest in advertising and places advertising controls in the wider context of information policy.

Information policy is not a term used by government. It is an analytical category, used to compare a range of measures aimed at similar objectives. These include controls over advertising and sponsorship, and public education programmes. Both sets of measures attempt to reduce the adverse consequences of alcohol or tobacco consumption through intervention in the market for information. Both involve the same participants, or closely related sets of organisations. For example, both the alcohol and advertising industries are involved in the provision of alcohol education, as are the medical Royal Colleges, government departments, Alcohol Concern, the Health Education Authority (HEA) and its counterparts in Wales, Scotland and Northern Ireland, and various pressure groups. These organisations are also involved in the (inter-related) debate over advertising and alcohol misuse. Advertising by producers can, it is claimed, undermine health education, by presenting positive images of drinking.

Government intervention in the information market can be justified on several grounds. From a rational choice perspective, the aim would be to reduce alcohol or tobacco-related problems by ensuring that consumers are provided with the information necessary to maximise their welfare. Governments can ensure that the demand for health information is met, either by providing the information directly or by changing the structure of incentives and sanctions so that it will be provided by others. An information policy based on these premises would include government funding for the Health Education Authority and voluntary organisations providing alcohol and tobacco education. It could also include encouraging industry to take responsibility for drink-driving publicity, printing health warnings on cigarette packets or drink containers, publicising the tar content of cigarettes and the alcoholic content of drinks and ensuring that advertisements do not actively mislead consumers about the consequences of smoking and drinking.

However, information policies can be adopted for other reasons. Most public education campaigns go beyond the provision of information and attempt to engineer changes in social behaviour. Campaigns on drinking and driving or cigarette smoking aim to persuade people to give up high-risk behaviours, often through the use of fear-arousal techniques, such as the portrayal of badly disfigured road accident victims in advertisements. These campaigns are essentially paternalistic, in that they are based on the premise that people are not the best judge of their own welfare where alcohol and tobacco are concerned and that some vulnerable groups, such as the young, need protection from advertising and promotion. This approach is reflected in the ethical codes governing advertising and sponsorship and also in the prominence given in some official reports to the concept of the 'presentation' of drinking or smoking in the media (Advisory Committee on Alcoholism, 1977). Presentation refers to the portrayal of alcohol and tobacco use on radio, the cinema and especially on television. From this point of view it is not just the messages contained in advertisements that give cause for concern but the way drinking and smoking are depicted in television drama and 'soaps'. For a prevention policy to be effective, it is argued, it should include controls over the media presentation of alcohol and tobacco, a policy involving the curtailment of editorial freedom.

It is hard to identify an underlying theoretical rationale for the government's information policy. Indeed it is hard to say whether there is any such thing as a consistent, government-wide policy. There are elements of both paternalist and rational choice models, with some departments, like

Health, favouring education aimed at behaviour modification while others, like Agriculture, favour improved consumer information.

There was a marked increase in government intervention in the information market throughout the 1980s and the British Government is now the second largest advertiser in the UK (Harrison, 1989). There was also an increased emphasis on mass advertising as a means of achieving health education and, to a lesser extent, on strengthening controls over alcohol and tobacco advertising. Health ministers claim that the Government's commitment to prevention is demonstrated by its funding of health education, and overall expenditure on the then Health Education Council increased, in 1980 prices, from £895,614 in 1969 to £6,991,992 in 1986.

The proportion of this expenditure devoted specifically to alcohol and tobacco education cannot be identified precisely, because much of it is hidden in other programmes, such as that concerned with the prevention of heart disease. But there was clearly a massive increase in funding for all categories of health education. This increase was accompanied by restrictions on the messages permitted in alcohol and tobacco advertisements. The Government stopped cigarette advertising on television in 1965 and from 1971 entered into a series of negotiations with the tobacco industry which, as Chapter 4 shows, resulted in increasing restrictions over non-broadcast tobacco advertising.

While increasing emphasis has been placed on the management of information, other forms of intervention, like price disincentives, have been relatively neglected. In order to gain any understanding of these developments we need to know more about the opportunities and constraints faced by policy makers. Our study of current prevention policy showed that important decisions were usually the outcome of negotiations within multi-organisational networks, composed of trade and professional associations, pressure groups and the relevant divisions within government departments (Tether and Harrison, 1988). This was the case in most policy areas, with the notable exception of indirect taxation, where the policy process is relatively insular and debate confined to Customs and Excise and the Treasury (see Chapter 4 of the first volume of this series, Maynard and Tether, 1989). In contrast, information policies are quite open to the participation of outside interests. Indeed where advertising policy is concerned government departments play a marginal role. This can result in the fragmentation of the policy process, with different aspects of the same problem being responded to in different ways, by different organisational networks. Accordingly, it was necessary to map out the government departments and other policy participants, and analyse organisational relations to see if they represent an impediment to the development of policy in this area (Harrison and Tether, 1987; Hjern and Porter, 1981).

THE GOVERNMENT DEPARTMENTS

This section identifies the administrative units within eleven government departments responsible for some aspect of alcohol and tobacco information policies and examines whether their various approaches form part of a coherent strategy. The eleven are the Department of Health, the Welsh, Scottish and Northern Ireland Offices; the Ministries of Defence and Agriculture; the Departments of Education and Science, Transport, Trade and Industry, and the Environment; and the Home Office. The next section comments on the degree to which these departments pursue compatible policies, and indicates ways in which non-governmental organisations influence the information policy debate.

Department of Education and Science (DES)

In England and Wales, the DES is the major department involved in health education policy in schools. Within the DES, responsibility for the development of policy concerning health education lies with Division B, one of four divisions in Schools Branch 3. This division is responsible for the national curriculum subject working groups and for the development of policy on a number of different subject areas. The task lies with a team of six administrators, who work closely with Her Majesty's Inspectorate (HMI). HMI is a separate, independent body which reports directly to the Secretary of State. Inspectors are appointed by the Queen to inspect and comment on the quality of education and have both a general responsibility for a number of schools in a locality and for specialist subject areas such as health education. Inspectors contribute to in-service courses for teachers and mount their own courses on specific topics, including health education.

The DES liaises closely with the Department of Health over health education matters and HM Inspectors used to sit as observers on several Health Education Council committees until that body was replaced, early in 1987, with the Health Education Authority. The DES is in touch with the Health Education Authority over health education in relation to alcohol and tobacco. A member of HM Inspectorate also sits as an observer on the Board of TACADE (the Teachers Advisory Council on Alcohol and Drug Education), one of the leading organisations in the field of alcohol and drug education. TACADE produces a range of materials to be used by teachers, youth workers and others engaged in educating young people about the risks of alcohol and other drugs.

UK health departments

The Department of Health has the lead responsibility for health education in relation to alcohol and tobacco use in England, with the Scottish, Welsh and Northern Ireland Offices having these responsibilities for their respective countries. At the Department of Health, health education is located in branch CPM1 of the Children, Maternity and Prevention Division. This branch liaises with other branches in the same division dealing with alcohol and tobacco-related problems, and with the Health Education Authority (HEA), which is funded by the Department of Health and is constituted as a special National Health Service Health Authority.

In Scotland, health education is provided by the Scottish Health Education Group (SHEG). Oversight of SHEG is vested in Division 5b of the Home and Health Department (SHHD) of the Scottish Office. The division is supported by professional groups in the Medical Services and the Nursing Services, two professional hierarchies located within the SHHD. The division can also draw on data supplied by the Chief Scientist's Office which is responsible for health-related research. The social work dimension of any alcohol policy issue is the responsibility of the Social Work Services Group located in the Scottish Education Department. Division 5b is also responsible for the health aspects of alcohol and tobacco consumption and drug misuse, and has a co-ordinating role within the Scottish Office in respect of these issues, although other administrative units retain lead responsibility in relation to their own interests.

Policy responsibility for health education in schools and other educational institutions rests with Division 2 of the Scottish Education Department (SED). Division 2 is concerned with alcohol and tobacco education as part of its broader concerns for curriculum and assessment issues. SED takes the view that alcohol and tobacco education have to be tackled in a broader programme of health education designed to teach children the skills to resist social pressures and make healthy choices in later life. In this, it follows the recommendations of the Scottish Health Education Coordinating Committee which brings together representatives of the SED, the SHHD and the SHEG. The Secretary of State for Scotland issues guidelines to local authorities on health education and much alcohol and drugs education is integrated into the Standard Grade Science Course in Scottish schools.

In Wales, health, the personal social services and educational provision are the responsibility of the Welsh Office. The Welsh Office has three Health and Social Services Policy divisions; Division 1 is responsible for health promotion including policy on primary care and related services, drugs, alcohol and tobacco, AIDS and other infectious diseases, public and environmental health, vaccinations, child abuse and aspects of child care. Drugs and alcohol are the responsibility of Branch 1 which is also responsible for policy on primary care and related services, health promotion generally, tobacco, dental health and fluoridation. The branch assumes a co-ordinating role within the Welsh Office in respect of alcohol and drug policy. Professional input to policy making is provided by the Nursing Division headed by the Chief Nursing Officer and the Health Professionals Group, headed by the Chief Medical Officer. The professional social work input is provided by a Social Work Services Division within the Housing, Health and Social Services Policy Group. Health education for young people involves the Education Department's Schools Division, Further Education Division and Educational Services Division.

In April 1987 the then Health Education Council's responsibilities in Wales were allocated to a new Welsh Health Promotion Authority, which also assumed the work of the Health Education Advisory Committee for Wales, which provided the Welsh Office and the HEC with advice on specific Welsh matters.

In Northern Ireland, health education is the responsibility of the Northern Ireland Office. Unfortunately, details of the Northern Ireland Office's alcohol and tobacco policy making responsibilities, structures and relationships have not been made public. The authors approached the Northern Ireland Office early in 1987, but although many enquiries elicited repeated assurances that information was being collected none was ever received (Tether and Harrison, 1988).

Ministry of Defence

The Ministry of Defence has extensive responsibilities for policies affecting the health and welfare of all men and women in the armed forces at home and abroad. The army, navy and airforce all have health education programmes, responsibility for which is shared between the personnel and medical officers. In both the personnel and medical functions, the organisational arrangements are designed to enhance inter-Service policy co-ordination. In the case of personnel issues, this is achieved mainly through the use of committees, the most important of which is the Principal Personnel Officers Committee, with its sub-committee on Alcohol and Drug Abuse. On the medical side, the chief vehicle for co-ordination is the tri-Service Defence Medical Services Directorate, with its Environmental Medical Research Unit providing the organisational focus for the medical interest in alcohol and tobacco-related issues. The Ministry of Defence makes wide use of health educational materials, many of which are produced in-house. In designing educational programmes, the Ministry liaises with the Department of Health and the DES to ensure that its policies reflect current thinking on priorities and make the best use of educational material. There are no contacts with other agencies and if the Ministry wished to contact the Health Education Authority it would do so through the Department of Health.

Department of Transport

The Department of Transport has responsibility for the Government's programme of public education on drinking and driving. Educational campaigns are planned by Branch 3 of the Road and Vehicle Safety Directorate, which is also responsible for the Highway Code. Publicity campaigns have been mounted by the Department of Transport since 1976 at an annual cost of between £0.55 million and £2.5 million. After each campaign there has been an attempt to evaluate the impact on public knowledge, attitudes and behaviour which has involved commercial consultants and the Education Section of the Government's Transport and Road Research Laboratory. While some campaigns have had an impact on public opinion, it appeared that the majority of those who were aware of the campaign's message got their information from editorial coverage on television and in the newspapers. A Department of Transport review concluded that mass advertising was not cost-effective and recommended that resources were shifted to other areas where spending could be shown to result in casualty reduction. The Department should, it was argued, promote editorial coverage on road safety in newspapers and magazines.

The Department of Transport is in close touch with other organisations involved in alcohol education, such as Alcohol Concern, TACADE and the Royal Society for the Prevention of Accidents, which receives a £500,000 annual grant from the Department.

Ministry of Agriculture, Fisheries and Food (MAFF)

MAFF is the sponsoring department for all sectors of the UK's alcohol industry. This involves identifying the interests of the industry and representing them within government, assisting with scientific matters and policy on regulation, such as controlling the composition of alcoholic drinks. Sponsorship responsibilities rest with the Alcoholic Drinks Division, which is divided into two branches, one of which, Branch A, deals with wine, while the other, Branch B, deals with all other alcoholic drinks. The Ministry has several responsibilities in relation to the provision of information about alcoholic drinks which have implications for prevention policies. The Alcoholic Drinks Division is concerned with the law on labelling drinks containers, particularly wine bottles. There is a large corpus of European legislation on wine labelling which is enforced in the United Kingdom by the Wine Standards Board. The Wine Standards Board, which is funded by MAFF and the Vintners Company, has inspectors who visit wine wholesalers and English vineyards to check the authenticity and accuracy of wine labels. The British Medical Association and others have suggested that alcoholic drinks containers should carry a health warning analogous to those found on cigarette packets. In responding to such suggestions, government ministers are advised by MAFF's Alcoholic Drinks and Standards Divisions.

European legislation governs the information provided about the alcoholic strength of drinks. To confirm with the European Directive on Food Labelling and similar regulations, the UK has been obliged to amend its food legislation so that the labels of all pre-packed alcoholic drinks declare the percentage of alcohol by volume. In England and Wales, regulations were drafted by MAFF's Standards Division, while the Scottish and Northern Ireland Offices were responsible for changes to legislation in their respective countries.

As the sponsoring department, MAFF has extremely close relations with the trade associations for the alcohol industry and less contact with organisations campaigning against alcohol misuse, such as Action on Alcohol Abuse (Triple A) and the British Medical Association (BMA), who tend to approach government through their contacts in the Department of Health. MAFF do include the health lobby in policy discussions on those occasions when new legislation is being considered and the Ministry has a statutory obligation to consult relevant interests. While MAFF does not exclude particular groups on political grounds, consultations are limited to those organisations known to MAFF. This can result in an uneven coverage of available opinion. For example, the BMA was one of 150 organisations included in the statutory consultations over the regulations on alcoholic strength labelling, as was the Oat and Barley Millers Federation; Triple A was not.

The Home Office

The Home Office has an indirect interest in information policy, through its responsibility to oversee the legislation relating to broadcasting. Division T1 of the Home Office's Broadcasting Department deals with the constitutional position of the Broadcasting and Cable Authorities. It is not involved in formulating the self-regulatory codes of practice governing the broadcast advertising of alcohol in the UK. The obligation to maintain codes of practice is laid upon the Independent Broadcasting Authority by the Broadcasting Act 1981, and on the Cable Authority by the Cable and Broadcasting Act 1984. They decide both on the appropriate contents of the codes and how they should be administered, although the Acts oblige them to consult with the Secretary of State from time to time. However, the legislation does give the Home Secretary power to ban a specific class or description of advertisement and this power was employed to end the advertising of cigarettes and cigarette tobacco on television in 1965. That power has not been employed in respect of any area of alcohol advertising.

The Home Secretary may request the broadcasting authorities to review the codes of practice governing alcohol advertising, as he did in 1988 following the establishment of the inter-departmental Ministerial Group on Alcohol Misuse. He may also request the broadcasting authorities to review their guidelines on the presentation of smoking and drinking in television programmes, as he did in 1988. The Home Office has, therefore, considerable influence over the way smoking and drinking are depicted on television and radio.

The Department of Trade and Industry (DTI)

The DTI was, until 1988, the sponsor for both the tobacco and advertising industries. In 1988 the Secretary of State for Trade and Industry decided that the DTI's relationship with industry should change, with more emphasis being placed on the promotion of competition and enterprise, and the term 'sponsorship' was no longer felt to be appropriate. Nevertheless, the DTI still maintains close links with the tobacco industry through the Consumer Market Division and has contact with both the Department of Health and the Department of the Environment over the regularly renegotiated voluntary agreements which govern the advertising and promotion of tobacco products.

Although the DTI's views are sought by other departmental parties to the agreement, the Consumer Market Division does not play a direct part in the negotiations surrounding the advertising of tobacco products and the DTI has no direct contact with the health lobby over either tobacco or alcohol. However, the DTI does have a peripheral interest in these negotiations because of its responsibilities for the advertising industry. Branch 2 of the Consumer Affairs Division is concerned with advertising issues including the self-regulatory control of advertising in the non-broadcast media. The DTI monitors the effectiveness of the present system, believes that it works better than any likely alternative and that its replacement by statutory controls would be less efficient and less effective. The Consumer Affairs Division is not involved directly with the negotiations over the voluntary agreements with the tobacco industry, but they intervened to arrange a meeting between the Department of Health and the Advertising Association so that advertisers could put their case for their 'right' to advertise tobacco products. The Department of Health had always negotiated with the tobacco industry but had never consulted advertising interests.

Department of the Environment

The Sport and Recreation Division of the Department of the Environment has an indirect role in the regulation of advertising, in that it has the lead responsibility for policy on sport and sports sponsorship. Both the alcohol and tobacco companies have made increasing use of sponsorship deals as restrictions over advertising have intensified since the mid 1970s. Sponsoring snooker tournaments and other televised sports has proved to be an extremely effective marketing strategy, and many health campaigners have objected on the grounds that the resulting television coverage is a way for companies to evade advertising restrictions. The tobacco companies, in particular, are accused of using sponsorship to circumvent the ban on advertising cigarettes on television. As a result of this pressure, sports sponsorship by the tobacco companies has been regulated by a code of practice since 1977, agreed between the Department of the Environment, the Department of Health and the Tobacco Advisory Council. This code obliges tobacco companies to include health warnings on all promotional signs and advertisements for sponsored events and sets limits for the total expenditure on sponsorship deals.

ORGANISATIONAL NETWORKS

There is no government department with responsibility for all aspects of information policy in relation to alcohol and tobacco. Instead, different departments have lead responsibilities for aspects of public education, health promotion, broadcasting, the advertising industry, self-regulation and the labelling of drinks containers or the provision of health warnings on cigarette packets and advertisements. Government has no overall strategy and, indeed, there are important differences between departments over crucial questions like the role of mass advertising in health promotion. The Department of Health is committed to greater expenditure on advertising through the Health Education Authority, while the Department of Transport has decided to phase out their annual drink-driving advertising campaigns by 1992, on the grounds that they are not demonstrably cost-effective.

Co-ordination takes place through informal, *ad hoc* discussions rather than through a formal planning process. In 1987, however, the Government established an inter-departmental Ministerial Group on Alcohol Misuse, which includes all of the departments identified in this chapter as having an interest in information policies, with the exception of the Ministry of Defence and the Northern Ireland Office. The Inter-Ministerial Group may lead to closer collaboration over alcohol-related issues. However, there is no equivalent body concerned with tobacco.

In formulating policy, government departments are in touch with professional, commercial and non-statutory organisations, some of which have access to scarce information or expertise, while others represent interests that decision makers have to take into account. These organisations vary in their proximity to government departments, the Department of Health having close links with Alcohol Concern and with Action on Smoking and Health (ASH), which it funds, but no contact with FOREST, a group which exists to defend 'the right of adults to consume tobacco products'. Some groups, like the National Chamber of Trade, have only a peripheral interest in the area and move into and out of these networks depending on the nature of the issue. Others, like the Advertising Association, have a permanent involvement in policy and well-developed links with the British Government and the European Commission.

There are three main clusters, or constellations, of organisations concerned with health education, drink-driving publicity and controls over alcohol and tobacco advertising. There is a certain amount of overlap between these networks, as many organisations have a role to play in relation to public education. Government, industry and the voluntary sector all fund public education campaigns. Governments are involved through the UK Health Departments and the Department of Transport, closely associated with the Health Education Authority, the Welsh Health Education Authority, the Scottish Health Education Group, Alcohol Concern, the Royal Society for the Prevention of Accidents, TACADE and ASH. Trade Associations for the alcohol industry also fund health education campaigns. The Brewers Society have cooperated with the Department of Transport in producing a video on drinking and driving to be shown in schools and, through its Social Aspects of Alcohol Committee, funds alcohol research and health education. The Scotch Whisky Association has a Research and Education Committee which funds research and gives grants to Alcohol Concern, the Scottish Council on Alcoholism and other bodies engaged in alcohol education for the young and for medical students. The Wine and Spirits Association has also established an educational trust, which produces videos, booklets and contributes to other educational campaigns. Only the tobacco industry is absent from the field, being obliged to distance itself from health issues at all times, although it does publish health warnings on advertisements and cigarette packets as part of its voluntary agreements with government.

In the past, the number of organisations involved in education led to conflicting advice and limited efficiency. Accordingly, the medical Royal Colleges and others agreed to promote consistent messages on such things as safe drinking limits. There is now greater unanimity over the advice being offered to the public over drinking. These moves towards greater co-ordination have been enhanced by the activities of TACADE, which attempts to co-ordinate the resources and training available on alcohol and drug misuse. Some areas of disagreement remain. The Department of Transport, in particular, feels that the Department of Education and Science could do more to facilitate education on drinking and driving in schools, while the Department of Health is clearly at odds with Transport over the value of mass advertising in preventing alcohol-related problems. There are also perennial debates about the objectives and scope of health education; what should health educators be trying to achieve and how should they get there? Where smoking is concerned there has been some conflict over the question of promoting harm reduction—'switch to a safer brand'—but increasingly education is aimed at persuading smokers to stop, on the grounds that there is, in reality, no such thing as a safe cigarette.

In relation to advertising controls there is firm support for a ban on tobacco advertising and promotion from the medical Royal Colleges, the British Medical Association (BMA), ASH and the Health Education Authorities. Support for a ban on alcohol advertising, by contrast, is weak and divided. The Royal College of Psychiatrists (1979, 1986) has argued that alcohol advertising should be curtailed if evidence emerges to link it with increased alcohol consumption, and this demand has received the support of the Royal College of Physicians (1987). Action on Alcohol Abuse, a campaigning body established by the medical Royal Colleges, has also called for a ban on alcohol advertising as part of a comprehensive alcohol control policy designed to reduce the per capita consumption of alcohol (Action on Alcohol Abuse, 1986). But support wavers. The BMA's 1987 annual conference reversed an earlier decision to campaign for a complete ban on alcohol advertising, following intensive lobbying by the advertising industry (Advertising Association, 1987).

The comparative weakness of the anti-advertising lobby may be because most of its members see advertising restrictions as just one of a range of measures they would like to see introduced, and success on this issue is not central to the achievement of their organisational objectives. Indeed, out of six major pressure groups, only the National Society of Non-Smokers placed a 'very high degree of priority' on the control of cigarette advertising (Harrison, 1986). Yet trade associations for the producers, like the Tobacco Advisory Council and the Scotch Whisky Association, for retailers, like the Retail Confectioners and Tobacconists Association, and for the advertising industry, like the Cinema Advertising Association and the Advertising Association, felt that defending advertising was the 'top priority'. Defending advertising is, of course, one of the central objectives of the Advertising Association, which believes that the 'main function of the Advertising

Association is to maintain the freedom of its members to advertise and carry advertising for all products and services which may be legally marketed' (Harrison, 1986).

The trade and the health lobbies each see the other as having more influence over government, and as being in a stronger position. FOREST saw the impediment to a 'fairer treatment of tobacco advertising' as pressures from the health establishment while the anti-smoking lobby believed that Ministers failed to implement the government's overall strategy of de-regulation because of fear of unfavourable publicity (Harrison, 1986). The Cancer Research Campaign, the former Health Education Council and the National Society of Non-Smokers all took a similar position, but believed that Ministers failed to take action against advertising because of the revenue consequences for government. The National Society of Non-Smokers and the Cancer Research Campaign cited commercial pressures on government as an impediment, to which the National Society of Non-Smokers added 'support for party funds' and the Cancer Research Campaign a 'lack of strong conviction' within the Department of Health (Harrison, 1986).

Two major networks of organisations can be identified in relation to advertising control issues. The first is linked predominantly with health organisations. The Health Education Authority is, as a special Health Authority within the National Health Service, linked to the Department of Health, but it also has close links with the BMA, the medical Royal Colleges and ASH. It is also in contact with the Coronary Prevention Group and with international organisations like the World Health Organisation, the International Union against Cancer and the US Surgeon General's Office. The Cancer Research Campaign is in contact with the HEA, the BMA and ASH. The National Society of Non-Smokers is in contact not only with the HEA, the BMA, ASH and the Department of Health, but also with several health charities including the Chest, Heart and Stroke Association, the British Heart Foundation, the Ulster Cancer Foundation, the Imperial Cancer Research Foundation and the Tenovus Cancer Campaign.

The second group centres on the Advertising Association, which represents advertising agencies, media organisations and large advertisers. The Advertising Association, which includes the Cinema Advertising Association, the Incorporated Society of British Advertisers and the Institute of Practitioners in Advertising amongst its members, deals with a range of commercial and government organisations such as the Brewers Society, the Wine and Spirits Association, the Tobacco Advisory Council, Department of Trade and Industry, the Department of Health, the Home Office, the European Commission, the National Consumer Council and the Consumers' Association. Only a few trade organisations, like the Retail Confectioners and Tobacconists Association (RCTA), stand apart from this network. The

RCTA deals directly with the Tobacco Advisory Council, the tobacco manufacturers, and government departments.

The Government's dependence on commercial organisations to administer their policy on the regulation of advertising means that collectively, under the aegis of the Advertising Association, these organisations have a considerable voice in determining what are considered to be feasible and legitimate policy options. They can persuade the Government to block European legislation or withdraw domestic legislation, and can influence policy over alcohol and tobacco advertising. The Advertising Standards Authority (ASA), which regulates non-broadcast advertising, is also influential. In 1974, when the then Department of Health and Social Security entered into negotiations with the Tobacco Advisory Council over a code of advertising practice, the ASA were able to veto some of the Department's proposals on the grounds that they could not be implemented within a self-regulatory system (ASA, 1974). By defining the constraints within which policy makers may operate, these organisations are able to influence the outcomes of policy decisions. Decisions are largely determined by the premises used in making them, and the ability to determine the constraints, norms and rules employed in decision making is an important source of power (Pfeffer, 1981).

The advertising industry is able to maintain its influence because of the high degree of consensus over regulatory issues, which enables the trade associations to speak and act in unison (see Chapter 1). Of all pro-trade organisations only one, FOREST, does not place a high priority on defending the freedom to advertise, although it is opposed to advertising restrictions: 'when all the threats to freedom of choice are taken into account, the advertising issue does not come near the top. We are mainly concerned with the right to continue to smoke in designated areas in public places' (Harrison, 1986). FOREST does not have any links with organisations concerned with advertising control.

Consensus over advertising self-regulation is promoted by frequent communication and close contacts between members of the Advertising Association, and by the cross-membership of Committees, Councils and Advisory Boards. The cross-membership of Committees or Boards of Directors has long been recognised as a co-ordinating device, enabling key organisations to pursue closely related strategies. The density of links between organisations is a marked feature of the advertising network. In 1987, the President of one of the leading UK advertising agencies, active in the campaign to defend tobacco advertising, was a member of the ASA Council. He was also a member of the International Advertising Association's World Council and World Board of Directors, Director General of the Periodical Publishers Association and Chairman of the

Communication, Advertising and Marketing Education Foundation, which were all represented on the Advertising Association's Council. He was a Council member of the Institute of Practitioners in Advertising and of the Advertising Association, which were both represented on the IBA's Advertising Advisory Committee.

Until recently, the Director General of the Advertising Association also sat on the IBA's Advertising Advisory Committee. The Independent Television Association (formerly known as ITCA), which is the trade association for the independent television companies, is a member of the committee that is responsible for drawing up the advertising code for the non-broadcast media (see Chapter 3). A chairman of the former ITCA Copy Committee was co-author, with the Advertising Association's Director of Research, of *The Case For Advertising Alcohol and Tobacco Products* (Henry and Waterson, 1981). In this and other publications, it was argued that the present advertising controls are effective, and that there is no case for further restrictions (Henry, 1980).

In 1983, the Chairman of the ITCA Copy Committee and the Advertising Association's Director of Research and Director General also sat on the Advertising Association's Alcohol Coordinating Group, which was set up in the early 1980s to counter any moves to introduce further restrictions on alcohol advertising. Other members of the Coordinating Group included the Scotch Whisky Association and the Gin Rectifiers and Distillers Association. A parallel group was established to defend tobacco advertising, bringing tobacco company representatives together with advertising and media interests (Advertising Association, 1984, p.21).

Not only are there close connections between the ITV Association and the Advertising Association, but the Advertising Standards Authority liaises closely with the Independent Broadcasting Authority. All of these organisations are involved in a continuing dialogue about advertising practices. Their views are remarkably similar. Like the ITV Association, the ASA Chairman has argued against stricter controls over products like alcohol: 'It is no part of the ASA's duty to establish a censorship on behalf of groups or organisations which believe that they know how to make us all better' (ASA, 1986, p.5). The Chairman of the ITCA Copy Committee and the Director General of the Advertising Association were both speakers, along with representatives of the IBA, of the IBA's Advertising Advisory Committee, and of the advertising agencies, at the IBA's first conference on advertising held in 1984 (IBA, 1984). And the construction of a consensus about the regulation of advertising is facilitated by the way that individuals move from one organisation to another. In 1980, for example, in his role as Chairman of the ASA, Lord Thomson of Monifieth, a former Labour Minister and European Commissioner, was condemning the European Commission's directive on misleading advertising. In 1981, Lord Thomson was appointed Chairman of the IBA and spoke out against the European Commission's interference in national advertising legislation (*The Times*, 1980, 1981).

The Advertising Association has considerable influence over government policy through the direct lobbying of MPs, peers of the realm, officials of political parties and of trade unions, journalists, civil servants in Whitehall and Brussels, and UK members of the European Parliament. The Association produces a Parliamentary Newsletter, which provides background information and comment on issues before parliament, and arranges 'briefings' for ministers and for 'leading MPs' of all parties. They also operate through the presentation of evidence to parliamentary select committees and the membership of departmental working parties. In 1978, for example, the Office of Fair Trading (OFT) established a working party to conduct research into the effectiveness of the ASA. Their partners on the working party were the Advertising Association and the Consumers' Association. The OFT Report, which was basically favourable to the ASA, suggested giving the Director General of Fair Trading reserve statutory powers to 'stimulate adherence' to the advertising code (DGFT, 1978). The response of the outgoing Labour Government was to set up a Department of Trade working party to consider the proposal. The working party, which reported back to the Minister of State for Consumer Affairs in 1980, also argued that the OFT be given the power to enforce the ASA's decisions (Department of Trade, 1980). Membership of the Department of Trade working party included the Advertising Association, the ASA and the OFT. According to its Director General, the Advertising Association is in contact with the OFT and the ASA 'most weeks of the year' (House of Lords, 1978, p.31).

The Advertising Association operates a Public Action Programme, aimed at influencing 'carefully selected groups of opinion-formers'. In order to reach these influential groups, the Association believes it must go beyond routine press relations and 'seek opportunities to put its message across' in publications read by members of 'target groups'. Its success in finding such opportunities can be seen by the way it placed a number of articles in newspapers and magazines, including the World Health Organisation's *World Health Forum*, as part of its 1986 campaign to defend alcohol advertising (Advertising Association, 1987). Individual briefings were arranged for selected writers and editors, from *The Spectator, New Society, The Director* and *The Observer*, and a number of journalists were said to 'now depend on the AA for a stream of alcohol-related research material' (Advertising Association, 1987, p.6). The Association also liaised with television and radio producers so that its representatives would appear on current affairs programmes when there was a likelihood that advertising issues would be raised. This carefully orchestrated campaign ensured that the Association's views were represented in public discussions of alcohol and tobacco advertising.

In exploiting every possible opportunity to promote its message, the Advertising Association operates as an extremely effective pressure group and has considerable skill in public relations. It has been far more active, and more successful, in defence of alcohol advertising and of the self-regulatory system of control than the health lobby has been in campaigning for its abolition.

CONCLUSION

Those concerned with health promotion have to operate in a rapidly changing world, a world in which there is increasing competition for the public's attention, with the growing importance of information technology and the introduction of new electronic media. As advertising has become such an important feature of contemporary society, engaged in by traditionally conservative financial institutions and by many professions, there has been a corresponding emphasis on the use of mass advertising as a means of communicating health information. This has been accompanied by pressure for greater controls over alcohol and tobacco advertising, often on the grounds that such advertising undermines health education. The self-regulation of alcohol and tobacco is discussed in detail in Chapters 3 and 4, together with an analysis of the costs and benefits of alternative policies.

Government has responded to demands for more alcohol and tobacco education by committing increasingly large sums of money to health education. It has also encouraged the alcohol and tobacco industries to adopt stricter codes of conduct governing their advertising. However, it is hard to identify the theoretical rationale for this policy; indeed there is no such thing as a consistent, government-wide information policy. Responsibility for different aspects of information policy is fragmented between at least fifteen administrative units in eleven government departments. Many administrators are unaware that their activities have implications for alcohol and tobacco policy and fail to exploit opportunities for health promotion. Some departments take different views over such questions as the cost-effectiveness of mass advertising as a means of communicating health information.

As in other areas of prevention policy, these government departments are linked into a series of organisational networks, which influence the policy debate (Harrison and Tether, 1987). The department with primary responsibility for advertising controls, the DTI, has much more contact with the advertising industry than with the health lobby. The advertising industry is extremely well organised and, through its umbrella organisation the Advertising Association, is able to operate as an effective pressure group. It maintains a high degree of consensus over regulatory issues, which enables the advertising agencies, the large advertisers and the media trade associations to speak and act in unison, thereby adding to their influence. The industry is united in its desire to oppose any further statutory regulation of advertising. The health lobby, in contrast, has been divided historically and has found it difficult to arrive at a consensus, particularly where alcohol is concerned. Few organisations campaigning over alcohol misuse place a high priority on banning advertising, or even agree that statutory controls over alcohol advertising are desirable. There is more support for a ban on tobacco advertising, but even here the health lobby is rather ineffectual, because it is not part of the advertising policy network.

Clearly, prevention policies involve complex issues that cut across the responsibilities of many government departments, posing particular co-ordination problems. Governments have tended to underplay these (DHSS, 1981) but in 1987 the need for improved collaboration was recognised with the establishment of an inter-departmental Ministerial Group on Alcohol Misuse. The Group was set up specifically to 'improve the co-ordination of alcohol policy'. There is no equivalent body concerned with tobacco policy, although many of the issues are the same. Regular meetings of the Ministerial Group are held, involving both ministers and senior civil servants, and this has resulted in several policy initiatives requiring cooperation between three or four departments. Such meetings can only proceed by consensus, however, which makes it difficult to deal with fundamental conflicts of interest between departments. Yet the conflict of interest between departments—between those charged with improving competition, or removing barriers to British business, and those concerned with health promotion—is one of the issues that has to be resolved before more effective information policies can be developed.

References

Action on Alcohol Abuse, (1986), *An Agenda for Action on Alcohol*, Action on Alcohol Abuse, London.

Advertising Association, (1984), *Annual Report and Accounts 1983*, Advertising Association, London.

Advertising Association, (1987), *The Advertising Association 1986/87*, Advertising Association, London.

Advertising Standards Authority (ASA), (1974), *12th Annual Report*, Advertising Standards Authority Limited, London.

Advertising Standards Authority (ASA), (1986), *Annual Report 1985-86*, Advertising Standards Authority, London.

Advisory Committee on Alcoholism, (1977), *Report on Prevention*, Department of Health and Social Security and the Welsh Office, London.

Department of Health and Social Security (DHSS), (1981), *Drinking Sensibly*, HMSO, London.

Department of Trade, (1980), *The Self Regulatory System of Advertising Control: Report of the Working Party*, Department of Trade, London.

Director General of Fair Trading (DGFT), (1978), *Review of the UK Self-Regulatory System of Advertising Control*, a Report by the Director General of Fair Trading, Office of Fair Trading, London.

Harrison, L., (1986), Organisations Involved in Advertising and Public Information Campaigns, Working Paper, ESRC Addiction Research Centre, University of Hull.

Harrison, L., (1989), 'The information component', in Robinson, D., Maynard, A. and Chester, R. (eds.), *Controlling Legal Addictions*, Macmillan, London.

Harrison, L. and Tether, P., (1987), 'Coordinating the UK's policy on alcohol and tobacco: the significance of organisational networks', *Policy and Politics*, 15, 77-90.

Henry, H., (1980), 'Advertising alcohol—an ITV view', *British Journal of Alcohol and Alcoholism*, 15, (3), 129-35.

Henry, H. and Waterson, M., (1981), 'The case for advertising alcohol and tobacco products,' in Leather, D. et al. (eds.), *Health Education and the Media*, Pergamon, Oxford.

Hjern, E. and Porter, D., (1981), 'Implementation structures, a new unit of administrative analysis', *Organisation Studies*, (2), 3, 211-227.

House of Lords, Select Committee on the European Communities, (1978), *Misleading Advertising*, 38th Report, Session 1977-78, HMSO, London.

Independent Broadcasting Authority (IBA), (1984), *Independent Broadcasting*, 40, 10-12.

Maynard, A. and Tether, P. (eds.), (1989), *The Addiction Market: consumption, production and policy development*, Avebury/Gower, Aldershot.

Pfeffer, J., (1981), *Power in Organisations*, Pitman, Boston, Mass.

Royal College of Physicians, (1987), *A Great and Growing Evil: The Medical Consequences of Alcohol Abuse*, Tavistock, London.

Royal College of Psychiatrists, (1979), *Alcohol and Alcoholism*, Tavistock, London.

Royal College of Psychiatrists, (1986), *Alcohol: Our Favourite Drug*, Tavistock, London.

Tether, P. and Harrison, L., (1988), *Alcohol Policies: Responsibilities and Relationships in British Government*, Addiction Research Centre Occasional Paper, Universities of Hull and York.

The Times, (1980), 8 May, 19.

The Times, (1981), 21 February, 15.

3 Alcohol advertising

LARRY HARRISON AND CHRISTINE GODFREY

As discussed in Chapters 1 and 2, the regulation of alcohol advertising in the United Kingdom is achieved through various codes of conduct which limit the ways in which the drinks industry may promote its products. Critics of this self-regulatory policy argue that these ethical codes are poorly enforced and that a statutory ban or restriction on the volume of advertisements would be preferable. Many see the elimination of alcohol advertising as an essential component of a multi-faceted control policy, aimed at reducing or stabilising total alcohol consumption (Royal College of Psychiatrists, 1979, 1986; Action on Alcohol Abuse, 1986; Royal College of Physicians, 1987).

The objectives of the self-regulatory policy have never been made explicit, but it is not aimed at restricting the volume of advertising and is not intended to reduce alcohol consumption. If the existing policy has a latent objective, it is to ensure 'socially responsible advertising' by preventing the promulgation of 'harmful' ideas and images of drinking. Advertisers are not supposed to associate drinking with driving, for example, or appeal to vulnerable groups like the young. This approach acknowledges that advertising is a legitimate activity, which should be permitted so long as its messages do not contradict or, in other ways, detract from the advice offered to the public on health education. Apologists for the advertising industry go further and claim that advertising actually supports health education, by encouraging consumers to switch to low alcohol beers, or less harmful cigarettes. In this way advertising becomes the 'ally of health education', as Sir Keith Joseph claimed in relation to the voluntary agreement over tobacco advertising (*The Times*, 1971). The development of controls over tobacco advertising is discussed in Chapter 4.

Self-regulation is sometimes presented as a way of achieving the same ends as an advertising ban at less cost to government, industry and the consumer. Yet the objectives of the two policies are actually quite different. An advertising ban, which is favoured by public health campaigners, can be classed as a consumption policy. Supporters of a statutory ban argue that advertising increases the total consumption of alcohol, and this leads to an increase in related harm. Curtailing advertising and promotion will, they argue, help prevent this. Advertising codes and health education, on the other hand, are information policies, measures which aim to reduce the adverse consequences of alcohol consumption through intervention in the information market. As such, they are supported by the alcohol and advertising industries which reject arguments for a link between total alcohol consumption and related harm, or, indeed, between advertising and any kind of alcohol-related problem. The alcohol industry included the statement that there was 'no evidence connecting (alcohol) misuse with the advertising of alcoholic drinks' in the 1985 edition of the British Code of Advertising Practice (Code of Advertising Practice Committee (CAP), 1985, p.80).

There is little doubt that this has been, and remains, one of the most controversial issues in alcohol policy. The Advertising Association has played a leading role in this debate, drawing on the available econometric evidence to support their argument that advertising does not influence levels of consumption (Waterson, 1981). Successive governments have accepted this view, claiming that there is insufficient evidence of a link between advertising and consumption, or between per capita consumption and the prevalence of harm (Department of Health and Social Security (DHSS), 1981). In this chapter, the debate over alternative alcohol advertising policies is re-examined. The first section describes the existing policy, and provides a detailed account of four distinct regulatory systems that govern advertising in different media, including innovations such as cable television and new data systems. The impact of the European Community (EC) on the current self-regulation codes is described in the second section. It should be noted that many of the arguments relating to the EC and new media relate also to tobacco advertising which is discussed in Chapter 4. In the third section, the costs and benefits of alternative policies are examined. Finally, impediments to changing the existing system are identified.

Chapter 1 provides a general description of the United Kingdom's self-regulatory system of advertising control which depends on four codes of conduct governing different media. These codes are the British Code of Advertising Practice (BCAP), the Independent Broadcasting Authority (IBA) Code of Advertising Standards and Practice, the Cable Authority Code and the Videotex Information Providers' Code. Alcohol advertising is covered by the general requirements of these codes and by a number of specific rules, contained in Appendix 2 of the BCAP, Rule 34 of the IBA and Cable Authority Codes, and Appendix 8 of the Videotex Information Providers' Code. These rules govern the day-to-day practice of alcohol advertising, define ethical practice and determine which ideas about drinking are regarded as unacceptable.

There are minor differences between the codes. In January 1988, they all prohibited references to alcoholic strength, the stimulating or sedative properties of a drink, or the suggestion that drinking enhances social or sexual success. All were agreed that advertisements should not show people drinking and driving, or operating dangerous machinery, although the videotex code failed to include a reference to machinery. Buying repeated 'rounds' of drinks was unacceptable in all advertising media, except videotex, while portraying 'solitary drinking' was prohibited only on television. The main difference between these codes is not in their content, but in the method of enforcement. The following section describes the administration of each system and the sanctions available to the regulatory authorities.

Administration of the IBA system

With regard to television, the definition of acceptable advertising practice is the formal responsibility of the IBA, guided by an Advertising Advisory Committee. Under the Broadcasting Act 1981, the Secretary of State for Home Affairs has the power to direct the Authority to exclude advertising for any class of project, or disallow specific advertising methods, but these powers are rarely used. Since 1954, when the original Independent Television Authority drew up the first code for television advertising, a government minister has overruled the Authority on only two occasions. In 1955, the Government prohibited 'advertising magazines', programmes devoted to advertising; and in 1965 the Postmaster General, the Minister then responsible for broadcasting, used his powers to direct the Authority to ban advertising for cigarettes and cigarette tobacco. As at January 1988, the Advertising Advisory Committee has ten members of whom four, the largest single group, are from the advertising industry. Three members represent consumer interests, one the medical, and one the pharmaceutical professions. There is an independent chair. The Committee is responsible for reviewing the Code of Advertising Standards and Practice and is consulted by the IBA on policy issues. There is also a separate Medical Advisory Panel, which advises on advertisements for medical, veterinary and surgical treatments.

The Code is administered by the IBA with the close cooperation of the programme companies and the Copy Clearance Secretariat of the Independent Television Association (ITV Association), the trade association for the television companies. Until government plans for a new radio authority are finalised, radio advertisements are checked by the ITV Association Copy Clearance Secretariat on behalf of the radio industry.

The procedure for regulating radio and television advertisements is complicated. Specialist staff at local radio and regional television companies are responsible for clearing the majority of local advertisements, but all financial advertisements, those directed at children, and those for alcoholic drinks, have to be referred to the Copy Clearance Secretariat of the ITV Association. Medical or pharmaceutical advertisements have to be submitted to the IBA's Medical Advisory Panel. National advertisers submit scripts directly to the Copy Clearance Secretariat, whose initial comments are endorsed or amplified by officers in the IBA Advertising Control Division. The advertisers are then informed of any amendments necessary to ensure conformity with the Code. Over 9,500 scripts for television and 10,700 scripts for radio advertisements were 'pre-vetted' in 1986, of which 22 per cent required revision (IBA, 1987a). Advertising agencies wait until their revised scripts are approved before proceeding with their production plans. The film, video or audio tapes are then submitted to the Copy Clearance Secretariat and the IBA Advertising Control Division for final amendments or clearance. In 1986, approximately four per cent of these completed advertisements required further amendments before being broadcast (IBA, 1987a).

The ITV Association distribute *Notes of Guidance* to advertisers, which interpret and amplify the provisions of the IBA Code. The Notes relating to the advertising of alcoholic drinks contain clauses that are not present in the formal Code (Henry, 1980). For example, the 'term tonic wine is not acceptable in sound or vision', and 'care should be taken that treatments featuring sportsmen being refreshed after activity do not give any impression that their performance is enhanced by drink'. The ITV Association guidelines are regarded as an extension of the formal Code by the IBA, and cannot be disregarded by advertisers. The IBA is not the sole source of advertising regulations, therefore, as the ITV companies have the editorial freedom to impose additional requirements on advertisers, or even to reject advertisements that comply with the IBA Code.

Among the additional requirements insisted upon by the ITV companies are important restrictions on alcohol advertisements. For example, although 'hard liquor' does not feature in the IBA's list of eighteen 'unacceptable products or services' (IBA, 1987b, p.4), the programme companies will not accept advertisements for spirits. The ITV Association *Notes of Guidance* explain that 'while there is not a ban on the advertising of hard liquor, it is not the policy of the programme companies to carry advertisements for whisky, gin, brandy, rum, vodka or drinks of equivalent strength. This does not apply to after-dinner liqueurs provided that they are advertised as such, and not as ordinary beverages' (Henry, 1980). This restriction on advertising spirits is unique to television and does not apply to commercial radio, nor to Oracle, the ITV teletext system (IBA, 1986; IBA, 1984a).

The IBA approach to advertising control emphasises prevention rather than remedial action, allowing no advertisements to be broadcast until they have been subjected to careful examination. The IBA has a legal duty to consider any complaint made to it about misleading advertisements, under the Control of Misleading Advertisements Regulations 1987, but it does not receive many public complaints, and very few of the complaints that are received are upheld. In 1986 the IBA received 3,483 complaints, relating to 1,480 commercials (IBA, 1987a). They upheld fifteen, just over one per cent. Only a small proportion of the offending 1,480 commercials were for alcoholic drinks. The IBA does not analyse public complaints by product category and cannot give a precise figure.

How this system will work in the future is open to question. In the White Paper *Broadcasting in the '90s*, the Government announced plans to replace the IBA and Cable Authority with a new body, the Independent Television Commission (ITC), which will exercise 'a light regulatory touch' (Home Office, 1988). The ITC will be responsible for issuing an ethical code governing advertising and sponsorship, but whether the new code will be as extensive, or enforced as rigorously, as the present code is not clear.

The regulation of viewdata systems

The revolution in information technology brings the prospect of an increase in direct-response advertising, whereby a customer responds to an invitation to purchase directly from an advertiser. Advertising and sales information, financial transactions and mail order purchases can be conducted by home computers linked to a central database. The possibility of ordering anything from an aeroplane or theatre ticket to a dozen cases of French wine through an electronic information system poses new problems for existing regulatory systems, and the lines of demarcation between the regulatory authorities can seem confusing to members of the public. The IBA Code and the copy clearance system apply to Independent Television's Oracle, which has carried advertisements since 1981, but Prestel, the British Telecom service, is governed by the ASA Code, as it is transmitted down telephone lines and is not technically a broadcast service (IBA, 1984a).

Oracle and Ceefax, the rival service run by the British Broadcasting Corporation, are known as *teletext* systems. They are broadcast by the same transmitters as television programmes, using part of the signal that is not required for other purposes. The data can only be de-coded by special apparatus within a television set. Prestel, on the other hand, is a *videotex* system. Videotex data is transmitted along existing telecommunications networks, and interpreted by a computer. Data can be received on screen, computer disc, tape, telex or direct print-out (Videotex Industry Association, 1983). The data on videotex are supplied by companies known as 'Information Providers', who sign a contract with a 'System Operator', like British Telecom, to lease pages or 'frames' on their system. They can sub-contract these frames to other firms, who are then known as 'Sub-information Providers' (Videotex Industry Association, 1983). Theoretically, the data can be provided by anyone possessing a computer linked to the central database, including the users themselves.

As teletext is considered to be a broadcast service, advertising on Oracle is controlled by the IBA Code, with explanatory guidelines for advertisers provided by the IBA. The interpretation of the Code is slightly more liberal than for programme advertising, as controversial advertisements can be kept on separate pages, where they will only be seen by viewers who actively seek them. Funeral directors and bookmakers, who are banned on television, are allowed to advertise on Oracle for this reason (IBA, 1984a, Part B, 1c, 1d). Cigarettes and cigarette tobacco are banned, however, and in place of the restrictions on the time of day when alcohol advertisements may be screened on television they are prohibited on 'editorial pages of special interest to children' (IBA, 1984a).

Advertising copy on British Telecom's Prestel is governed by the CAP Committee in the same way as copy in a newspaper or magazine. The Advertising Standards Authority (ASA), which supervises the BCAP, accepted responsibility for Prestel because they believed it could be classified as a print medium: it is possible to obtain a computer print-out of Prestel advertisements. This means that ASA investigators are able to verify public complaints. The ASA will not accept responsibility for other videotex services, because of the difficulty of applying rules and procedures that were designed with the non-broadcast media in mind to a new medium, 'electronic publishing', that shares some of the characteristics of broadcasting, and some of the characteristics of print, while differing from both.

Videotex systems differ from other media because information is constantly being deleted or modified, and there may be no permanent record of controversial messages. Videotex provides instant access to information at any time of the day or night from anywhere in the world. While radio and television can restrict certain advertisements and programmes to times when children are unlikely to be watching, information on videotex is always available to anyone in the home. As videotex systems are interactive, they can be used for the direct purchase of goods and services by any person with access to the computer terminal, making them an important medium for direct response advertising.

There has been a rapid development of such systems in France, and it is already possible for French customers equipped with a computer terminal and a credit card, to buy wine directly from the château and have it delivered to the front door. This may be a beneficial development for many consumers, reducing opportunity and transaction costs, but it also carries a number of risks. Juveniles may make unwanted purchases and adult customers may buy on impulse, or on the basis of inadequate or misleading information. Also, reducing the transaction costs associated with buying alcohol may lead to a rise in consumption and related problems.

It is clearly important to develop safeguards for videotex users, but the approach adopted for broadcast systems, which involves all advertisements being checked before they are transmitted, cannot be applied to a system based on a telecommunications network. It is virtually impossible to monitor all information before it is made available to the public, because of the capacity of modern computer databases and the fact that data is being supplied and continuously updated from so many sources at once. For this reason, the Videotex Industry Association (VIA) has drawn up its own code of practice, the Videotex Information Providers' (VIP) Code, which has detailed regulations covering credit transactions and the direct sales of goods and services (VIA, 1983). The VIP Code contains special appendices dealing with advertising of alcoholic drinks and cigarettes, and applies to all advertising on public videotex systems. This leaves out the private or 'closed user group systems', which are operated by companies selling goods directly to agents or customers. These would be extremely difficult to regulate in practice.

The VIP Code is the most extensive and detailed set of regulations to have been adopted by any trade association, and the twenty-seven rules governing cigarette advertising are more stringent than those covering any other medium. The rules for alcoholic drinks are similar to those found in the BCAP, though less detailed. The VIA procedure for resolving public complaints is essentially one of arbitration and conciliation. Complaints about information on videotex systems are made, in the first instance, to the System Operator and Information Provider. If a complainant is dissatisfied with their response and the companies are members of the VIA, the Chief Executive of the VIA is called upon to arbitrate. If the Information Providers do not accept his decision, the seven members of the VIA Complaints Committee examine the case and reach a majority verdict. Where complaints are upheld, Information Providers may still appeal to the Council of the VIA, but the Council's decision is final (VIA, 1983).

The weakness of the VIA system is that not all Information Providers are members of the trade association, although there are a number of sanctions that can be applied to those who refuse to accept the VIA's ruling (VIA, 1983). The System Operator may be asked to insert a warning notice, or 'blank off' the offending frames, or make access difficult in other ways. Publishers of videotex directories may be asked to include a list of 'defaulters' in their next edition, and the System Operator may be asked to cancel the Information Provider's contract. They could also be expelled from the Association. Although 'electronic publishing' is inherently more difficult to control than broadcasting, the sanctions available are broadly comparable to those used by publishers in other media.

The administration of the cable television authority system

Cable television allows viewers to receive a large number of channels, including satellite broadcasts, relayed to their television sets by cable. Unlike most European nations, Britain permits advertising on cable television, both in programme breaks and on special channels devoted to classified advertisements. Under the terms of the 1984 Cable Television Act, the Cable Television Authority is required to draw up a code of advertising practice in consultation with the IBA (Section 2, clause 46). The Authority is advised by the same Advertising Advisory Committee as the IBA, and its Code and Programme Guidelines are based on those developed by the IBA, and embody the same restrictions on alcohol and tobacco. There are important differences between the two systems, however, because cable programmes can be sponsored by companies willing to underwrite programme costs, a form of advertising prohibited on radio and television. Under the Cable Authority's rules on sponsorship, alcohol companies can sponsor or commission programmes, and include a short copyline promoting their product, whereas tobacco companies are not allowed to publicise cigarettes or cigarette tobacco, and the use of a tobacco company's house name cannot be used in programme credits if it indirectly publicises cigarettes (Cable Authority, 1987).

Like the IBA, the Cable Authority operates a copy clearance system. Under this system, the programme providers or cable operators send scripts for alcohol advertisements to the Authority for clearance. The Authority does not check the finished product on a routine basis, but they do select particular products or services for closer scrutiny, requesting video tapes for all commercials in these categories that have been screened in the previous four weeks. In January 1988, this work was performed by Advertising Control Officers, but there were plans to establish a Cable Copy Panel, involving representatives of the cable operators and programme providers.

Under the control of Misleading Advertisements Regulations 1987, the Cable Authority has a duty to consider any complaints about advertising on cable television, unless they appear 'frivolous or vexatious'. Programme providers or cable operators have to forward copies of public complaints to the Cable Authority. When a complaint is upheld, the Authority has the power to direct the cable operator to stop the transmission of the offending advertisement. By a strange anomaly in the legislation, advertising on text-only cable services is not regulated by the Cable Authority, and it is unclear whether it is covered by any of the existing codes. Complaints about text-only cable services may have to be made directly to the Director General of Fair Trading (DGFT).

In 1987, the DGFT was given specific responsibility for investigating public complaints over advertisements which do not come within the jurisdiction of the IBA or Cable Authority, alongside powers to seek an injunction in the courts restraining the publication of misleading advertisements. The DGFT intends to use these powers only as a last resort in exceptional cases, or where normal means of persuasion have been exhausted. There is a remote possibility that these reserve powers could open the door to greater judicial intervention in advertising control, as the DGFT could become a route to appeal over complaints that have not been upheld by the ASA or CAP Committee. The Director General is obliged to consider the public interest in reaching his decision, but he must also have regard to the desirability of encouraging the self-regulatory control of advertising. It is unlikely, therefore, that he will exercise his discretion in a way that could be seen as undermining the self-regulatory authorities, by, for example, frequently challenging alcohol or tobacco advertisements in the courts.

Administration of the ASA system

Advertising in media other than videotex, radio, broadcast and cable television is covered by the British Code of Advertising Practice (BCAP). Apart from a few exceptions, such as advertisements addressed to the medical profession and to business investments, magazines printed in Britain for export and telephone sales promotion techniques, the Code covers advertising in all newspapers, magazines, posters, brochures, circulars and in the cinema. It also covers advertisements on video tapes, Prestel, balloons and banners towed by aircraft.

The BCAP is drawn up by the Code of Advertising Practice Committee (CAP). In 1987, fifteen of the twenty-one organisations that nominated representatives to CAP were also members of the Council of the Advertising Association. CAP co-ordinates the activities of the media associations in enforcing the Code, and it also handles intra-industrial disputes (CAP, 1985). Overall administration and the investigation of public complaints are the responsibility of the Council of the Advertising Standards Authority Limited (ASA), a non-profit making limited company. Both the ASA and CAP are financed by the industry through a 0.01 per cent surcharge on non-broadcast advertising expenditure, the levy being collected by an independent body, the Advertising Standards Board of Finance. The ASA Council has ten members, more than half of whom have to be drawn from outside the advertising industry.

Complaints from members of the public are investigated by the ASA Secretariat's case officers, who make a recommendation to the Council of the ASA. The Council makes the final decision. If the complaint is upheld, the advertiser is asked to withdraw the offending advertisement. In cases of non-compliance, the ASA Council can issue a 'media notice', informing the trade associations that the advertisement has contravened the Code, and asking publishers to refuse to sell further space to the advertiser. In 1986, media notices had to be issued on nineteen occasions (ASA, 1987). The fact that a media notice had been issued was published, along with the findings in all other cases heard by the Council, in theASA's monthly case reports.

The BCAP is also enforced by the Direct Mail Services Standards Board, a member of the CAP Committee. The Board was established by the Post Office in 1983 as a means of providing an incentive for direct mail companies to observe advertising standards. Direct mail represents an increasingly important part of the postal business, the volume of direct mail advertising having grown from 540 million items in 1975 to 1,401 million in 1986, an increase of 260 per cent (Waterson, 1987). Companies that contribute to the Advertising Standards Board of Finance surcharge, and satisfy the Board that they only provide services to clients who comply with the BCAP, receive official recognition and are able to display the Board's symbol. They also receive a one per cent discount from the Post Office on their annual mail bill.

In their 1983 advertisements, the ASA publicised the fact that over 7,500 people had written to them in the previous year. The annual number of complaints has remained fairly constant since then, but less than half of these complaints are fully investigated. Complaints are rejected for a variety of reasons, the commonest being the absence of any apparent breach of the Code. Well over 1,000 complaints are dismissed on these grounds each year. A further 500 complaints concern broadcasting and are forwarded to the IBA, and about 500 complaints refer to cases already investigated. In approximately 1,000 cases, the ASA considers insufficient evidence has been produced and requests further details from the complainant (ASA, 1985). The proportion of complaints accepted for further investigation fluctuates from year to year, but it is never more than 40 per cent. Table 3.1 shows that in 1984 it was 38.1 per cent and in 1986, 31.8 per cent.

Table 3.1

Public complaints investigated by the ASA, 1980–86

	Number of complaints received	Number pursued	% of complaints pursued
1980	6533	2209	33.8
1981	6145	1778	29.0
1982	7690	3114	40.5
1983	7548	2911	38.6
1984	7733	2943	38.1
1985	7308	2542	34.8
1986	7820	2489	31.8

Source: ASA *Annual Reports*.

According to the ASA Annual Reports, public complaints about alcohol advertisements are comparatively rare. It is difficult to assess this claim, as the ASA does not record the total number of alcohol complaints received, as opposed to the number selected for investigation. It is possible that a large number of complaints about alcohol advertisements are received, but the proportion investigated is lower than average. This is unlikely, however, as all regulatory agencies report a similar lack of public concern about alcohol advertising.

In addition to investigating public complaints, the ASA monitors advertisements on a systematic basis. The Authority analyses a representative sample of publications and conducts a number of spot checks on certain product categories, including alcoholic drinks. The monitoring exercises have produced no evidence of widespread breaches of the Code by alcohol advertisers. In 1986, for example, over 550 advertisements for alcohol drinks were scrutinised and only one gave rise to concern (ASA,

1987). This is in marked contrast to the claims made by many public health campaigners, who believe that some companies consistently breach the BCAP by aiming alcohol advertisements at young people (Action on Alcohol Abuse, 1986).

The effectiveness of self regulation

The codes of practice that govern alcohol advertising are similar in content, but differ in the way they are administered and in the sanctions available to the regulatory authorities. Advertisements cannot be transmitted on broadcast and cable television unless cleared by the IBA or Cable Authority. Videotex is much more difficult to control, because of the nature of electronic information systems. In serious cases, the VIA would advise members to obstruct public access to offending information, but some time would elapse between the initial complaint and action being taken to enforce the VIA's ruling. The only other sanctions available to the VIA are to persuade publishers of videotex directories and system operators to exclude offenders.

The ASA faces similar problems in relation to the non-electronic media. The Authority can publicise the names of recalcitrants in their monthly reports and require publishers to reject offending advertisements. An advertisement could be seen by thousands of people before being withdrawn, however, and the possibility of adverse publicity may not deter the minority of advertisers who are determined to gain a competitive advantage by going beyond the restrictions embodied in the Code. The ASA monthly case reports have a limited circulation amongst the general public, and media notices do not affect those publishers who are not members of one of the trade associations. This includes the publishers of 'soft-porn' magazines, who are not members of the Periodical Publishers Association (DGFT, 1978). In the early 1980s, several soft-porn magazines had audited circulations in excess of 300,000 and a high proportion of the advertising was for alcoholic drinks. In these cases, the only recourse is to complain directly to the publisher, or approach the DGFT, who can seek an Order in the High Court restraining publication.

Codes of practice are only effective if they are widely observed. There is considerable disagreement about whether alcohol advertisers break the rules as a matter of routine. The regulatory authorities believe there is little cause for concern, while public health campaigners claim there is widespread evasion and non-compliance. The debate is difficult to resolve as there is little empirical evidence. There has been no independent review of the enforcement of the IBA Code and only two independent evaluations of the work of the ASA, both of which were conducted in the 1970s and neither of which examined alcohol advertising in any detail. In 1974, an investigation conducted by the Consumers' Association on behalf of the Bureau Européen des Unions de Consommateurs found that 14 per cent of advertisements in the British national press appeared to be in breach of the BCAP (BEUC, 1974). In 1978, the OFT found that the failure rate in national publications had remained at 13 per cent, in spite of the re-organisation of the ASA in 1974 following the BEUC report (Director General of Fair Trading, 1978). The majority of infringements discovered by the OFT were relatively minor, but the proportion of expensive, full-page advertisements that violated the Code was significantly higher. The OFT considered that 17 per cent of all large advertisements, that is those covering one quarter page or more, were in breach of the Code. The ASA did not accept these figures, believing that the proportion of gross violations of the Code was nearer to one or two per cent of all printed advertisements (ASA, 1979).

The small number of complaints reported by all regulatory bodies might appear to support the claim that alcohol advertisers observe the rules conscientiously. At the very least they seem to demonstrate little public dissatisfaction. The low number of complaints about alcohol advertisements does not, however, necessarily mean that the public are satisfied with existing advertising practices. Complaint statistics are not a reliable indicator of public dissatisfaction, because complaining is an activity that imposes costs on the individual and tends to be reserved for expensive purchases where consumers have suffered directly (Pickering and Cousins, 1986). For example, the ASA receive the greatest number of complaints about advertisements for cars, holidays and computers (ASA, 1986).

Public attitudes to alcohol advertising generally are not well documented. In contrast with the many polls that have been conducted on tobacco advertising, public opinion on alcohol advertising has rarely been canvassed. The data that exist do not suggest that a large proportion of the public find alcohol advertising offensive, or believe that its regulation would be effective. For example, a 1978 MORI survey for the Brewers Society presented respondents with suggestions of 'ways in which the levels of drunkenness could be reduced' and asked them which would be effective. Only ten per cent thought that a ban on advertisements for drink on television would be effective, nine per cent thought tighter controls on how drink can be advertised would be effective and seven per cent favoured a ban on all advertisements for drinks. A repeat poll in 1981 produced similar responses. Another MORI poll in 1980 asked respondents whether they would support or oppose a series of policy options. Of the sample, 46 per cent said they would support a ban on alcohol advertisements on television, but only 29 per cent supported a total ban on all advertising. Research conducted by the North Western Regional Health Authority asked respondents whether they thought various policy options for the prevention of alcohol abuse were 'a good idea'. Different types of advertising policy received quite different responses. For example, 72 per cent thought that alcohol advertising should be banned in cinemas where children's films were being shown, and 70 per cent thought that alcohol advertisements should be taxed and the proceeds used for health education. However, only 40 per cent thought that it was a good idea to ban alcohol advertisements on television. Similar findings were apparent in Wood's survey *Beliefs About Alcohol* (1986) in which 37 per cent thought it would be a good idea to impose a ban on television advertising for alcohol, whilst 46 per cent thought it unnecessary.

The current self-regulatory system applies to advertising, but not to sales promotion and sponsorship. The absence of controls over the practice of sports sponsorship, in particular, is a serious deficiency. Although the alcoholic drink industry is now one of the main sources of sponsorship funds for British sports organisations, there has been nothing to parallel the campaign against the tobacco companies' involvement in sports sponsorship. Individual sportsmen and women have objected to contracts that oblige them to promote alcoholic drinks, but the Central Council for Physical Recreation and other sporting organisations are firmly opposed to any attempt to restrict sponsorship. There is no voluntary agreement controlling sports sponsorship by the brewers and distillers as there is between the Government and the tobacco industry. This is discussed in Chapter 4. Neither are there clauses in any of the Codes of Advertising Practice specifically forbidding an association between alcohol and sport, although there are provisions that forbid an association with 'physical performance'.

The Brewers Society recommends that members apply the principles of the advertising codes when arranging sponsorship. It has also recommended that members avoid the sponsorship of motor racing. The Brewers Society cannot force members to follow these recommendations, however, and individual brewers have advertised their association with football teams in ways which clearly flout the spirit of the advertising codes. If the presentation of alcohol is considered an important component in prevention policy, then the question of associating healthy sporting activities with alcoholic drinks would need to be reconsidered.

EUROPEAN ADVERTISING POLICY

In the preceding section, prevention policy was discussed in relation to the United Kingdom's self-regulatory system for controlling advertising. This section considers the implications of European Community (EC) policy for national advertising controls.

The European Commission is seeking to standardise the present variety of European advertising regulations in order to remove any barriers to the establishment of a common market for broadcasting by 1992. There have been a number of attempts to persuade members of the EC to adopt standardised advertising controls. In 1970, the International Code of Advertising Practice was recommended for use in the EC by the European Council of Ministers. The International Code has either been adopted, or used as the basis for a national advertising code, in most of the 21 countries represented on the European Council. The machinery of enforcement is remarkably similar in each country. Complaints are considered by a tripartite body composed of advertisers, agencies and media representatives. In Denmark, Italy, France and the UK, the advertising interests are joined by members from outside the industry, such as representatives of consumer organisations, while in Belgium and the Netherlands they are not.

The national codes vary in terms of comprehensiveness, some making no specific references to alcohol. However, wines and spirits are covered by a separate International Code of Ethics for Advertising Wines and Spirits, adopted by the trade in the 22 countries represented by the Fédération Internationale des Industries et du Commerce en gros des Vins, Spiritueux, Eaux-de-vie et Liqueurs, or International Union of Wine, Spirits, Brandy and Liqueur Industrialists and Wholesalers, usually known by the initials of the French title, FIVS. This organisation, which was set up to defend the commercial interests of the companies involved, covers the wine-producing members of the EC, together with other major producers such as Australia and the USA. The Code was submitted to the European Commission and approved in 1980.

The timing of the FIVS initiative, and the inclusion of a statement opposing any restriction on the advertising of spirits on television, may have been an attempt to anticipate and forestall any regulation of advertising by the European Commission in the light of the current plans for Direct Broadcasting Satellites (DBS). The advent of DBS means that transnational corporations are able to circumvent the national regulation of advertising.

Few advertising campaigns are designed with an international audience in mind; beer and cider advertisements are aimed at local and regional audiences. Nevertheless, evidence from countries that receive foreign television programmes already suggests that some sections of the alcohol industry are quite prepared to use international broadcasting to evade national restrictions. Austria does not permit the advertising of wine on television, for example, but cannot prevent Bavarian stations beaming wine advertisements across the border with the prices quoted in Austrian schillings (*Sunday Times*, 1982).

In the early 1990s, the satellite broadcasts that will be received in Britain, in addition to those transmitted by the satellites allocated to Britain, are likely to originate in France, Ireland and Germany. All of these countries have a code of practice governing television advertising and the provisions are fairly similar. Like most EC countries, they ban the advertising of cigarettes, matrimonial agencies and fortune tellers. There are some inconsistencies; the Federal Republic of Germany permits the advertising of spirits, while Ireland and the UK do not. French television used to prohibit the advertising of pastis, whisky, vodka, gin and geneva, while permitting rum and cognac. In 1980 the European Court of Justice ruled that this was discriminatory. Now, under the 'Diverse Measures for Social Order' legislation passed in 1987, France prohibits all television advertising of alcoholic drinks.

In an attempt to resolve these anomalies before satellite television becomes popular, the Council of Europe produced another Code of Conduct in February 1984. This Code was approved by the governments of all 21 member countries. Not only are advertisers bound by the laws of the country of transmission, but by the laws of any other country which can receive the broadcast (*The Times*, 1984).

The Council of Europe's Code was criticised by many broadcasting companies for being too lax. The focus was on formal legislation when many countries have adopted self-regulatory systems. It would not be an offence under the Council's scheme to broadcast advertisements that contravene national codes of conduct. As a result, the broadcasting authorities, including the British IBA, have endorsed an alternative code produced by the European Broadcasting Union (EBU). The EBU, better known as Eurovision, has instructed its members to strengthen their internal rules to avoid the international broadcasting of cigarette advertisements. Restrictions on the advertising of alcohol are also to be strengthened, where necessary, in order to avoid contravening the regulations in individual European nations (IBA, 1984b). Negotiations are presently continuing in the Council of Europe over a convention on Transfrontier Broadcasting and these negotiations may well form the basis for an international agreement.

The European Commission favours statutory controls over advertising. The Commission produced a draft directive in 1975, requiring all member states to adopt statutory controls over unfair and misleading advertising. In Britain, the Advertising Association led a campaign against the European directive, claiming that the principle of self-regulation would be destroyed if consumers had recourse to a judicial system (*The Times*, 1978). In 1980, the British Government assured the ASA that they would not agree to any European regulations that 'undermined' the present system (ASA, 1981, p.6). The final draft of the directive on misleading advertising, binding on all members of the EC, was adopted on 30 June 1984 after ten years of negotiations (Council of the European Communities, 1984). The British Government succeeded in its bid to have the directive amended to protect the self-regulatory system, and the Department of Trade and Industry has found ways to comply with the directive by giving the statutory responsibilities for investigating public complaints to the DGFT, the IBA and the Cable Authority, which will cause minimum disruption to established procedures.

However, pressure for European standardisation is intensifying. The European Commission sees the present patchwork of advertising codes and regulations as a barrier for the free movement of goods and services across European frontiers. In 1984, the Commission issued a Green Paper, *Television Without Frontiers*, which recommended, amongst other things, a common approach to controls over tobacco and alcohol advertising (European Commission, 1984, paras. 31, 32). As the majority of member states banned tobacco advertising on television, the Commission argued that it would be 'consistent with the health policies of the Community to make this prohibition general in all Member States'. Only a minority of states prohibited alcohol advertising, however, and the Commission held that this was not the best approach for the Community 'at the present time'. It would be better to develop, 'at Community Level', a code of practice to define unacceptable forms of alcohol advertising (European Commission, 1984, para. 32).

A revised draft directive outlining the code for alcohol advertising was issued in 1988 (European Commission, 1988, article 10). The code is less extensive than any of the British codes, containing six clauses against the IBA's eleven. Member states will be free to impose stricter standards than this, or even to ban alcohol advertising, but only in relation to broadcasts originating on their own territories. It will not be possible to exclude advertising on satellite channels. This means that by the 21st century it will be impractical, if not impossible, for individual member states to have national policies on alcohol advertising which differ from those favoured by the majority of EC members.

ALTERNATIVE ALCOHOL ADVERTISING POLICIES

The preceding sections included a detailed description of the UK's self-regulatory system of advertising control and the way in which new codes of practice were developed in response to technological innovation. One widely canvassed alternative to the present system has been a statutory ban on alcohol advertising. There is, however, a range of possible alternatives, including strengthening existing voluntary codes or some other form of regulation such as taxing advertising expenditures. In this section, alternative advertising policies and their economic effects are considered.

To evaluate any change in advertising policy, it is necessary to consider what benefits such a change in policy would bring and at what cost. A first step in this process is to examine the objectives of advertising policies. Existing alcohol advertising policy described in the first section has been concerned with controlling information, rather than with influencing alcohol consumption directly. The proponents of an advertising ban suggest that it would reduce alcohol consumption. In this section, we review the existing evidence on the link between alcohol advertising and consumption, and the relevance of this research to predicting the outcome of a complete advertising ban, or of alternative policies. The advertising industry and the trade have argued that consumers would not benefit from a ban, but instead would lose valuable information. A number of other concerns have been expressed on the possible effects of a ban on the advertising and alcohol industries. The potential costs of different advertising polices are also discussed in this section.

The relationship between advertising, alcohol consumption and policy options

Measuring the effect of advertising on consumption poses a number of problems, and great care is necessary in the evaluation of material presented by both health and trade lobbies. Comparing the trends in consumption of alcohol and levels of advertising can be very misleading since such simple correlations do not allow for the effects of other variables on consumption, such as price and income. One method which has been used to attempt to isolate advertising effects is to construct demand models, as described in Chapter 2 of the first volume of this series (Maynard and Tether, 1989).

There are a number of particular difficulties in attempting to measure the effect of advertising within these models. A major problem is that of obtaining reliable data on advertising expenditures. Unlike data on consumption, prices and income, no official advertising statistics are collected. The data available from private surveys cover press and TV advertising only. Cinema and poster advertising is excluded, as is expenditure on sponsorship. A second concern is to specify how advertising affects consumption and whether the determining factor is the level of expenditure or some volume measure of advertising messages received. Also, it may be argued that the effect of advertising can last more than one period, so that some measure of the stock of advertising should be used. Another more technical concern is the direction of causality between alcohol consumption and advertising. Firms may set advertising budgets in line with sales and hence consumption may be a factor in determining advertising expenditure. If advertising has an effect on consumption and vice versa, feedback effects between advertising and consumption occur. Misleading results on the effects of advertising could then be obtained from estimates of demand models which did not take this feedback into account.

A number of studies have included advertising variables in their examination of the determinants of alcohol consumption. McGuinness (1980) specified a model in which total per capita alcohol consumption was related to the prices of beers, spirits and wine, income, the number of licensed premises and to the advertising of beer, spirits, wine and cider. Advertising was measured in this study as the volume of messages. In this analysis, only the coefficient for spirits advertising was found to be significant, and this coefficient was used to predict that a one per cent fall in spirits advertising in 1975 would have resulted in a 0.13 per cent fall in the consumption of alcohol. A fall of one per cent in all advertising expenditure in 1975 was predicted to reduce alcohol consumption within the range of 0.2 to 1.0 fluid ounces of pure alcohol per person, other things being equal.

The specification of the McGuinness model was, however, criticised by Walsh (1982) who re-estimated the model for beer, spirits and wines, cider and perry consumption separately. In each of the equations, the separate advertising variations for the different types of drink were included. This meant that the model allowed for both own- and cross-beverage alcohol advertising effects. It could be hypothesised, for example, that a rise in spirits advertising with no change in beer advertising would increase spirits consumption, but lower beer consumption. Walsh estimated the model in two forms, using alcohol consumption measured by volume and also by expenditure. The results suggested that beer advertising did influence beer consumption, the coefficient on the variable being significant in both the volume and expenditure equations. The elasticities for volume and expenditure measures for 1975 were 0.10 and 0.12 respectively. Similarly the coefficient of spirits advertising was found to be statistically significant with 1975 elasticities being 0.21 for volume and 0.25 for expenditure. These estimated elasticities imply that a ten per cent rise in spirits advertising would increase the volume of alcohol consumed as spirits by 2.1 per cent and spirits expenditure by 2.5 per cent. For wine, however, the level of wine advertising was not found to be significantly related to wine consumption, but there were significant cross-beverage advertising effects.

Using all the coefficients on these cross-advertising effects, Walsh calculated that a ten per cent increase in the volume of beer advertising would increase beer consumption by one per cent, but lower spirits and wine consumption by 0.5 per cent and 2.0 per cent respectively, with the overall effect on alcohol consumption being only 0.2 per cent. A ten per cent rise in spirits advertising, in contrast, was calculated to raise both spirits and wine consumption (two per cent and three per cent respectively) and lead to an overall increase in alcohol consumption by one per cent.

McGuinness (1983) later re-estimated his model in a disaggregated form but obtained fewer significant coefficients on the advertising terms. Beer advertising again had a statistically significant coefficient in the equation for beer consumption. The 1979 estimate of the elasticities suggested that a ten per cent rise in beer advertising would increase the volume of beer consumption by 1.6 per cent. Cider advertising was, however, found to be negatively related to beer consumptions, although the coefficient was small. The 1979 elasticity was estimated at -0.02. For wine, none of the coefficients on the advertising terms were significant. For spirits consumption, the wine advertising coefficient was significant and suggested that in 1979 a ten per cent rise in wine advertising would have reduced spirits consumption by 1.5 per cent.

Another study which examined the influence of advertising on different alcoholic drinks was carried out by Duffy (1983). This study differed in a number of ways from the work of McGuinness and Walsh. Quarterly data were used instead of annual data, and no licensing variable was included. Advertising was also treated in a different way. Duffy included in each of his equations the influence of own advertising, for example, beer advertising in the beer equation, and also a term measuring all other advertising. A drop in all other advertising, while beer advertising remained constant, might be hypothesised to increase beer consumption.

In Duffy's model, beer advertising was found to be significantly related to beer consumption, although the elasticity was small at 0.07 for beer advertising only and 0.09 for beer advertising relative to all other advertising. There was no evidence that advertising affects wine consumption and the evidence for spirits consumption was mixed. When the model was re-estimated to allow for the effect a change in the level of consumption might have on advertising, i.e. a simultaneous effect, the coefficients for wine advertising were still found to be insignificant. Significant effects for both beer and spirits were found with elasticities of 0.2 and 0.1 approximately.

The Duffy and McGuinness models were re-estimated using annual data and subjected to statistical evaluation (Godfrey, 1988). This study focused on the role of licensing and is described in more detail in Chapter 6. The results as they relate to the effects of advertising on consumption are now described.

For the volume measure of spirits consumption, there was some evidence that spirits advertising has some influence on spirits consumption with significant elasticities, evaluated for 1980, being in the range 0.18 to 0.25, suggesting that a ten per cent decline of spirits advertising would reduce spirits consumption by at most 2.5 per cent. There was no evidence that the level of the rest of advertising significantly influenced the demand for spirits in the Duffy model, although, in general, the signs on the coefficient were negative. Nor were any significant cross-beverage effects found in the acceptable forms of the McGuinness model.

The results for spirits expenditure indicated no significant effects of advertising on consumption and the elasticities estimated were very small in value. There was some evidence of cross-beverage advertising effects with significant negative elasticity of beer advertising in one equation (-0.34), and a positive and significant value for wine advertising in another (0.26).

The results for wine volume, as with previous studies, cast some doubt on the role of advertising on the demand for wine. No significant advertising elasticities for either wine or other advertising variables were found and the estimated elasticities were small. In contrast, there were significant coefficients when consumption was measured in terms of expenditure. The largest 1980 elasticity estimate was 0.56. Some cross-beverage advertising effects were also found in the McGuinness models, both beer and spirits advertising, in general, being negatively associated with wine expenditure, the significant coefficients yielding elasticity estimates of -0.24 and -0.25 respectively.

In most other studies, the relationship between advertising and consumption seemed to be strongest for beer consumption. For both expenditure and volume measures, feedback with consumption was detected for the advertising and licensing variables. Re-estimating the models with the appropriate techniques yielded coefficients that were, in general, imprecisely estimated and therefore the effects of advertising on beer consumption cannot be accurately quantified. It is, however, interesting to note that, in some forms of the Duffy model, the 'rest of advertising term' was found to have a significantly negative effect on demand. This suggests that if advertising on goods other than beer rises, beer consumption would fall.

Duffy has also estimated other models of alcohol demand. The effects of advertising on different types of wines and spirits were examined (Duffy, 1982). The results suggest that wine advertising does influence the different types of wine products, that is, heavy wine, light wine, sparkling wine and British wine. The coefficients on the ratio of own-advertising to other forms of wine advertising were significant in all four equations, but were small. For different types of spirits expenditure on advertising was found to be significant for whisky and brandy, but not for gin and vodka.

In another study which concentrated on the interrelationships between the demand for beer, spirits, and wine, cider and perry, Duffy (1987) estimated a sub-system demand model including advertising terms. Duffy found small advertising elasticities and considered the cross-product effects of advertising negligible. During the period of his study, 1963-1983, beer advertising grew relatively more than spirits and wine advertising and all other advertising. From his estimates, Duffy suggests beer consumption has been stimulated by the relative rise in its own advertising and also the relative decline in spirits and wine advertising, but the overall effect is small. On average it was less than 0.01 per cent per annum. The rate of growth of spirits consumption suffered from both the relative decline in its own advertising and the rise of beer advertising. Overall, taking into account non-alcohol advertising, Duffy concluded that drinks advertising appeared to have raised the growth rates for all types of alcoholic drink at the expense of other goods, but the effects were quite small. Selvanathan (1987) also included advertising terms for the different types of alcoholic drinks within a sub-system demand model. He concluded that advertising had an insignificant effect on the consumption of alcohol as a whole.

These empirical results are supported with evidence from other countries. Bourgeois and Barnes (1979), for example, found some evidence that total alcohol advertising has effects on beer consumption in Canada. For wine, the broadcast advertising variable was found to be positive and significantly related to the consumption of wine, but the coefficient for print advertising was not significant. For spirits, both print and broadcast variables were found to be significant, but the print variable was negatively related to consumption. As the authors state, these results suggest some degree of substitution between beer and spirits, and the need to disaggregate the advertising terms.

It should be noted, when considering these reported results, that statistical insignificance does not necessarily imply that the variable in question has no effect on consumption, but merely that it is imprecisely estimated. In general, however, there is some agreement on the effects of advertising from all empirical studies. It cannot be concluded that advertising does not influence consumption, but the results discussed above would lead to the conclusion that any effect is small. All own-beverage elasticities were considerably less than one and imply that a ten per cent reduction in advertising would result in consumption falling by less than three per cent. There is also some evidence of cross-beverage advertising effects which suggests that advertising policies for each beverage cannot be considered in isolation. A number of difficulties arise in predicting the effects of alternative advertising policies. For example, estimating the effects of no advertising expenditure, that is, a ban, is outside the normal range of predictions from such demand models and a simple extrapolation from advertising elasticities would not allow for any additional effects of a ban which may alter the social acceptability of drinking.

In some other countries, researchers have tried to measure directly the effects of advertising regulations. Ornstein and Hannsens (1985) included four advertising control dummies in their analysis of the demand for alcohol in the USA. Two controls were related to regulation concerning the prohibition of poster advertising and of retailer novelties. The third and fourth type of regulation considered the prohibition of price advertising on posters or in print. For spirits, the last two dummies were found to be significant and positive, and the authors' finding supported earlier conclusions that, in the absence of price advertising, prices were approximately three per cent higher. There were some differences in the results for beer. The poster-price advertising dummy was significant and positive, but not the print-price advertising dummy. The other two dummies were insignificant.

Hoadley, Fuchs and Holder (1984) also considered the effects of different advertising control laws across US States on spirits consumption. Their conclusion was that the 'restrictions on mass media advertising, on novelty items and on exterior signs were found to have no discernible effect on consumption, while limits on the use of price in advertisements seemed to have a small (if any) effect'.

Two Canadian studies have considered the effect of alcohol advertising bans in particular Provinces and concluded that the bans did not have an effect on consumption. Smart and Cutler (1976) outline, however, the difficulties of implementing an advertising ban and evaluating its effects over a short period. One problem is the difficulty of controlling advertising from other areas, or other countries. With new technologies, as discussed in the earlier part of this chapter, such cross-boundary effects become even more difficult to control. Any change in advertising policy also promotes considerable media coverage and publicity against restrictions. How this increase in media coverage effects consumption and therefore counteracts the possible effects of an advertising ban are difficult to determine. The authors of this study also point to other factors which may hinder the effectiveness of an advertising ban. They noted that, in the case of British Columbia's legislation, there was some evidence of both a lack of community support for the ban and an uncertainty that the ban would be retained if the Government changed. Similar factors were found in an evaluation of the Manitoba ban on beer advertising in the electronic and print media (Ogborne and Smart, 1980). This ban was for one beverage, beer, and did not affect out-of-state material. Such case studies indicate the difficulties in framing legislation to have the desired outcome, as was described in Chapter 1. Further, such legislation cannot be guaranteed to be effective unless there is strong and public concern about the issue. Although there have been some empirical studies on the link between advertising and consumption, there has been less attention paid to the possible relationship between advertising and alcohol-related problems. In one US study, a model linking alcohol consumption, alcoholism and alcohol-related mortality was developed (Schweitzer et al., 1983). The results of this study suggested that a prohibition of advertising would result in a shift from beer consumption to spirits consumption, and this shift would decrease alcoholism by over 15 per cent. The details of this model have been criticised (Maynard, 1983), but developments of models of this kind could prove useful in policy analysis (Godfrey and Maynard, 1988).

Most studies of the effects of alcohol advertising have considered the effects of the whole population and there has been less analysis of particular groups which may be of policy concern. Strickland (1983) used a survey of teenagers to investigate advertising within the framework of social learning theory. Advertising was, however, found to have only a 'meagre' effect on the level of consumption. Other studies have been concerned not only with direct advertising, but also with the portrayal of alcohol in the media. How such portrayal affects social learning is, of course, very difficult to determine. Stricter advertising policies may change media portrayal and this is one of the effects of changing policy which cannot necessarily be predicted from existing studies.

Current policy has been aimed at the information content of advertising; the relationship between advertising, information and health behaviour is even more difficult to quantify than the relationship between advertising and consumption. The results from the studies reviewed in this section, therefore, only provide limited evidence for evaluating alternative policies.

Costs of advertising policies

If the benefits of an advertising policy are uncertain, so are the potential costs to consumers, governments, the alcohol industry and the advertising industry. The advertising industry, in particular, has emphasised the possible detrimental effects of an advertising ban (Waterson, 1981). In this section, the costs of alternative advertising policies to different groups and how these costs influence the policy debate are considered.

The advertising industry. One of the largest potential losers from a complete ban, or restrictions, on advertising expenditures is the advertising industry. As can be seen from Table 3.2, alcohol advertising expenditure on press and TV has grown substantially over the last 20 years, both in real terms and as a percentage of total advertising on consumer goods. In 1984, alcohol advertising accounted for approximately ten per cent of all advertising, but only seven per cent of all consumers' expenditure. Of the total, the largest proportion it still spent on beer. Of the total alcohol advertising expenditure in 1984, some 83 per cent was spent on television advertising. The imposition of a TV ban on beer, cider and wine advertisements could have serious consequences for TV companies and the advertising industry.

Table 3.2

Press and TV alcohol advertising expenditure 1963–87

Year	Total alcohol advertising expenditure—constant prices (1980) £m	Advertising on alcohol as a percentage of total advertising on consumer goods %
1963	52.35	6.2
1965	52.80	5.9
1970	59.71	8.0
1975	61.26	9.9
1980	75.96	9.0
1981	78.11	8.5
1982	94.78	8.6
1983	114.57	9.4
1984	110.35	9.6
1985	100.40	8.3
1986	111.00	9.4
1987	119.91	9.7

Source: *Statistical Review of Press and TV Advertising,* Legion Publishing Services; *Quarterly Digest of Advertising Expenditure,* Media Expenditure Analysis Ltd.

The advertising industry has, however, not only been concerned with the possible loss of advertising revenue from alcohol. It has been suggested that a ban may have a domino effect and lead to further restrictions for other commodities. The advent of satellite broadcasting and computer-based technology also bring uncertainty to the advertising and media industries. It is, therefore, not surprising that the Advertising Association has in the past played such a prominent role in organising opposition to advertising restrictions and will continue its lobbying activities.

The alcohol trade. Forecasts of the effect on consumption of reducing advertising expenditure, or altering the information contained in the advertisements discussed in the previous section, are calculated assuming everything else is held constant, under the economists' 'ceteris paribus' assumption. In the face of advertising controls, however, producers may well change their behaviour which in turn may affect consumption. The main reason that individual firms advertise is in order to increase sales and profits. Clearly a firm that is efficient in an economic sense will maximise profits and to do this will increase advertising to the point where the marginal revenue from advertising, that is the extra profit obtained from increased sales, equals the marginal cost, that is the cost of the extra advertising.

Advertising decisions by any one firm may, however, be influenced by the advertising of rival firms. Clarke (1985) suggests that the association between the number of firms and advertising intensity may be comprised of two offsetting effects. Increased numbers of rival firms may imply greater price competition and less advertising intensity. Conversely, as the number of firms fall, advertising may increase. Increasing concentration, however, also implies that firms will take more account of the actions of rival firms. Any of the firms will realise that an increase in advertising would increase their own sales at the expense of their rivals who would then likewise increase advertising. Knowing such effects would occur may result in less advertising in markets with only a few firms.

It is important to explore the relationship between advertising and competition in order to predict the effects of any advertising control policy. Governments may be concerned that high levels of advertising will affect competition between firms and, therefore, health and competition policies may not necessarily conflict. The alcohol industry and, in particular, the brewers are large advertisers. The brewing industry is also concentrated and dominated by six large groups, although the re-emergence of regional and small local breweries has decreased the concentration of the industry in recent years (Booth, Hardman and Hartley, 1986).

If the advertising in the alcohol market is assumed to be influencing competition, there would be an economic case for advertising controls irrespective of health concerns. There would be two possible objectives of such an advertising policy. The first would be to correct for any undue distortion of consumers' preferences by excessive advertising; this would have the effect of reducing demand for the product. The second purpose of the policy would be to increase competition in the market. Such competition would be expected to reduce prices and any monopoly profits. If prices were reduced, however, demand would be expected to rise. The overall effect on consumption from these two offsetting effects will depend on the relative sizes of the overall advertising and price elasticities for the product.

The second assumption is that firms in the alcohol industries are not advertising excessively and are not enjoying monopoly profits. In this situation, a restriction of advertising may hinder competition and may raise prices in the long run. Hence such a policy would not, in these circumstances, have adverse consequences for health objectives. In the absence of competition by advertising, however, firms may compete on price or other non-price means. If an advertising policy has the effect of reducing costs, it may be acceptable to existing firms. This may help explain the willingness of the spirits industry to agree not to advertise on TV. Also, as discussed in Chapter 1, such agreements may limit competition from overseas competitors. Further, any restriction on alcohol advertising may well differentially affect the on- and off-licence markets. The ability of brewers to tie their tenants to their own brands, for example, may be stronger if advertising is severely restricted. In this situation, a health policy may be in conflict with a more general industry policy designed to promote competition.

Whatever the market situation, producers may mitigate any effects of an advertising policy. One issue is the likelihood of greater price competition. This possibility may suggest that an advertising policy cannot be pursued alone and, for example, may need to be accompanied by a tax policy. An alternative policy is to limit the effect which any reduction in advertising may have in reducing manufacturers costs, for example, by taxing alcohol expenditures. Advertising is, however, only one form of marketing and, as Chapter 4 shows, when faced with advertising restrictions firms may react by increasing other marketing activities, such as the number of sales personnel or the range of promotional activities.

The form of the policy change may have additional consequences. As was discussed in Chapter 1, the producers may gain additional benefits from the close collaboration with each other, and with the Government, arising from the negotiations involved in voluntary agreements. They also may be able to limit the adverse consequences for their profitability. This will not necessarily conflict with a health policy and the government may gain other health benefits from the negotiations. It is clear that the industry prefers voluntary agreements to legislation, and an advertising and sponsorship ban may well severely curtail their commercial activities.

Consumers. The advertising industry has claimed that an advertising ban would deprive consumers of important product information, restrict consumer choice by leading to a smaller number of brands and, in particular, make it difficult to introduce low alcohol drinks (Advertising Association, 1987). On the other hand, consumers may be considered to gain from enforced codes of practice concerning the contents of advertisements, especially if future codes contained directives to provide information on the strengths and contents of drinks, and also the harmful effects of misuse.

Costs and benefits to consumers are likely to vary between policy alternatives. Advertising bans may result in lower consumption and less serious alcohol-related problems. Also, with tighter advertising codes or increased regulation on the content of advertisements, consumers may gain information and still enjoy considerable choice among brands.

Governments. As discussed in Chapter 1, regulation involves political and monetary costs for governments. The present system of voluntary codes has involved few costs to government, the burden being borne by the trade, advertising industry and broadcasting authorities. Present policy has concentrated on the deregulation of industry, part of the support for this emphasis being the argument that one of the hidden costs of regulation is that regulators become captured by the regulated (Stigler, 1971; and Chapter 5 of this volume). Alternative advertising polices would mean greater involvement by governments, and possible increases and shifts in the burden of administrative costs.

Governments will be concerned with political implications of policy changes. For example, the changes in information technology described in the first section suggest that individual national governments may lack the means to control advertising across all media. This lack of control may affect a government's credibility if the public regarded it as being ineffective. The importance of public opinion in enabling policy change and determining its effectiveness was illustrated by the Canadian experience of the advertising ban in British Columbia (Smart and Cutler, 1976).

CONCLUSION

An examination of the development of current advertising policies and of the possible effects of alternatives suggests that there are a number of impediments to the use of advertising controls as part of a co-ordinated approach to the prevention of alcohol-related problems. There is little evidence that the present self-regulatory system has prevented either misleading information or alcohol-related problems. The effectiveness of alternative advertising policies to control information or consumption is also subject to debate. Empirical studies suggest that any decreases in advertising expenditure will at best result in small decreases in consumption, although the effect of a complete ban is uncertain.

One major impediment to change is uncertainty about the net benefits of alternative policies. Costs and benefits are especially difficult to evaluate when the objectives of alternative policies are unclear and information and consumption objectives may conflict. Advertising is only one form of marketing, so that restricting marketing in one way may induce producers either to circumvent agreements or to find alternative means to fulfil their own objectives of increasing market share and profits.

Technological innovation and the EC goal of achieving one internal market by 1992 present further obstacles to the development of a comprehensive national advertising policy. Satellite broadcasting and computer-based technology are extremely difficult to control and policy making competence has shifted to the European Commission. The European Commission is attempting to standardise national advertising controls but it has proved extremely difficult to persuade all member states to adopt strict controls over alcohol advertising. However, there is an increasing awareness of alcohol-related problems and their costs throughout the European Commission, which may help to minimise these impediments.

The evolution of controls on tobacco advertising and sponsorship, with the growing acknowledgement of the adverse effects of smoking, is considered in the following chapter.

References

Action on Alcohol Abuse, (1986), *An Agenda for Action on Alcohol*, Action on Alcohol Abuse, London.

Advertising Association, (1987), *The Relationship Between Advertising and Alcohol Misuse,* Submission to the Ministerial Group, Advertising Association, London.

Advertising Standards Authority (ASA), (1979), *16th Annual Report*, ASA, London.

Advertising Standards Authority (ASA), (1981), *18th Annual Report*, ASA, London.

Advertising Standards Authority (ASA), (1985), *Annual Report (1984-85)*, ASA, London.

Advertising Standards Authority (ASA), (1986), *Annual Report (1985-86)*, ASA, London.

Advertising Standards Authority (ASA), (1987), *Annual Report (1986-87)*, ASA, London.

Booth, M., Hardman, G. and Hartley, K., (1986), 'Data Note 6, The UK alcohol and tobacco industries', *British Journal of Addiction*, 81, 825-830.

Bourgeois, J.C. and Barnes, J.G., (1979), 'Does advertising increase alcohol consumption?', *Journal of Advertising*, 19 (4), 19-29.

Bureau Européen des Unions des Consummateurs (BEUC), (1974), *A study of advertising in the U.K. and the Federal Republic of Germany*, Paper prepared for the Environment and Consumer Protection Services of the EEC, BEUC, London.

Cable Authority, (1987), *Code of practice on programme sponsorship*, Cable Authority, London.

Clarke, R., (1985), *Industrial Economics*, Blackwell, Oxford.

Code of Advertising Practice Committee (CAP), (1985), *British Code of Advertising Practice*, 7th edition, CAP, London.

Council of the European Communities, (1984), 'Directive on misleading advertising', *Official Journal of the European Communities*, L250, 19 September, 17-20.

Department of Health and Social Security (DHSS), (1981), *Drinking Sensibly*, HMSO, London.

Director General of Fair Trading (DGFT), (1978), *Review of the U.K. self-regulatory system of advertising control: a report by the Director General of Fair Trading*, Office of Fair Trading, London.

Duffy, M., (1982), 'An econometric study of the demand for various types of wines and spirits in the United Kingdom', *International Journal of Advertising*, 2, 245-264.

Duffy, M., (1983), 'The demand for alcoholic drink in the United Kingdom, 1963-1968', *Applied Economics*, 15, 125-140.

Duffy, M., (1987), 'Advertising and the inter-product distribution of demand: a Rotterdam model approach', *European Economic Review*, 31 (5), 1051-1070.

European Commission, (1984), *Television Without Frontiers*, the Green Paper on the establishment of the Common Market for broadcasting, COM(84)300 final/2, European Commission, Brussels.

European Commission, (1988), *Proposals for a council directive ... concerning the pursuit of broadcasting activities*, COM(88)154 final, European Commission, Brussels.

Godfrey, C., (1988), 'Licensing and the demand for alcohol', *Applied Economics*, 20, 1541-1558.

Godfrey, C. and Maynard, A., (1988), 'An economic theory of alcohol consumption and abuse', in Chaudron, D. and Wilkinson, H. (eds.), *Theories of Alcoholism*, Addiction Research Foundation, Toronto.

Henry, H., (1980), 'Advertising alcohol—an ITV view', *British Journal of Alcohol and Alcoholism*, 15, (3), 129-135.

Hoadley, J.F., Fuchs, B.C. and Holder, H.D., (1984), 'The effect of alcohol beverage restrictions on consumption: a 25-year longitudinal analysis', *American Journal of Drug and Alcohol Abuse*, 10 (3), 375-401.

Home Office, (1988), *Broadcasting in the '90s: Competition, Choice and Quality*, Cm.517, HMSO, London.

Independent Broadcasting Authority (IBA), (1984a), *The IBA Code for Teletext Transmissions*, IBA, London.

Independent Broadcasting Authority (IBA), (1984b), *Independent Broadcasting*, IBA, London.

Independent Broadcasting Authority (IBA), (1986), *Independent Radio Advertising Guidelines*, IBA, London.

Independent Broadcasting Authority (IBA), (1987a), *Annual Report and Accounts, 1986-7*, IBA, London.

Independent Broadcasting Authority (IBA), (1987b), *The IBA Code of Advertising Standards and Practice*, IBA, London.

Maynard, A., (1983), 'Modelling alcohol consumption and abuse: the powers and pitfalls of economic techniques', in Grant, M., Plant, M. and Williams, A. (eds.), *Economics and Alcohol*, Croom Helm, London.

Maynard, A. and Tether, P. (eds.), (1989), *The Addiction Market: consumption, production and policy development*, Avebury/Gower, Aldershot.

McGuinness, T., (1980), 'An econometric analysis of total demand for alcoholic beverages in the UK, 1956-1975', *Journal of Industrial Economics*, September, 85-109.

McGuinness, T., (1983), 'The demand for beer, spirits and wine in the UK, 1956-1979', in Grant, M., Plant, M. and Williams, A. (eds.), *Economics and Alcohol*, Croom Helm, London.

MORI Polls, (1978, 1980, 1981).

Ogborne, A.C. and Smart, R.G., (1980), 'Will restrictions on alcohol advertising reduce alcohol consumption?', *British Journal of Addiction*, 75, 293-296.

Ornstein, S.I. and Hanssens, D.M., (1985), 'Alcohol control laws and the consumption of distilled spirits and beer', *Journal of Consumer Research*, 12, 200-213.

Pickering, J. and Cousins, D., (1986), 'The benefits and costs of voluntary codes of practice', *European Journal of Marketing*, 16, (6), 31-44.

Royal College of Physicians, (1987), *A Great and Growing Evil: The Medical Consequences of Alcohol Abuse*, Tavistock, London.

Royal College of Psychiatrists, (1979), *Alcohol and Alcoholism*, Tavistock, London.

Royal College of Psychiatrists, (1986), *Alcohol: Our Favourite Drug*, Tavistock, London.

Schweitzer, S.O., Intriligator, M.D. and Salehi, J., (1983), 'Alcoholism: an econometric model of its cause, its effects and its control', in Grant, M., Plant, M. and Williams, A. (eds.), *Economics and Alcohol*, Croom Helm, London.

Selvanathan, E.A., (1987), *Advertising and Consumption: A New Approach with an Application to Alcohol*, Discussion Paper 87.15, Department of Economics, The University of Western Australia, Perth.

Smart, R.G. and Cutler, R.E., (1976), 'The alcohol advertising ban in British Columbia: problems and effects on beverage consumption', *British Journal of Addiction*, 71, 13-21.

Stigler, G.J., (1971), 'The theory of economic regulation', *Bell Journal of Economics and Management Science*, 2, (1), 3-21.

Strickland, D.E., (1983), 'Advertising exposure, alcohol consumption and misuse of alcohol', in Grant, M., Plant, M. and Williams, A. (eds.), *Economics and Alcohol*, Croom Helm, London.

Sunday Times, (1982), 12 December, 15.

The Times, (1971), 17 March, 1-2.

The Times, (1978), 8 March, 20.

The Times, (1984), 25 February, 4.

Videotex Industry Association (VIA), (1983), *Videotex information providers' code of practice*, VIA, London.

Walsh, B.M., (1982), 'The demand for alcohol in the UK: a comment', *Journal of Industrial Economics*, 30 (4), 439-446.

Waterson, M., (1981), *Advertising and Alcohol Abuse*, Advertising Association, London.

Waterson, M. (ed.), (1987), *Advertising Statistics Yearbook 1987*, Advertising Association, London.

Wood, D., (1986), *Beliefs About Alcohol,* Research Report No.5, Health Education Council, London.

4 Tobacco advertising

PHILIP TETHER AND CHRISTINE GODFREY

Tobacco advertising, like alcohol, is governed by a number of self-regulatory agreements. As well as codes of practice developed between different media and the industry, the government and the tobacco industry have regularly negotiated a number of voluntary agreements concerning advertising, sports sponsorship and product modification. Chapter 1 contains a review of the general advantages of voluntary agreements (compared to legislation) for both the regulators and the regulated. In this chapter, the development of the self-regulatory system for tobacco advertising and sponsorship is outlined, and the specific advantages and disadvantages of this approach for advertising control examined.

The self-regulatory approach to the control of tobacco advertising in the UK is believed to be inadequate by many groups concerned with the health consequences of smoking. These groups argue that such agreements allow manufacturers to continue advertising a dangerous product which is clearly inimical to health and that such advertising sustains and promotes consumption. They demand what they see as the only effective regulation on tobacco advertising—its complete abolition by law. The tobacco companies disagree. They claim that advertising does not lead to increased consumption, but sustains brand shares of the market. As Chapter 3 makes clear, the same claim is made by the manufacturers of alcoholic beverages and in both cases the producers are generally supported in their arguments by the advertising industry.

This chapter examines these rival claims with the aim of clarifying policy alternatives. The first section examines the components of the complex, self-regulatory system governing the advertising of tobacco in the UK, the details of which are little known and little understood by many in the tobacco advertising debate. The second section reviews the available econometric evidence to establish whether self-regulation or the most frequently canvassed alternative, a statutory ban on all tobacco advertising, is likely to have greater net benefits.

THE SELF-REGULATORY SYSTEM

The self-regulatory system governing the advertising and promotion of tobacco products in the UK has seven separate elements embodied in four codes of practice and three voluntary agreements. These components are:

- the Independent Broadcasting Authority (IBA) Code of Advertising Standards and Practice
- the Cable Authority Code
- the Videotex Industry Code
- the British Code of Advertising Practice
- a series of regularly, re-negotiated voluntary agreements between the tobacco industry and government on the advertising and promotion of tobacco products
- a separate, though interlocking, series of agreements on product modifications, and finally,
- a series of voluntary agreements on the sponsorship of sport by tobacco companies in the UK.

However, the provisions of the Cable Authority Code are virtually identical with those of the IBA Code, and the Videotex Industry Code governs material which is not primarily directed at consumers although, as Chapter 3 suggests, it may have implications in the future for alcohol advertising. Broadly, the remaining five components of the self-regulatory system were developed in the 1970s, following a decade of high-profile publicity concerning the dangers of smoking, although elements of this self-regulatory system were in place earlier.

The complex, self-regulatory system for tobacco goods is the product of on-going bargaining processes involving a variety of groups and organisations with conflicting concerns and interest in tobacco advertising. Each component of the self-regulatory system has developed from, and is the current product of, these competing interests and points of view. Negotiated policy making of this kind has been characterised by Lindblom (1965) as partisan mutual adjustment. Groups and organisations are partisan in that they pursue their own interests. They are, however, capable of mutual adjustment in that they adapt to the decisions made by other agencies or attempt to influence them through negotiation, bargaining and manipulation. The policy that emerges from this essentially political process may not be the best judged in terms of some external standard, but it will be agreed and hence feasible. Lindblom's model of partisan mutual adjustment is both descriptive and prescriptive in that it purports not only to describe what happens but to recommend it as a democratic way of making policy.

The incremental, negotiated and agreed development of the self-regulatory system is not a vehicle for the government's advertising policy in respect of tobacco products; rather, it is the policy. The system is the result of conflicting pressures and forces, rather than any detailed rational plan in the minds of policy makers. As in other policy areas characterised by incrementalism, government has no hidden agenda or plan. The then Department of Health and Social Security articulated a broad tobacco policy to discourage the uptake of smoking, to encourage those who have started to stop and to limit the hazards for those who do start and cannot stop (DHSS 1980). This statement did not precede the self-regulatory system, although elements of the self-regulatory system such as health warnings and product modifications are clearly encompassed in this broad statement.

However, as described more fully in Chapter 3, the current voluntary system is on the brink of major changes. Preparations are under way for the completion of the EC Internal Market by 1992. Draft Directives on tar yields and tobacco product labelling are currently under consideration and, if adopted, they will probably need to be implemented through legislation. Thus the voluntary system is under question. The basic policy issue addressed in this chapter concerns the impact of control over tobacco advertising, whatever the mechanics of this control, as opposed to its total ban. The four main areas of the present system are now considered in more detail: the IBA code, the British Code of Advertising Practice, the voluntary agreements and the work of the Independent Scientific Committee on Smoking and Health.

The IBA code of advertising standards and practices

The earliest, unified self-regulatory Code of Practice governing an area of the media dates from the introduction of commercial television. The IBA has a statutory responsibility, reaffirmed in the Broadcasting Act 1981, to maintain and enforce a Code of Practice covering all advertising on commercial television and independent radio. The Code's many provisions cover topics such as programme independence from advertisers, subliminal advertising, good taste and price claims. It is administered by the IBA with the aid of the Independent Television Association (ITV Association). The scripts of all advertisements, apart from certain kinds broadcast by one commercial radio station only, are pre-vetted by representatives of the IBA and ITV Association. The system is buttressed by the IBA's Advertising Advisory Committee which contains representatives of consumers and advertisers who advise on the content of the Code, and a Medical Advisory Panel composed of doctors who comment on advertisements which have medical implications.

Although the IBA Code has a statutory basis, it can be regarded as essentially voluntary since interference by government is rare and the various bodies and committees forming the regulatory network have effective control over its contents. However, government did use the Code's statutory basis to enforce a ban in 1965 on televised cigarette advertising. In 1973, this prohibition was extended to the new, independent radio network. These prohibitions are the only statute-based restrictions on the advertising of tobacco products in the UK. The advertising of cigars and pipe tobacco is still allowed on independent television and radio, although cigar and pipe tobacco advertising are the subject of two supplementary Codes of Conduct which form part of the voluntary agreements reached between the tobacco industry and government. The Minister to whom the IBA is now responsible is the Home Secretary and any government could, if it wished, use its statutory powers to end all advertising of all tobacco products in the commercial broadcast media.

The British Code of Advertising Practice

The 1965 ban on the televised advertising of cigarettes displaced a hastily constructed, voluntary code of practice agreed in 1962 when the debate over tobacco advertising between the tobacco companies and the IBA's predecessor, the Independent Television Association (ITA) was at its fiercest. In addition to introducing restrictions on the times at which cigarette advertisements could be broadcast, the Code laid down that such advertisements would not:

- overemphasise the pleasure obtained from smoking
- feature the conventional heroes of the young
- appeal to pride or manliness
- utilise fashionable social settings
- feature romantic situations in such a way as to link those pleasures with those of smoking.

Although the statutory ban rendered these provisions redundant in respect of televised advertising, they were significant since the tobacco companies intended they should cover not only broadcast but also non-broadcast advertising. After the television ban, the provisions remained as part of a voluntary Code of Practice administered by the Tobacco Advisory Council (TAC) in respect of all advertising in the non-broadcast media. They form the basis of the various provisions concerning tobacco advertising in the British Code of Advertising Practice, which was developed in conjunction with the advertising industry.

Debates in the late 1950s and early 1960s over advertising in general, and tobacco advertising in particular, played a major part in shaping the advertising industry's own self-regulatory structures. This system had been developed over the previous 40 years to promote and maintain professional standards among advertising practitioners. The advertising industry's principal trade association is the Advertising Association (AA) which incorporates media, advertiser and advertising agency interests. It was formed in 1926 and 'one of its first tasks was to establish a special Vigilance Committee to oversee advertising standards and practices. The Association regarded this regulatory function as being extremely important and established a committee in the absence of any external pressure' (Baggott and Harrison, 1986, p.146). As a result of the fierce criticism of advertising standards, the AA decided in 1961 to establish a Code of Advertising Practice (CAP) Committee to oversee the design and implementation of the British Code of Advertising Practice (BCAP), the first edition of which was published in that year. The aim was to reduce the growing pressure for statutory controls over advertising standards and to demonstrate that not only were professional standards being maintained but would, henceforth, be seen to be maintained. The BCAP was modelled on the International Code of Advertising Practice (ICAP) first published in 1937 by the International Chamber of Commerce. It was the first attempt in the UK to distil the principles underlying the many codes then operated by press and magazine publishers and to synthesise them into a coherent body of regulations.

However, critics pointed out that advertising interests remained in full and effective control of the BCAP. As a consequence, the Advertising Standards Authority (ASA) was established in 1962. As was pointed out in Chapter 3, the task of the ASA is to provide outside scrutiny of the CAP Committee which retains ultimate responsibility for amendments to the Code and its observance by the organisations represented. ASA members participate in CAP Committee activities, including the regular up-dating of the Code and the ASA investigates complaints concerning alleged infringements of the BCAP from the public and publishes an Annual Report and monthly Case Reports. The ASA and the CAP Committee share a joint secretariat although 'day-to-day work, however, is organised so as to avoid problems arising as a result of the distinct functions of the Authority and the Committee' (CAP Committee, 1985, p.14). Concern over the close links between the ASA and the CAP Committee led, in the 1970s, to government action designed to reinforce the ASA's independence. With the backing of consumer groups, the Minister for Consumer Protection and the Director General of Fair Trading persuaded the advertising industry of the advantages of increasing the lay membership of the ASA and of shifting responsibility for its funding from the AA to a new body, the Advertising Standards Board of Finance Ltd (ASBOF) which was established in 1974 with powers to fund the ASA's operations from a surcharge of £0.01 levied on advertising expenditures.

In 1975, the TAC handed oversight of its voluntary code on tobacco advertising in the non-broadcast media to the ASA which incorporated it into the BCAP as Appendix 1: 'Advertising of Cigarettes, of the components of manufactured cigarettes and of hand-rolling tobacco'. The Introduction to the 'Cigarette Code' contains the following statement:

> 'The essence of the Code is that advertisements should not seek to encourage people particularly the young, to start smoking or, if they are already smokers, to increase the level of smoking or to smoke to excess; and should not exploit those who are especially vulnerable, in particular young people and those who suffer from a physical, mental or social handicap.' (CAP Committee, 1985, p.57)

The core provisions of the Cigarette Code remain those framed by the TAC in 1962, although there have been a considerable number of additions and refinements.

Advertisements for all tobacco products are the only category of advertisements which must be pre-vetted by the advertising industry's own self-regulatory machinery. This is done in the health sub-committee of the CAP Committee. The health sub-committee is one of four sub-committees, all of which offer pre-publication advice on advertising copy on different ranges of products. Each contains an element of external scrutiny in that one member of the ASA Council sits on each of the four sub-committees. The Cigarette Code and the associated pre-clearance procedures operated by the CAP Committee, were adopted as part of the voluntary agreements, the first of which was reached in 1971, between the tobacco manufacturers and government. However, although these agreements may have implications for the Cigarette Code, it remains an independent component of the self-regulatory system and the CAP Committee emphasises that neither it nor the ASA are parties to the bi-lateral aspects of those voluntary agreements concerned with product modification and research, and the location of advertisements and health warnings. Health warnings, providing one of the most visible signs of the self-regulatory systems at work, were introduced in 1971 in the first of a series of bi-lateral agreements reached between the tobacco industry and government concerning the advertising and promotion of tobacco products.

Voluntary agreements: advertising, promotion, health warnings

Following the ban on cigarette advertising on television, the tobacco companies invested heavily in gift coupon schemes. These were not designed to advertise the product. Rather, they were a marketing strategy which, by offering inducements to purchase, reduced the cost of the product and introduced competition by price. The companies' total advertising budget in 1962 was £13 million, but by 1966 they were spending about £41 million on advertising and promotion (Royal College of Physicians, 1971). About half of this expenditure was on gift coupon schemes. The then Minister of Health, Kenneth Robinson, sought to restrict the growth of gift coupon schemes and tobacco advertising in the non-broadcast media. A voluntary agreement was drafted but negotiations broke down. Legislation was then prepared but the proposed laws were opposed in Cabinet by Richard Crossman who feared that their introduction, following hard on the heels of Barbara Castle's breathalyser, would saddle the Labour Government with the reputation of being a kill-joy determined to deprive the working class of all their pleasures (Crossman, 1976). Any prospect of legislation was abandoned when the Ministry of Health was incorporated into the new Department of Health and Social Security (DHSS) in 1968 with Crossman as its first Secretary of State.

However, concern over the tobacco companies' freedom to advertise a product of proven hazard continued to generate calls for more controls and a series of Private Members Bills sought to regulate tobacco advertising. The first voluntary agreement was reached against a background of well-publicised Parliamentary agitation over two Private Members Bills which sought to restrict tobacco advertising. Sir Keith Joseph, Crossman's Conservative successor at the DHSS, was ideologically averse to legislation in this area but, under pressure to act, he was not above using the threat of legislation. After initial opposition he tabled amendments to one of the Private Members Bills which was sponsored by Sir Gerald Nabarro, as a lever to extract a voluntary agreement from the companies. Although the Bill was lost thanks to what Nabarro called a 'malignant minority' of MPs representing constituencies with tobacco interests, the Secretary of State's plot was successful. As a result of his voluntary agreement, the first health warnings appeared on cigarette packets. These read 'Warning by HM

Government: Smoking Can Damage Your Health' and the words, 'Every packet carries a Government Health Warning'.

This first voluntary agreement was revised in 1977, 1980, 1982 and 1986. Successive agreements have developed and elaborated the provisions concerning health warnings (which are known as the Labelling Code) and identified fresh areas of concern. The health warnings have grown larger and more varied. Restrictions on advertising budgets have been introduced and progressively tightened. Tobacco advertising in cinemas has been phased out and one tobacco product, cigarillos, which survived the advertising ban on television has now been removed. Two supplementary Codes of Conduct governing the television advertising of cigars and pipe-tobacco and promotional campaigns have been negotiated. The BCAP's Cigarette Code has been refined and an emphasis on young people and women has led to the tobacco industry setting funds aside to promote compliance with the law on tobacco sales to minors and to restrictions on advertising in magazines with a large, young, female readership. In addition, tar limits have been reduced. These tar limits are not negotiated as part of the voluntary agreements on tobacco advertising, promotion and health warnings. Rather they are the subject of separate, bi-lateral negotiations between the tobacco industry and government, although the result of these negotiations is incorporated into the Labelling Code in order that information on tar levels appears on packaging along with health warnings.

Independent Scientific Committee on Smoking and Health

The establishment of the Independent Scientific Committee on Smoking and Health (ISCSH) was announced in 1970 by Sir Keith Joseph together with the details of the first voluntary agreement on health warnings. ISCSH started its work in 1973 under the Chairmanship of Dr. (later Lord) Hunter. It currently has eleven members plus Government representatives and supporting officers. In 1987, members included a clinical pharmacologist, three professors of community medicine, a pathologist, a toxicologist and a chest physician specialising in dust diseases as well as the Chairman Sir Peter Froggatt. A chemistry advisor is supplied by the Laboratory of the Government Chemist and a representative of the Scottish Home and Health Department also attends its meetings.

Announcing the Committee, Sir Keith Joseph indicated that it:

'would receive information related to research in the use of tobacco, and substitute smoking materials.... The Department would be ready, through the Committee, to assist the industry to develop acceptable ways of monitoring the safety of the ingredients in smoking products.... Details of the constituents of each brand of cigarette would be supplied to an authority to be determined;

(and that) information on tar and nicotine should be published if the Secretary of State so decided.... The Scientific Committee.... would advise what should be published and how.' (House of Commons, 1971a)

One of the Scientific Committee's first tasks was to construct guidelines for testing synthetic tobacco substitutes which were then being mooted. The voluntary agreement which was struck between the tobacco manufacturers and Health Ministers in 1977 vested responsibility for approving substitutes and additives to tobacco in the Scientific Committee and the manufacturers undertook to follow the guidelines set up by the Committee in making submissions. The proposed addition of tobacco substitutes required the repeal of the Pure Tobacco Act 1842, which controlled additives and adulterations. This Act required nothing to be added to the tobacco (except water) in order that it could be taxed by weight. As a result of EC intervention, tax is now charged on the finished product and not the tobacco, a change which facilitated the promotion of tobacco substitutes.

Once the Act was repealed, the Scientific Committee took over responsibility for authorising substitutes and additives. The substitutes were promoted by Imperial Tobacco in partnership with Imperial Chemical Industries (ICI) which jointly developed a tobacco substitute known as New Smoking Material (NSM), and Gallahers and Rothmans which cooperated with the (American) Celanese Corporation to develop another substitute known as Cytrel. The Scientific Committee judged that products containing substitutes may be no more damaging to health than similar products containing tobacco only and could prove to be less injurious (ISCSH, 1975, p.3). The products were launched in 1977, but proved a commercial flop. The tobacco industry blamed the failure on the health lobby. Health educationalists and others were certainly vocal in their opposition to NSM and Cytrel. They pointed out that combustion of any organic material releases carcinogens and that 'safer' could easily become 'safe' in many smokers' minds. However, it is unlikely that the health lobby was as influential as the tobacco companies claimed to believe. The principal cause of their failure was consumer resistance:

'they were not significantly lower in tar than any of the nineteen low tar brands currently on the market; they were no cheaper than 'ordinary' cigarettes (the government had seen to that, to protect its revenue); and most important of all, smokers just did not like them.' (Taylor, 1984, p.97)

After the failure of tobacco substitutes, modification of tar yields was sought through filtration and ventilation. Tobacco is much the same in all cigarettes and blending has only a very minor influence on tar levels. However, tar yields are affected by the structure of the filter and the porosity of the paper and some tobacco 'rods'—the manufacturers' name for the cigarette exclusive of the filter—are ventilated with small pin holes. The Health Departments of the UK publish six-monthly tar tables on the basis of data supplied by the Laboratory of the Government Chemist which carries out tests on cigarette samples from the Customs and Excise which are analysed on a monthly basis. There is full collaboration between the Laboratory of the Government Chemist and industry chemists who undertake parallel analyses. The publication of official tar tables from 1973 put pressure on the industry to conclude a series of tar yield agreements with the Health Departments based on recommendations by the Scientific Committee and successive agreements have resulted in reducing tar levels. The first tar table contained five categories as shown in Table 4.1.

Table 4.1

Tar table 1973

Designation 1973	Range
Low tar	0 – 10 mg tar/cigarette
Low to middle tar	11 – 16 mg tar/cigarette
Middle tar	17 – 22 mg tar/cigarette
Middle to high tar	23 – 28 mg tar/cigarette
High tar	29 + mg tar/cigarette

By 1986 the tar table had been reduced to four categories defined as in Table 4.2.

Table 4.2

Tar table 1986

Designation 1986	Range
Low tar	0 – 9 mg tar/cigarette
Low to middle tar	10 – 14 mg tar/cigarette
Middle tar	15 – 17 mg tar/cigarette
High tar	18 + mg tar/cigarette

The Scientific Committee is an important component of the self-regulatory system and the tar banding agreed with the tobacco industry has, since 1977, been incorporated into the Labelling Code, thus ensuring that tar categories are displayed on all cigarette packaging and optionally on advertisements.

Since its inception, the Scientific Committee's work has focused on ways of making tobacco less harmful, firstly through the possible use of tobacco substitutes and subsequently through reduction in tar yields and more general changes in cigarette design. Its first three reports reflect this concern (ISCSH, 1975, 1979, 1983). However, in its fourth Report (ISCSH, 1988), the Scientific Committee reviewed the evidence relating to passive smoking which had first been raised in the Committee's Third Report. The Scientific Committee is in the difficult position of seeking to make a dangerous product less harmful, even when that still means dangerous. Its members are well-aware of this problem, hence their decision to develop a broader interest in the health consequences of tobacco consumption.

Sports sponsorship by tobacco companies

In the mid 1960s, the tobacco industry responded to the ban on cigarette advertising on television with increased expenditure on other sources of promotion, including sports sponsorship. Sports sponsorship is the 'direct financial or other assistance provided to sports organisations, clubs or individuals, involved in sport. It includes providing money for a specific event or series of events in return for advertising and publicity.... If sponsorship is fully integrated into a marketing plan, a sponsor has a number of opportunities to exploit the investment in an area such as television, press and public relations' (Tether and Robinson, 1986, p.69).

The promotion of sporting events by tobacco companies associates a substance of known hazard with the healthy lifestyle which sport implies. The issue, from a public health point of view, is what effect this association is likely to have on participants and spectators and is sports sponsorship by tobacco companies compatible with public health goals? The impact of this indirect advertising on the sports-minded young is of particular concern, since they are 'a specific target for the promotion of sport. The promotion of sports has built around the promotion of heroes. They are inseparable. Spectators go to a match to see figures that are larger than life, who are out on their own in possessing skills which they could never match. Such philosophy is pitched at youth' (*Australian Business,* 1981). In the light of these comments, it is instructive to note that the rules of the cigarette code of the BCAP make two indirect and one direct references to the relationship between tobacco, advertising and sporting events. They are:

'2.9 Advertisements should not include or imply any person or testimonial for, or recommendation of, the product by any well-known person of distinction in any walk of life, nor should they claim directly or indirectly the recommendation of a particular brand by any group or class of people engaged in an activity or calling which particularly attracts public adoration or emulation.

2.13 Advertisements should not feature heroes of the young.

2.14 Advertisements should not imply that smoking is associated with success in sport. It should not depict people participating in any active sporting pursuit, or obviously about to do so, or just having done so, or spectators at any organised sporting occasion.' (CAP Committee, 1985)

The first sports sponsorship agreement was negotiated in 1977, following criticism that the tobacco companies were using sponsorship to circumvent the agreement on advertising which, through the Cigarette Code, bans any association with sporting activity. The agreement was re-negotiated in 1982 and again in 1986.

The implementation of voluntary agreements on sports sponsorship has been accompanied by increasingly less critical public attitudes to sponsorship by tobacco companies. Table 4.3 shows that in polls between 1975 and 1984, the proportion of respondents expressing disapproval of sports sponsorship by the tobacco industry fell by 38 per cent.

Table 4.3

Attitudes towards sports sponsorship by tobacco companies

	Approve %	Disapprove %	Don't know %
1975[a]	24	70	–
1980[b]	34	49	17
1980[c]	67	33	–
1984[c]	59	32	–

a. *The Times*, 8.9.75
b. Gallup Political Index, November, 1980
c. National Opinion Polls

It is possible that concern over the funding of sporting activities generally has weakened public resistance to the implications of associating sport with tobacco. However, amongst other restrictions, the voluntary agreements have gradually curtailed the amount of funding provided directly to the sporting activity. The voluntary agreements have limited expenditure on sporting events, firstly to 1976 levels and in the last agreement to the 1985 level. They have also set a ceiling on advertising which promotes sponsored events, restricted the movement of sponsorship money to hitherto unsponsored sports and introduced health warnings on all press, poster and cinema advertising for, and static promotional signs at, sponsored events. These restrictions are not trivial. In 1985, tobacco companies spent £8 million sponsoring snooker, Grand Prix motor racing, League football, darts and other events. Pegging sponsorship expenditure to 1985 levels means 'in effect, a cut of 8 per cent' (*Daily Telegraph*, 25 March 1986, p.1). The ceiling placed on the advertising of sponsored events is currently set at 20 per cent of total expenditure. This is an important move since hidden expenditure and the advertising of sponsored sporting events is high. In evidence to an enquiry in New Zealand, it was claimed that for every dollar spent on sponsorship, three more were spent by sponsors on promoting the fact of their sponsorship (Tether and Robinson, 1986, p.69).

The 1982 agreement by the tobacco companies to include current Government health warnings in their press, poster and cinema advertising for sponsored events and on static promotional signs at such events, links the sports sponsorship agreements with the Labelling Code in the advertising, promotion and health warnings agreement. However, the gap between the sports sponsorship agreement and the Cigarette Code of the BCAP (with its anti-sport clauses) is recognised by both the voluntary agreements and the CAP Committee. Although the former emphasises that 'The display of sponsors' signs and other aspects of publicity relating to sponsored sporting activities should be compatible with the Cigarette Code contained in the British Code of Advertising Practice', they also observe that 'Advertisements for sponsored sporting activities will not, however, simply on account of the observance of any requirements of this agreement, be deemed also to be cigarette advertising and therefore subject to requirements of other voluntary agreements relating to such advertising' (Department of the Environment, 1987, p.4). For its part, the CAP Committee emphasises that neither the ASA nor the Committee are 'parties to the separate Voluntary Agreement between the tobacco industry and the Minister for Sport on the sponsorship of sport' (CAP Committee, 1985).

The future of sports sponsorship by tobacco companies may lie more with the television companies than the Government. Television provides sponsors with a large audience. Both the ITV companies and the BBC have their own codes of practice governing coverage of sponsored events which are designed to limit free advertising.

In March 1987, the IBA announced that it had decided not to televise any new tobacco-sponsored sporting events although existing commitments would be honoured. The corporate view appears to be that such a development is both logical and desirable, given current attitudes towards smoking and the fact that commercial television companies have long been unable to show cigarette advertising on television. The BBC's position is more complicated, if only because it carries most of the major sponsored events. As well as having a duty to provide a public service, it has a world-wide reputation as a televisor of sport to protect. The BBC and independent television companies reserve the right to cover over advertisements for cigarette brands. The display of house or brand names on participants, officials, vehicles, equipment and animals likely to come within shot of the television cameras is prohibited. In addition, the voluntary agreements specify the number and size of signs allowed around or in the play area or arena for a range of sports, for example, curling, cycling, bowls and darts. However, it is claimed that some tobacco companies have broken both the spirit and the letter of the voluntary agreement.

Snooker tournaments appear to have given particular concern to the television authorities. Some tobacco companies have, it is claimed, covered the competition hall with signs and the decoration of the venue has obviously been deliberately designed to echo their products. It is alleged that at one tournament a number of signs were clustered within camera shot, and the Government health warning could not be read by viewers. It is also alleged that the warnings have become smaller and smaller until they are virtually indecipherable. The tobacco companies reject the claim that the agreement on sports sponsorship has been abused, arguing that house names (as opposed to brand names) are not tobacco advertising. Nevertheless, when the third sports sponsorship agreement was announced, the BBC's Board of Governors issued a statement accepting it as a base-line, but they specifically reserve the right to impose further editorial restrictions to ensure that BBC air time is not used to sell cigarettes. As a result, the BBC's own code of practice has been tightened.

ALTERNATIVE ADVERTISING POLICIES

The scope and content of voluntary agreements on tobacco advertising and sports sponsorship described above have expanded considerably over the last twenty years. The codes have included measures to control misleading information, protect particular groups and to introduce health information such as health warnings on cigarette packets.

It is clear from the earlier analysis that the bargaining process for these agreements has involved trading off advertising controls with other aspects of smoking policy such as agreements on tar levels. The nature of the agreements may affect consumption and the harm associated with smoking. In assessing the costs and benefits of current policy compared to any alternatives such as legislation or a complete advertising ban, it is necessary to consider the value of any indirect benefits arising from voluntary agreements as well as the direct costs and benefits. In this section of the chapter, available evidence on the costs and the benefits of both present and alternative policies is reviewed in order to assess the impediments to a preventive based advertising policy for tobacco products.

Tobacco advertising, consumption and government policies

A considerable amount of money has been spent campaigning directly against advertising restrictions both in the UK and overseas. In a campaign to challenge proposals to ban advertising in Western Australia, it was stated that the tobacco industry spent nearly $3 million on the campaign, for a population of approximately 1.3 million, compared with the expenditure of $300,000 promoting the policy proposals by the Western Australian Government (Castleden et al, 1985). As well as lobbying costs, however, the advertising industry has put resources into producing reports (Waterson, 1984) and the tobacco companies have also commissioned or supported research on the issue. The Metra Report (1979), for example, was commissioned by two tobacco companies. In recent years, there has been some attempt by the health lobby to produce research reports supporting their view that advertising does influence consumption habits, such as that by Chapman (1986).

Differences in the empirical findings of the various studies mean that it is not clear whether or not advertising increases the aggregate level of tobacco consumption. Government ministers have taken advantage of the belief that the link between total consumption and advertising is not proven in order to defend present policies and counter arguments for further restrictions. For example, Mr John Patten, then Under Secretary of State for Health and Social Security, stated in 1983: 'There is as yet no clear evidence that banning advertising would have any direct effect on overall cigarette consumption and hence on the nation's health' (House of Commons, 1983). Similar views have been expressed by other ministers and on more specific issues such as the effect of advertising in children's smoking habits. However, the link between advertising and consumption cannot be examined in isolation from the other factors which influence tobacco consumption. Tobacco consumption is related to such variables as prices, income and health effects. Unless the influence of these factors is correctly specified, it will not be possible to obtain accurate effects of advertising on tobacco consumption. Without taking into account changes in other factors, therefore, attempts by both sides of the lobby to consider differences in consumption between countries with different advertising policies, or changes in consumption before and after a policy change, have to be treated with caution.

A number of studies in the UK have attempted to investigate the link between advertising and aggregate tobacco consumption controlling other factors. McGuinness and Cowling (1975), for example, specified a model in which cigarette expenditure was dependent on the price of cigarettes, the level of disposable income, the previous quarter's level of cigarette expenditure, the stock of advertising messages and the health education effect. They hypothesised that health shocks, such as the publicity surrounding the reports of the Royal College of Physicians, had the effect of reducing the effectiveness of advertising messages. The model was estimated with quarterly data relating to the period 1957 to 1968. Using Johnston's (1980) corrected figures, their results suggest that advertising does have a positive and statistically significant effect on consumption. The short run impact of advertising was calculated as 0.08 before the 1962 Royal College report, and 0.07 after it. Long run estimates were larger, at 0.09 before the report and 0.08 after it. Such results would suggest that a 10 per cent fall in advertising would result in a fall of consumption of less than 1 per cent.

In the Metra Report (1979), commissioned by Imperial Tobacco and Gallaher, it was claimed that analysis of the McGuinness and Cowling model and other models led to the conclusion that there was no evidence of a relationship between advertising and cigarette sales. The authors of the Metra Report suggested that the McGuinness and Cowling model was unstable when extended to newer data. There are, however, many reasons for the differences in results between the two studies. The Metra study had access to industry data and only data for one variable, personal disposable income, was common to both studies. Differences in estimates of coefficients when data and variable definitions varied are not proof of the inadequacy of the McGuinness and Cowling model.

Radfar (1985) also re-estimated the McGuinness and Cowling model using data from 1965 and 1980. He found the model was stable when account was taken of later health shocks, which was not done in the Metra Report. Radfar did find significant advertising effects varying between 0.09 in the short run and 0.15 in the long run. Radfar's estimates suggest that a 10 per cent fall in advertising would result in a 1.5 per cent fall in consumption, all other variables remaining constant. There are a number of technical problems in obtaining correct tests of significance from the McGuinness and Cowling model. This is discussed further elsewhere (Godfrey, 1986a).

In a study using a different model and annual data, Witt and Pass (1981) also found a significant advertising effect. Their model related the number of cigarettes to the price of cigarettes, disposable income, current levels of press and television advertising expenditures, and a set of health scare dummies. The estimates suggest an advertising elasticity of 0.07 which would, other things being equal, imply a 0.7 fall in the number of cigarettes consumed after a 10 per cent fall in advertising expenditure.

Results from these and other studies have differed not only in estimated advertising effects but also in estimated effects of variables such as price and income. The use of different models and data makes comparisons of results difficult. Also, few of the results mentioned above were calculated using data published after 1975. Estimated equations of the demand for tobacco have been obtained using a general model with advertising terms, which includes several models in the literature as special cases (Godfrey, 1986b). Statistical tests were applied to find the simplest model with assumptions which were consistent with the data.

The results of research on the role of advertising are not conclusive. For some measures of cigarette consumption, an adequate model could be constructed without an advertising term, but for other measures advertising significantly affects consumption. Short-run advertising elasticity estimates were generally in agreement with the results from previous studies, being in range of 0.07 to 0.11. However, the long-run estimates, which range from 0.23 to 3.5, were much larger than previous results. One general conclusion which can be drawn from this research is that it is dangerous to use untested models for predicting the effects of alternative advertising policies.

Evidence on the link between advertising and aggregate consumption from non-UK studies is equally mixed. Chetwynd et al. (1988), in a study of aggregate demands for cigarettes in New Zealand using quarterly data, found significant advertising elasticities of 0.07. These estimated elasticities are similar to UK estimates. Two other recent studies found positive, but small and statistically insignificant, effects of advertising on consumption (Bishop and Yoo, 1986; Yucelt and Kaynak, 1984). Two earlier US studies found small, but statistically significant, advertising effects (Fujii, 1980; Young, 1983).

The results discussed above could be used to extrapolate the effect of a 100 per cent reduction of expenditure, that is, an advertising ban. So, for example, using the long-run advertising elasticity of 0.23, it would suggest that an advertising ban might result in a 23 per cent reduction in cigarette expenditure. There are several limitations involved in forecasting any large policy changes, even with well-founded and tested empirical models. Estimated models are based on existing data variations and the estimates may break down in the event of a major policy change, even if this was not as dramatic as an advertising ban. Even if the relationship between advertising and consumption remained constant over large changes, an advertising ban may have additional effects on consumption compared to a large reduction in advertising expenditure. In the Marsh and Matheson (1983) survey, 44 per cent of smokers felt that 'smoking can't really be dangerous or the

Government would ban advertising'. Such attitudes may suggest that a ban would change the way individuals perceive the health risk. Absence of advertisements may also help the process of stopping smoking and reduce the relapse rate. It should also be noted that the estimates of changes in consumption resulting from a change in advertising are made assuming all other factors remain constant. Possible reactions of the industry to such restrictions are considered later in this chapter.

However, existing empirical work, which has concentrated on the aggregate effects of advertising on total consumption, is subject to certain limitations. There may be problems in aggregating over different groups of consumers. The disaggregated studies which have been undertaken, such as those by Atkinson and Skegg (1973) and Townsend (1983, 1987), suggest that the effects of price and other variables may vary between different groups. Such disaggregated studies, however, need a rich data set which is sometimes difficult to acquire. Work in the US using cohort data has suggested that teenagers may respond differently to price, health information and advertising from the rest of the population (Lewit, Coate and Grossman, 1981). The young and their decision to start smoking are of particular policy interest, but this is another area where the lack of available data thwarts tight analysis.

Also, existing analyses have not considered the content of advertising, and whether existing or new information policies would affect consumption. So, for example, it would not be possible to infer from such results the effects of a policy with a stricter enforcement of the voluntary codes, of more prominent and effective health warnings. The effect of a tombstone policy which imposes strict restrictions on the content of advertising copy is also difficult to predict. Warner et al. (1986) discuss other policy options. Nor is it possible from such empirical results to measure whether existing advertisements provide valuable information to consumers. Some other empirical work that has examined such aspects of advertising is therefore of interest.

Several authors have tried to measure whether advertising or sports sponsorship alters individuals' perception of the good. Work in the UK and elsewhere does suggest that children are aware of cigarette brands from sponsored events (Aitken, Leather and Squair, 1986). Even with more obscure advertisements where brand names are not displayed, children have been shown to be able to correctly identify the brands being advertised (Aitken, Leather, O'Hagan and Squair, 1987). Also children who smoke were shown to take more notice of cigarette advertisements than non-smokers of the same age (Aitken et al., 1987; Chapman and Fitzgerald, 1982). As the authors suggest, this does not necessarily imply that advertisements have prompted children to start to smoke. Nevertheless they are capable of interpreting the information which is being portrayed in advertisements.

Other researchers have tried to measure the effects of a specific policy change. In general, these studies have been for non-UK data, but their analyses do indicate some of the difficulties in forecasting the effect of a major policy change when other factors also change. So, for example, the Canadian study by Smart and Cutler (1976) of the effects of the advertising ban in British Columbia, indicated the difficulties involved in making such a ban effective.

Another example of these difficulties was provided by the 1971 ban on TV advertising of cigarettes in the US. Prior to the ban, the Fairness Doctrine had ensured that health messages were broadcast in proportion to cigarette advertisements. There has been some disagreement on differentiating the effects of the TV ban and the loss of health education messages. Both Hamilton (1972) and Schneider et al. (1981) found that the health information broadcasts had been more effective in reducing consumption than the advertising messages had been in increasing consumption. Hamilton suggested that the net effect of the policy had, therefore, been to increase consumption. Baltagi and Levin (1986), however, found no support in their empirical analysis for the hypothesis that the ban in advertising increased per capita cigarette consumption.

McLeod (1986) examined the effect of the Australian ban on cigarette advertising in the electronic media in 1976. He estimated a demand model of cigarettes and included a dummy for each year after the ban was introduced. The estimated coefficients of the dummies, in general, indicated a fall in consumption but only the coefficient for the year 1976/77 was significant. McLeod suggests that this advertising ban produced a short-lived effect of a five to six per cent reduction in consumption. Whether this drop in consumption is attributed to the advertising ban, or a more general health information effect, is of course open to question.

A difficulty in forecasting the effect of an advertising ban, or any other alternative to voluntary agreements, is in measuring the indirect health information benefits that may have accrued from present policies. Most of the UK studies of tobacco demand reviewed in this chapter have found significant health effects. It is, however, impossible to distinguish the role of health warnings, for example, from the more general effect of increased awareness of health risks.

One interesting cross-national study attempted to analyse the relationship between different governments' policies and the level of tobacco consumption (Cox and Smith, 1984). Comparisons between the countries were made by estimating separate demand functions for each country over the same time period. Countries were grouped according to whether policies were mainly legislative in nature or voluntary as in the UK. Coefficient estimates were hypothesised to reflect these unobservable policy variables. The study concluded: 'In general the results of the foregoing analysis tend to support the feelings of many commentators in the health field that the strategy of voluntary agreements is an inadequate response to the problems generated by tobacco smoking.' There are, however, a number of statistical difficulties with this type of analysis. Only two of the fifteen countries considered had well-established legislative policies. Another problem is that the model for each country was estimated with constant coefficients over the whole period and the hypothesis that these coefficients may be different before and after a major policy change was not tested. This work, despite its limitations, attempts to address cross-country comparisons in a more rigorous way than much of the material released by lobby groups.

The thrust of the tobacco industry's arguments against advertising restrictions is that there is no relationship between advertising and the level of total consumption. It has been shown from the review of previous studies and empirical work presented in this section that no such firm conclusions can be drawn. Nor is the aggregate relationship between advertising expenditure and consumption the only interesting policy issue. Some groups may be particularly important and if, for example, it can be shown that the young would particularly benefit from an advertising or sponsorship ban, this may be a sufficient basis for a policy change. Information objectives of advertising policies are also not considered in the aggregate analysis.

The difficulties of forecasting the effect of a major policy change have been considered and a number of side effects of such policies outlined. The effects of some supply side responses from the industry on the outcomes of policies are now considered.

Advertising policies and the tobacco and advertising industries

A number of different groups may lose from advertising policies including the tobacco industry, advertising agencies, and distribution networks. It is important to consider both how such groups have reacted to current advertising agreements and how they might respond to alternative policies. Clearly the first voluntary agreements described in the first section of the paper altered the advertising strategies of tobacco companies. Increases in poster advertising and sports and arts sponsorship prompted the Government to widen the scope of voluntary agreements. Tobacco companies have also diversified their marketing activities into travel firms, clothes and refurbished shop fronts to display logos. Faced by a ban on formal advertising, firms may react by extending these and other activities not necessarily prohibited by a ban.

The effects of post-voluntary agreements on the full promotional activities of tobacco companies are difficult to determine. Data are not available on advertising for cinemas, posters or sponsorship. Some data are published on press and TV advertisements and these are given in Table 4.4. Despite advertising policies, the real value of tobacco advertising on press and TV has quadrupled since 1955. The peak, however, was reached in 1965 before the TV ban on cigarettes took effect. The following year saw a drop in tobacco advertising expenditure and a drop in the proportion spent on cigarettes. The proportion of tobacco advertising devoted to cigarettes rose, however, in the late 1970s only to fall after 1981. In 1984, about 74 per cent of tobacco advertising was spent on the press and this amount was about 4 per cent of the total press advertising expenditure surveyed.

Table 4.4

Tobacco advertising expenditure, 1955-87

Year	Total tobacco advertising expenditure £m—constant prices (1980 = 100)	Cigarette advertising expenditure as a percentage of tobacco advertising expenditure
1955	10.4	78.4
1960	20.6	79.5
1964	75.8	80.8
1965	79.9	75.1
1966	55.6	65.7
1967	48.9	59.8
1968	56.3	67.6
1975	37.5	69.7
1980	48.9	81.8
1981	40.3	74.8
1982	47.6	72.6
1983	49.5	71.9
1984	43.5	70.4
1985	48.2	77.6
1986	46.1	74.4
1987	40.4	75.4

Source: *Statistical Review of Press and TV Advertising,* Legion Publishing Services; *Quarterly Digest of Advertising Expenditure,* Media Expenditure Analysis Ltd.

Dependence on tobacco advertising revenue may mean that the media, as well as the advertising industry, might form part of a lobby opposing policy changes and that media willingness to cover health issues may be effected (Whelan et al., 1981; Jacobson and Amos, 1985).

The available statistics do indicate that advertising activities, although subject to restrictions, are still sizeable. The size of advertising budgets may reflect the degree of competition between tobacco companies. It is useful to consider how firms would compete in the absence of advertising or if advertising were severely curtailed, and what effects other forms of competition might have on tobacco consumption. The UK tobacco industry is highly concentrated and is dominated by four large multinational companies. These four firms have accounted for 93 per cent of the sales of cigarettes in the UK since 1984 (Booth, Hardman and Hartley, 1986). There is little, if any, evidence that present restrictions have influenced competition within the industry and the level of concentration has been high for the last 30 years. Voluntary agreements to limit expenditure on some forms of advertising may therefore be welcomed as marketing costs can be reduced uniformly across the industry. Indeed companies may be willing to trade off concessions, for example, health warnings, for such gains.

Profitability of the tobacco industry has risen during the period since 1970 and is usually above the 'all industry' level. Booth, Hardman and Hartley (1986) give several explanations for this record on profitability, including the high degree of concentration which may suggest some monopoly power in the industry. Another feature of the structure of the tobacco industry has been that it has responded to falling cigarette sales by diversifying into other markets, for example, financial services and the leisure industry. As Booth et al. (1988) suggest, such diversification is an obvious method by which firms can protect themselves and their shareholders from government prevention policies. Three of the four tobacco companies are among the top 40 enterprises in the UK and the fourth is in the top 100. Such large firms may represent very powerful pressure groups.

One feature of the tobacco market since 1984 has been a growth of the consumption of generic brand low-cost cigarettes, mainly imported. Although still only a small proportion of total consumption, imports of such cigarettes rise considerably between 1983 and 1985. Godfrey and Powell (1987) discuss this further. One reason for the low cost of these cigarettes is the absence of advertising costs. The industry has used the growth in imports to argue that further controls of advertising would damage the UK industry and the balance of payments. The determinants of total trade in tobacco goods are, however, complex. Declining UK consumption has caused a decline in imported tobacco, and the industry responded to falling home markets by exporting more cigarettes. The total trade in tobacco manufacture has, therefore, either been in surplus or equilibrium since 1979 (Godfrey and Powell, 1987). The present Government policies do not favour protectionism and so it may be thought desirable to have a more competitive market in the UK. Increasing competition resulting from high levels of imports may weaken the political power of the industrial lobby and ease the introduction of preventive policies such as advertising controls.

If firms do not use advertising as a means of competing for market share, other methods such as the lower prices of generic brands may become a more general strategy. Any gains, therefore, arising from controls in advertising may be offset from increasing consumption arising from lower prices.

To sum up, there is little evidence that tobacco companies have suffered losses as a result of the development of advertising policies described above, and indeed they may have gained from some parts of the agreements. A complete ban on advertising may have much larger effects on the industry's structure and profitability.

CONCLUSION

The threat of legislation, as shown in the first section of the paper, has played some part both in governments' ability to ensure agreement with the tobacco industry and in the industry's observance of codes of practice. The coverage of the voluntary agreements between the government and the tobacco industry has been expanded to include levels of expenditure, the location of advertising, sports sponsorship and product modification. Along with the introduction of health warnings, such measures have had some influence on the general decline of cigarette smoking, although their exact contribution is difficult to quantify. See Chapter 2 in the first book of this series, Maynard and Tether, 1989.

There has, however, been considerable debate about the need for further restrictions. Public opinion, as measured by opinion polls, has consistently been in favour of a ban on cigarette advertising. In 1963, for example, 45 per cent of respondents in a Gallop poll agreed with the suggestion that all advertising for cigarettes should be suppressed, compared with 38 per cent who disagreed and 17 per cent who did not know. By 1982, public opinion had hardened. In a poll commissioned by the DHSS, 57 per cent of respondents approved of a ban on advertising, compared with 20 per cent who disapproved and 20 per cent who were indifferent (Leedham, 1987). Also there seems to be less scope for achieving indirect health benefits from further modification. As indicated in Chapter 1, however, any legislative alternative can be costly to governments.

There are a number of difficulties in forecasting the costs and benefits of alternative advertising policies. Empirical evidence suggests that reductions in expenditure may reduce consumption, but only by a small amount. As discussed above, extrapolating the results from existing studies to forecast the effect of a complete ban is hazardous. Most forecasts are calculated assuming everything else remains constant. If the reduction or removal of advertising promotes price or other competition, offsetting effects on consumption may occur. Without a clearer indication of the benefits of an advertising ban or legislation to restrict advertising, considerable impediments remain to a change in advertising policies. In the future, changing technology will, as discussed in the case of alcohol in Chapter 3, make any control whether voluntary or legislative more difficult to implement.

References

Aitken, P.P., Leather, D.S. and Squair, S.I., (1986), 'Children's awareness of cigarette brand sponsorship of sports and games in the UK', *Health Education Research*, 1, 203-211.

Aitken, P.P., Leather, D.S., O'Hagan, F.J. and Squair, S.I., (1987), 'Children's awareness of cigarette advertisements and brand imagery', *British Journal of Addiction*, 82, 615-622.

Atkinson, A.B. and Skegg, J.L., (1973), 'Anti-smoking publicity and the demand for tobacco in the UK', *Manchester School of Economics and Social Studies*, 41, 265-82.

Australian Business, (1981), 24 September 1981, 4.

Baggott, R. and Harrison, L., (1986), 'The politics of self-regulation: the case of advertising control', *Policy and Politics*, 14, (2), 143-159.

Baltagi, B.H. and Levin, D., (1986), 'Estimating dynamic demand for cigarettes using panel data: the effects of bootlegging, taxation and advertising reconsidered', *The Review of Economics and Statistics*, 68, 148-155.

Bishop, J.A. and Yoo, J.H., (1986), 'Health scares, excise taxes and advertising ban in the cigarette demand and supply', *Southern Economic Journal*, 52 (2), 402-411.

Booth, M., Boakes, R., Hardman, G. and Hartley, K., (1988), 'Data Note 14, Mergers in the U.K. alcohol and tobacco industries', *British Journal of Addiction*, 83, 707-714.

Booth, M., Hardman, G. and Hartley, K., (1986), 'Data Note 6, The UK alcohol and tobacco industries', *British Journal of Addiction*, 81, 825-830.

Castleden, W.M., Newish, D.J. and Woodward, S.D., (1985), 'Changes in tobacco advertising in Western Australian newspapers in response to proposed Government legislation', *The Medical Journal of Australia*, 142, 305-308.

Chapman, S., (1986), *Cigarette Advertising and Smoking: A Review of the Evidence*, British Medical Association Inprint, London.

Chapman, S. and Fitzgerald, B., (1982), 'Brand preference and advertising recall in adolescent smokers: some implications for health promotion', *American Journal of Public Health*, 72, 491-4.

Chetwynd, J., Coope, P., Brodie, R.J. and Wells, E., (1988), 'The impact of cigarette advertising on aggregate demand for cigarettes in New Zealand', *British Journal of Addiction*, 83, 409-14.

Code of Advertising Practice (CAP) Committee, (1985), *British Code of Advertising Practice,* 7th edition, CAP Committee, London.

Cox, H. and Smith, R., (1984), 'Political approaches to smoking control: a comparative analysis', *Applied Economics*, 16, 569-582.

Crossman, R.H.S., (1976), *Diaries of a Cabinet Minister*, Vol. 2, Hamish Hamilton and Jonathan Cape, London.

Daily Telegraph, (1986), 25 March, 1.

Department of the Environment, (1987), *Sponsorship of Sport by Tobacco Companies in the UK*, HMSO, London.

Department of Health and Social Security (DHSS), (1977), *Prevention of Health*, HMSO, London.

Department of Health and Social Security (DHSS), (1980), *On the State of the Public Health for the Year 1978*, HMSO, London.

Fujii, E.T., (1980), 'The demand for cigarettes: further empirical evidence and its implications for public policy', *Applied Economics*, 12, 479-489.

Godfrey, C., (1986a), 'Government policy, advertising and tobacco consumption in the U.K. A critical review of the literature', *British Journal of Addiction* 81, 339-346.

Godfrey, C., (1986b), *Price and Advertising Elasticities of the Demand for Tobacco*, Working Paper, ESRC Addiction Research Centre, University of York.

Godfrey, C. and Powell, M., (1987), *Budget Strategies for Alcohol and Tobacco Tax in 1987 and Beyond*, Discussion Paper 22, Centre for Health Economics, University of York.

Hamilton, J.L., (1972), 'The demand for cigarettes: advertising, the health scare and the cigarette advertising ban', *Review of Economics and Statistics*, 56, 401-411.

House of Commons, (1971a), *Parliamentary Debates*, Vol. 816, Col. 212, 29, HMSO, London.

House of Commons, (1971b), *Parliamentary Debates 1970-71*, Vol. 819, Cols. 340-4, HMSO, London.

House of Commons, (1983), Mr. John Patten in reply to parliamentary question, *Parliamentary Debates, 1983-84*, Vol.48, Col.432, HMSO, London.

Independent Scientific Committee on Smoking and Health (ISCSH), (1975), *Tobacco Substitutes and Additives in Tobacco Products*, (First Report), HMSO, London.

Independent Scientific Committee on Smoking and Health (ISCSH), (1979), *Developments in Tobacco Products and the Possibility of 'Lower-Risk' Cigarettes*, (Second Report), HMSO, London.

Independent Scientific Committee on Smoking and Health (ISCSH), (1983), *Third Report*, HMSO, London. 58E7

Independent Scientific Committee on Smoking and Health (ISCSH), (1988), *Fourth Report*, HMSO, London.

Jacobson, B. and Amos, A., (1985), *When Smoke Gets in your Eyes: Cigarette Advertising Policy and Coverage of Smoking and Health in Women's Magazines*, British Medical Association Inprint, London.

Johnston, J., (1980), 'Advertising and the aggregate demand for cigarettes. A comment', *European Economic Review*, 14, 117-125.

Leedham, W., (1987), 'Data Note 10, Alcohol, tobacco and public opinion', *British Journal of Addiction*, 82, 935-940.

Lewit, E.M., Coate, D. and Grossman, M., (1981), 'The effects of government regulation on teenage smoking', *Journal of Law and Economics*, 24, 545-569.

Lindblom, C., (1965), *The Intelligence of Democracy*, Free Press, New York.

Marsh, A. and Matheson, J., (1983), *Smoking Attitudes and Behaviour*, HMSO, London.

McGuinness, T. and Cowling, K., (1975), 'Advertising and the aggregate demand for cigarettes', *European Economic Review*, 6, 311-328.

McLeod, P.B., (1986), 'Advertising bans, tobacco and cigarette consumption', *Economic Letters*, 20, 391-396.

Maynard, A. and Tether, P. (eds.), (1989), *The Addiction Market: consumption, production and policy development*, Avebury/Gower, Aldershot.

Metra Consulting Group, (1979), *The Relationship Between Total Cigarette Advertising and Total Cigarette Consumption in the UK*, Metra, London.

Radfar, M., (1985), 'The effect of advertising on total consumption of cigarettes in the UK', *European Economic Review*, 29, 225-231.

Royal College of Physicians, (1971), *Smoking and Health Now*, Pitman Medical and Scientific Publishing Co. Ltd, London.

Schneider, L., Klein, B. and Murphy, K.M., (1981), 'Governmental regulation of cigarette health information', *Journal of Law and Economics*, 24, 575-612.

Smart, R.G. and Cutler, R.E., (1976), 'The alcohol advertising ban in British Columbia: problems and effects on beverage consumption', *British Journal of Addiction*, 71, 13-21.

Taylor, P., (1984), *Smoke Ring: The Politics of Tobacco*, The Bodley Head, London.

Tether, P. and Robinson, D., (1986), *Preventing Alcohol Problems: A Guide to Local Action*, Tavistock, London.

Townsend, J., (1983), *Cigarette Tax and Social Class Patterns of Smoking*, Paper presented at the Fifth World Conference on Smoking and Health, Winnipeg, Canada.

Townsend, J., (1987), 'Cigarette tax, economic welfare and social class patterns of smoking', *Applied Economics*, 19, 355-365.

Warner, K.E., Ernster, E.V., Holbrook, J.H., Lewit, E.M., Pertschuk, M., Steinfeld, J.L., Tye, J.P. and Whelan, E.M., (1986), 'Promotion of tobacco products: issues and policy options', *Journal of Health Politics, Policy and Law*, 11, (3), 367-392.

Waterson, M.J., (1984), *Advertising and Cigarette Consumption*, 5th edition, The Advertising Association, London.

Whelan, E.M., Sheridan, M.J., Meister, K.A. and Mosher, J.F., (1981), 'Analysis of coverage of tobacco hazards in women's magazines', *Journal of Public Health Policy*, 2, 28-35.

Witt, S.F. and Pass, C.L., (1981), 'The effects of health warnings and advertising on the demand for cigarettes', *Scottish Journal of Political Economy*, 28, 86-91.

Young, T., (1983), 'The demand for cigarettes: alternative specifications of Fujii's model', *Applied Economics*, 15, 203-211.

Yucelt, U. and Kaynak, E., (1984), 'A study of measuring influence of advertising and forecasting cigarette sales', *Managerial and Decision Economics*, 5, (4), 213-218.

5 Legislation: the policy networks

PHILIP TETHER, WENDY LEEDHAM AND LARRY HARRISON

Chapter 1 argues that legislation and self-regulation are not such distinct processes as might first appear. Both government and outside interests are incorporated into the policy process, making it possible for particular interests to dominate in both cases. This chapter uses two examples of policy regulated by legislation to illustrate the range and diversity of policy participants and relationships in the policy process. The chapter shows that the implementation of policies to reduce alcohol or tobacco consumption using legislation must acknowledge the influence of the diversity of interests and decision making processes which are often ignored when calls are made for 'tougher' regulation.

The two examples are explored using the concept of 'policy networks', described in Chapter 2. They highlight the notion that legislation may be concerned with policy issues that may involve either conflicting interests or a consensus of opinion; and may have policy outcomes which are either clear or unclear. The 'map' of current UK activity around liquor licensing and drink-driving is described, detailing the network of relations between organisations and their 'stances' on the debates about existing and recent changes in legislation. These discussions of the policy networks provide the context for the more detailed analysis of liquor licensing and drinking and driving in Chapters 6 and 7.

LIQUOR LICENSING

In this section, the diversity of interests and decision making processes involved in regulation using legislation are illustrated using the example of liquor licensing. The map of policy participants in liquor licensing issues presents a wide range of interests and organisations appearing in different places at different times, but with the Home Office as the government department at the heart of the policy network. The Home Office has an obvious concern with the maintenance of public order and law enforcement. Liaison between the Home Office and other agencies serves to give policy makers access to views on the desirability of various policy options, rather than to gather information about potential policy outcomes. Interest group views on reform of the licensing law, for example, were translated into action by a government sympathetic to the principles of deregulation and based on limited evidence of policy outcomes from Scotland (see Chapter 7 of the first volume of this series, Maynard and Tether, 1989).

Liquor licensing matters are the particular concern of a Liquor Licensing Section within a division of the Criminal Justice and Constitutional Department of the Home Office, employing in 1988 a small staff of one Principal, with three officers and clerical support. The Liquor Licensing Section has close links with two Home Office forums seeking to stimulate the development of crime prevention measures, the Standing Conference on Crime Prevention (SCCP), and the Crime Prevention Unit (CPU). The major issues of concern for these forums are the public order implications of reforming licensing law. A Principal from the Diversion of Offenders Section of the Criminal Policy Departments with specific responsibilities for alcohol issues links the Criminal Policy Department with the CPU and exercises a specific co-ordinating role in respect of any crime prevention matters which have an alcohol dimension. The Principal also monitors other departmental policies which might have implications for the criminal justice system. The SCCP has considered alcohol-related subjects; in 1986 one of the five reports presented was entitled *The Prevention of Violence Associated with Licensed Premises* (Home Office, 1985a). The Home Office Research and Planning Unit has also studied the relationship between alcohol and city centre disorder (Home Office, 1985b).

Home Office oversight of alcohol policy has been enhanced by the 'alcohol' Principal's role as joint secretary to the inter-departmental Ministerial Group on Alcohol Misuse. Government-wide co-ordination on crime prevention issues is promoted by an Inter-Departmental Group on Crime Prevention, with ministerial members drawn from the Departments of Health, Energy, Education and Science, the Environment, Transport, Employment, Trade and Industry, together with the Treasury, the Health and

Safety Executive and the Scottish, Welsh and Northern Ireland Offices. The Group is served by civil servants from the Liquor Licensing Section and where appropriate, the 'alcohol' Principal from the Diversion of Offenders Section.

The Home Office also liaises with other government departments on proposals to reform licensing law, principally the Department of Health (DoH) over health issues, and the Department of the Environment (DoE), the Ministry of Agriculture, Fisheries and Food and Department of Trade and Industry (DTI) on trade and employment issues. The tourist industry, which has been at the forefront of the campaign to relax the liquor licensing hours in England and Wales, is sponsored by the DoE. Although the DoE Small Firms and Tourism Division includes a branch which liaises with other departments over reform of liquor licensing hours, the lead on this topic has been taken since 1985 by the Enterprise and Deregulation Unit (EDU) which moved with Lord Young from DoE to the Department of Trade and Industry. The EDU is a central task force with staff drawn from a variety of government departments and business organisations. It is responsible for promoting deregulation throughout Whitehall. Every department has nominated officers responsible for pursuing deregulation objectives and many departments have their own deregulation units.

The Home Office is also the focus for a number of non-departmental interests in the liquor licensing policy network. Its law enforcement responsibilities mean that the police are the major non-departmental group consulted in relation to a wide range of policy issues, including liquor licensing, alcohol and crime and road safety. The Home Office is the sponsoring department for the police and there are established channels to assist the two-way flow of information and exchange of views. Links with the police are maintained principally through the Association of Chief Police Officers (ACPO) which has about 275 members, holding ranks above Chief Superintendent in England, Wales and Northern Ireland. Discussion and debate on pedestrian drunkenness, public order and licensing matters find their way into government, more specifically, to the Police Division of the Home Office, by way of a set of joint committees.

Continuing, lower-level, day-to-day contact between ACPO and the Home Office is maintained by six committees with specific areas of responsibility. These are maintained by the twice-yearly Central Conference of Chief constables, which acts as a forum for ACPO-Government discussions. As such, it is chaired by the Permanent Under Secretary in charge of the Home Office's Police Division. Other members of the Central Conference include the Deputy Under Secretary and all the Assistant Under Secretaries in the Police Division. The twice-yearly Central Conference considers major policy issues of mutual concern to the ACPO and Home Office.

Members of the Central Conference Standing Committees are drawn from both the ACPO and the Home Office, and thus provide the ACPO with a 'transmission belt' making its views known to government, and vice versa. The relationship between the Home Office and the main police organisation is extremely close and allows for constant exchanges. Only a few other groups, such as the Justices' Clerks' Society and the Magistrates' Association, have such close contact and none has such complex organisational connections.

ACPO also maintains links with a small range of other organisations, although not on an institutionalised basis. These include the National Association for the Care and Resettlement of Offenders (NACRO) and the National Association of Victim Support Schemes.

The Constitutional Department in the Home Office has close links with the Magistrates' Association (MA) and the Justices' Clerks' Society, two interest groups whose members work directly with the liquor licensing law. The MA, representing 25,000 magistrates in 57 branches, does not have any formal organisational links with government. However, it is approached by the Home Office for its views on proposed legislation, and the MA may approach Government to make its views known. Contact with the department takes place by letter and consultation. The MA's views on aspects of liquor licensing laws are considered by the Legal Committee, one of the MA's Standing Committees, which in 1981 incorporated a previously separate Licensing Committee as a result of the proposed changes in permitted hours. Policy recommendations go from Standing Committees to the MA's Council for a final decision.

The MA does not campaign publically, but the MA Council attempts to influence the practice of magistrates by sending circulars to Branch Secretaries, by the officers attending branch meetings and by the publication of a journal. Prior to the 1988 Licensing Act, the MA did not oppose a 'rationalisation' of existing laws. The option for permitted hours that they favoured was for drinking establishments to be open for nine hours, decided at the discretion of the licensee, within fixed limits. The hours decided upon should be displayed outside the licensed premises.

The Justices' Clerks' Society is also consulted by the Home Office on liquor licensing reform, and in 1983 published proposals for *Licensing Law in the Eighties* (Justices' Clerks' Society, 1983), which addressed two major areas of liquor licensing—the rise in drunkenness and drink-related offences, the outdated complexity of the licensing law and the inordinate amount of time being spent in court on licensing matters. The Society's views on proposals for liquor licensing reform broadly supported the suggested

11.00am-1.00pm opening hours provided that this period is an option and that licensees are required to notify their Chief Constable and the Clerk to the (Licensing) Justices, and are required to publicise their opening hours outside the premises. They have also made proposals aimed at loosening the perceived administrative burdens on licensing justices, such as the replacement of yearly renewal of licences by two-tier licences renewable after five years (Justices' Clerks' Society, 1983).

The Home Office Constitutional Department also contains a division which is responsible for shops law which has a close and obvious connection with liquor licensing. The Liquor Licensing Section also maintains contact as necessary with other groups, such as the Retail Trade Consortium, the Brewers Society and the Restaurateurs Association of Great Britain. Contact with the various tourist boards is through their sponsoring department, the DoE.

Although the Home Office can be regarded as the focus of the liquor licensing policy network, the DTI and DoE have a major interest in liquor licensing issues, through their links with the tourist industry. The tourist industry saw the English and Welsh licensing laws as a major constraint on its development. The English Tourist Board and the British Tourist Authority are largely independent bodies, although at present financed by government, and have lobbied energetically for changes to a law which they believed had a detrimental effect on the tourist industry.

The tourist industry is sponsored by the DoE, a responsibility which is located in the Small Firms and Tourism Division (SFT). The SFT Division, which is headed by an Under Secretary, has three branches; two of the three are concerned with promoting small businesses and the third with tourism. The branch concerned with tourism is divided into three sections, one dealing with matters relating to the English Tourist Board, another with the British Tourist Authority and the third (SFT3C) liaises with other government departments over key issues like education and training and the reform of liquor licensing hours. As mentioned above, the lead on liquor licensing issues has been taken since 1985 by the Enterprise and Deregulation Unit, currently located in the DTI. The DoE has its own deregulation unit in the Senior Management Support Unit, plus a number of regional enterprise units concerned with enterprise and deregulation at the local level. These units are able to report to the EDU on the restrictions faced by local businesses. The Small Firms Services, a series of nine regional centres offering advice and counselling to local businesses, also relays complaints about restrictive regulation to the EDU. Close links exist between the SFT Division and the EDU, which used to be based in the DoE, largely because both pursue similar objectives with regard to policy on deregulation and on small businesses. Those in the EDU who liaise with the Home Office are still in frequent contact with their colleagues in SFT3C over liquor licensing issues. Although the DoE is no longer at the centre of the network of deregulation units throughout Whitehall, it maintains close links with the DTI and it is represented on the inter-departmental Ministerial Group on Alcohol Misuse.

The DTI's major interest in liquor licensing issues is in ensuring that competition is promoted within British industry and that restrictive business practices are subject to effective safeguards. Branches 4 and 5 of the General Policy Division of the DTI are together responsible for the overall development and application of UK competition policy and for liaison with the main competition authorities—the Office of Fair Trading and the Monopolies and Mergers Commission (MMC).

Section A in Branch 4 is concerned with mergers, monopolies and anti-competitive practices. Section B is responsible for the general development of competition policy. Section C is temporary, and has been established to conduct a review of law and policy on mergers and restrictive practices, with the intention of creating a more favourable 'competition climate'.

Branch 5 has two Sections. Section A is responsible for policy on restrictive trading practices legislation and for interest in European Community (EC) competition policy and in international aspects of competition policy generally. Section B in Branch 5 is responsible for newspaper mergers and it has a number of general 'sponsorship' duties in relation to the MMC. For example, the Section handles appointments to the MMC and co-ordinates briefing and Governmental submissions. It also has a co-ordinating role in referrals to the MMC of nationalised industries and other public bodies under Section 11 of the Competition Act 1980.

Branches 4 and 5 in the General Policy Division work closely with the Enterprise and Deregulation Unit (EDU) which itself has an informal structure, with each Principal being responsible for liaising with a group of departments.

The liquor licensing policy network also includes a complex of different interest and pressure groups whose activities feed into governmental policy making through various channels. The Brewers Society, the caterers and tourist trade, the Campaign for Real Ale (CAMRA) and the publicans form the major coalition who have argued in favour of liquor licensing reform. A concerted campaign for flexi-hours was launched in 1984 with the creation of the Flexi-Law Action Group (FLAG) involving these interests. Despite early divisions between the Brewers Society and the National Union of Licensed Victuallers (NULV) and the National Association of Licensed House Managers (NALHM) about what 'reform' might mean, the most authoritative statement of FLAG's view appears to have been made by the

Brewers Society in a letter to Triple A (Action on Alcohol Abuse), a pressure group established by the medical Royal Colleges:

> 'The Brewers Society and the National Union of Licensed Victuallers have a joint policy to seek an amendment to licensing law in England and Wales that would retain 'permitted hours' as at present but add provision to allow individual licensees to select the hours most suited to the hours of their trade and apply to the Licensing Justices for a 'variation' to cover such hours. It is proposed that the maximum should be 12 hours between 10.00am and 12.00 midnight (14 hours in special circumstances). Licensing Justices would consider each 'variation' application, hear objections and decide to grant, or not grant the application on its merits, using their local knowledge.' (Action on Alcohol Abuse, 1985)

It is important to note that the FLAG 'umbrella' does not cover certain 'alcohol interests'. The Scotch Whisky Association claims to have no views on the desirability of liquor licensing reform. Moreover, off-licences, which already enjoy longer permitted hours than the on-licence trade (except on Sundays) have shown little interest in reform. Their interest is centred more around reform of the Sunday Trading laws promised in the 1987 Conservative manifesto (Conservative Central Office, 1987). The larger off-licence retailers have made it clear that they will press for an extension of permitted hours on Sundays if general trading is allowed in the future.

The Brewers Society has regular discussions with the Home Office and the DTI on matters concerning licensing as and when specific issues arise. However, it also has more permanent consultative status since it is a member of the Brewing Sector Working Party—a consultative body which works under the auspices of the National Economic Development Office (NEDO). This body can be used as mean of influencing policy. Its latest report, for example, called once again for a relaxation of licensing laws to assist the development of the industry (Brewing Sector Working Group, 1983). The brewers also have an opportunity to influence government through the British Tourist Authority (BTA). The infra-structure of the BTA includes representatives of the hotel and restaurant trade, the brewers and the Government. It has kept licensing matters under review for a number of years. The BTA is a useful channel for pressure on liquor licensing. It has statutory duties to promote and develop tourism, and to advise Ministers on how this might best be achieved. These responsibilities give BTA considerable weight, especially within the DTI. This Department has, in recent times, shown considerable sympathy towards the argument for licensing law liberalisation.

If the DTI has been a major focal point for trade pressure on reform, the DoH provides the target for those groups which oppose liberalisation in general. For example, the Advisory Committee on Alcoholism (ACA), set up to recommend action on the problem of alcohol misuse, had a strong psychiatric and 'public health' membership. In one of its three reports (ACA, 1977) the Committee recommended a moratorium on licensing law reform until such time as it was certain that changes would not worsen the situation. To date, the Health Departments have opposed all attempts to liberalise the law. 'Public health' organisations such as the Royal College of Psychiatrists and the Royal College of Nursing have argued against any reforms in what they allege is our present state of ignorance. Alcohol Concern (1986) argued that 'limiting pub hours restrains the consumption of alcohol and thereby contributes significantly to reducing alcohol problems'. Triple A did not oppose the nine 'permitted hours' being made more flexible but it did reject the call for more 'drinking time'. Opposition to longer drinking hours is supported by another 'public health' interest, the temperance societies. Despite their long history, these societies are not moribund and the UK Alliance—the political wing of the national organisation—actively opposed liberalisation.

The 'map' of policy participants and networks illustrates that there are channels for influencing policy, given the uncertainty of the outcome of relaxation of legislation, but that these are not equally accessible to all interests. If pressure group power is measured by consultative status and closeness to government, the brewers are well placed through the membership of NEDO and the BTA and their links with the Department of Trade and Industry. So are the police, although it should be observed that the latter, along with the Justices' Clerks' Society and the Magistrates' Association, tend to avoid controversial issues and have taken up highly ambiguous positions on the question of 'permitted hours'. However, the views of the Home Office are all-important. On the subject of licensing law, it regards pressure from other organisations as simply that—pressure. It believes that, apart from the police, they have little to offer in the way of real information and research evidence on the effects of licensing laws. The Home Office civil servants regard themselves as the 'experts' and ministers have insisted in the past that they will not introduce changes until further evidence of any possible effects becomes available. However, the Conservative Government has been committed to the principles of deregulation, and calls for relaxation of the licensing laws have been concordant with policy developments in other areas. Evidence on the effects of relaxation was sought and produced by the Office of Population Censuses and Surveys (Goddard, 1986) and this has been used to justify policy decisions.

DRINKING AND DRIVING

In this section, the drink-driving issue is used to illustrate the network of policy participants and decision making processes in drink-driving legislation. The drink-driving policy networks differ from those concerned with liquor licensing by virtue of there being more agencies with specific areas of responsibility and activities who are in regular, informal contact with each other. The network serves to collect data which feed directly into policy making and also to disseminate information and education about existing policy. The centrality of the law enforcement issue gives police views a considerable influence with decision makers. The greater technical and scientific input into the policy debate gives policy makers more opportunities to move towards rational choices.

The two government departments with responsibility for aspects of alcohol consumption and transport safety in the drink-driving policy network are the Department of Transport and the Home Office. Despite the centrality of the Home Office's law enforcement responsibilities in the drink-driving issue, the Department of Transport is the focus of the policy network. It is responsible for road accidents and related legislation; alcohol consumption in the merchant navy; sponsorship of the Civil Aviation Authority, which in turn is responsible for alcohol consumption in civil aviation; and alcohol consumption and railway safety. The Department is organised so that different aspects of policy are the responsibility of five policy directorates, the Road and Vehicle Safety (RVS) Directorate, Marine and Ports Directorate, Railways Directorate, Civil Aviation Policy Directorate, and the Aircraft Accident Investigation Branch. Each directorate is headed by an Under Secretary and brings together divisions which deal with similar modes of policy or related areas of policy. The Road Safety Division has responsibility for drink-driving issues and is broken up into three branches (RS1, RS2 and RS3). RS1 previously had the main responsibility for the drink-driving campaigns directly funded by the Department, whilst RS2 was responsible for the Highway Code, but this responsibility was transferred to the specially created RS3 branch. The Principal heading RS1 Branch has the leading interest in alcohol, road safety and related legislation, and is responsible for overall policy on the identification and management of drivers with a drink problem.

A separate unit within the RVS Directorate, the Driver and Vehicle Licensing Centre (DVLC), is involved in drink-driving issues through its concern for drivers with a medical disability. The Road Traffic Act 1974 requires drivers, insurers or courts to notify the Secretary of State of any disability which may affect the licence holders competence to drive. Approximately 600 notifications per day are sent to the Medical Advisory

Branch of the DVLC, some of which are alcohol-related. Problem drinkers can be referred to the DVLC without having committed an offence or been involved in an accident. The DVLC is also responsible for administering the High Risk Offender (HRO) procedure. The HRO procedure was introduced in 1983 and applies to all offenders who have already incurred two disqualifications for drinking and driving within a ten year period, where the blood/alcohol concentration was in both cases 200 mgs/100 mls or over. The DVLC advises all offenders where they can obtain help for their drinking problem and informs them that they will be required to undergo an examination at the end of a three year disqualification period to re-establish their competence to drive.

The Government's Transport and Road Research Laboratory (TRRL) provides research support to the UK's Transport Departments. Three of the TRRL's four sections are involved with drink-driving issues and it plays a central role in the formulation of drink-driving policy. TRRL's Data Section maintains an accident data base and is responsible for statistical analysis. The Medical Section researches the behavioural characteristics of drinking drivers. The Education Section is responsible for the development and evaluation of public education. The TRRL has a direct link with Ministers involved in policy formation through its research function. It is able to undertake specific programmes of research to meet the requirements of policy makers in the Department of Transport, and the Scottish, Welsh and Northern Ireland Offices. As part of its general remit, the TRRL collates the drink-driving statistics for Great Britain which are published annually by the Department of Transport. TRRL's data collection function also provides the technical information required to feed into the development of policy. For example, it receives information from Coroners and Procurators Fiscal on the proportion of road users killed in road accidents and found subsequently to have exceeded the legal blood/alcohol limit.

The Department of Transport's Civil Aviation Policy Directorate liaises with the non-departmental public body that has the statutory responsibility for safety standards in civil aviation—the Civil Aviation Authority (CAA). The Secretary of State is responsible for the Air Navigation Orders governing civil aviation, but the Department's lack of technical competence in these matters means that it is the CAA that advises the Minister on legislation. The Air Navigation Orders declare that no-one may pilot an aircraft while under the influence of alcohol or drugs. However, the CAA is able to influence airline policy through its control of airlines' qualifying certificates. To operate in the UK an airline must possess an Air Operators Certificate issued by the CAA. To qualify for the certificate, the airline must comply with CAA requirements, one of which is that the airline must instruct its aircraft crews to abstain from alcohol for at least eight hours before reporting for duty.

Problem drinking amongst air crews is monitored by the Medical Department of the CAA through regular medical examinations. If a drink problem is identified, the pilot's licence is withdrawn by the CAA, although it may be reinstated if he or she is rehabilitated.

The Aircraft Accident Investigation Branch also has an interest in alcohol and air safety. The Branch reports directly to the Secretary of State and is completely independent. The Branch employs 29 Accident Inspectors, who investigate about 250 accidents per year. Pathologists measure the blood/alcohol concentrations of pilots in all fatal air traffic accidents, and the Branch has the powers to make recommendations for more stringent controls over pilots' drinking, but has never considered it necessary to do so.

The Railway Inspectorate acts in a similar way, although it is administratively part of the Department's Railways Directorate. The Chief Inspections Officer has direct access to Ministers on railway safety matters. But it is the Board of British Rail that has the statutory responsibility for safety and complete discretion over operational matters. Following a train crash in 1984 when it was found that the driver's judgement had been impaired by alcohol, the inspecting officer recommended that powers to breathalyse train crews be introduced, but this has not been accepted by British Rail.

The numerous drink-driving interests in the Department of Transport are not linked through any formal structures. There are close and informal contacts between the Road Safety Division and the DVLC, but no formal machinery for co-ordinating policy on alcohol and safety around other forms of transport. Discussions between the railway, marine and aviation sections take place on an *ad hoc* basis on specific issues. Each Directorate has had different views on the use of legal breath/alcohol or blood/alcohol limits since 1967. The Marine Directorate believe that it would be inappropriate to impose similar restrictions on seafarers, as the ship is effectively the seafarer's home. The Civil Aviation Authority considers the introduction of blood/alcohol limits for pilots unnecessary.

The Department of Transport is in contact with other departments in the drink-driving policy network through an Inter-Departmental Advisory Committee on Road Safety. The Committee is chaired by the Under Secretary in charge of the Road and Vehicle Safety Division and it includes representatives from the DoH, the Department of Education and Science (DES) and the Home Office. A Working Group was established to examine drink-driving issues, but is presently held in abeyance. RS1 Branch of the Road Safety Division has frequent contact with the Home Office, DoH and to a lesser degree the DES. In the Home Office this is mainly through the section concerned with road traffic legislation (FS Division). Although there is frequent contact with the DoH, the DoH does not have drink-driving issues as part of its remit, and this has been a source of friction between the two departments in the past. The Department of Transport would like the DoH to be actively involved in the treatment and rehabilitation of drivers suspended under the High Risk Offender procedure.

The Department of Transport also established the Road Traffic Law Review, a Departmental Committee of Enquiry, to examine whether the law could be made simpler, more effective and more acceptable to the public (Department of Transport and Home Office, 1988). Representatives from the Home Office, the Department of Transport and the University of London constituted the Review Committee, which reported in 1988.

The Road Safety Division has some contact with the DES over drink-driving education in schools and with the relevant sections of the Welsh, Scottish and Northern Ireland offices. The Department collaborates directly with the alcohol industry over drink-driving education material, bypassing their sponsoring department, MAFF. The CAA does not have contacts with other government departments, neither does the Railway Inspectorate nor the Accident Investigation Branch.

The Department of Transport is in touch with a wide range of organisations over alcohol and safety issues, mostly on an informal, telephone contact basis, but there are some formal consultations. Probably the most important contact is the Royal Society for the Prevention of Accidents (RoSPA) which receives an annual grant from the Department. This was £500,000 in 1985. RoSPA's Road Safety Committee includes representatives from the Road Safety Division, the TRRL, the DoH, the Automobile Association, the Royal Automobile Club and the Pedestrians' Association. The TRRL is involved in direct contacts with many outside bodies, including local authorities, Road Safety Officers, both individual and corporate, the Casualty Surgeons' Association and the Association of Chief Police Officers. Close links with the police are ensured by the practice of seconding a serving police officer to the TRRL at the Department of Transport's expense. The Department of Transport is also linked to the police and the Home Office through ACPO's Traffic Committee of the Central Conference, which deals with drink-driving issues. A representative of the Road Safety Division is permanently appointed to ACPO's Traffic Committee of the Central Conference.

Close links with medical interests are maintained through the Medical Committee on Accident Prevention (MCAP). MCAP is a charitable trust which receives grants from the DoH and the Department of Transport. The MCAP has both a Transport and an Alcohol committee and brings together representatives of the TRRL, the BMA and the Royal Colleges. The MCAP has been influential on drink-driving policy, a former Chairman, Dr. Andrew Raffell, having sat on the Blennerhassett Committee which reported on its examination of drink-driving legislation in 1976 (Department of Environment, 1976).

The Department of Transport also has contact with parliamentary bodies, such as the House of Commons Select Committee on Transport, the All Party Group on Transport Safety, and the influential Parliamentary Advisory Committee on Transport Safety (PACTS). The fifty strong All Party Group provides another important forum, having associate members from many of the same medical, police, road safety and motoring organisations that serve on RoSPA's committees. The broad-based nature of PACTS ensures not only that recommendations are based on the most up-to-date research evidence available, but that they are related to cost and practical considerations. PACTS is a Trust and is self-sufficient from grants and membership subscriptions. It briefs members of both Houses of Parliament, mainly on aspects of road and air transport, though it also serves as a forum for discussion on all aspects of transport safety.

The Health and Safety Executive (HSE) is another connection in the organisational network concerned with alcohol and transport safety. Members of the Railway Inspectorate attend the HSE management board and the Inspectorate is in touch with HSE initiatives on alcohol and work policies. Detailed discussions take place between the railway unions and management in the Health and Safety Commission's Railway Industry Advisory Committee, which is chaired by the Chief Inspecting Officer of Railways. The Commission, which has union representatives, provides all sides of industry with another opportunity to discuss alcohol and safety issues.

The Home Office is responsible for police enforcement of drink-driving laws, through its FS Division, one of eight Divisions within the Police Department. This Division contains three sections dealing with the Police Dependents Trust, Police Training and Road Traffic. The Road Traffic Section is headed by a Principal assisted by four officers and clerical support. Although it deals with a wide range of traffic law issues, approximately 50 per cent of its time is spent on drink-driving law enforcement matters such as approval of evidential breath-testing machines, monitoring test and conviction rates, and providing an input into drink-driving policy debates. The Road Traffic Section is involved in internal Home Office consultations over alcohol issues as appropriate. It is also in regular contact with the Road Safety Division in the Department of Transport which is responsible for such matters as environmental safety measures, the Highway Code and the Department of Transport's drink-driving campaigns. The Principal in charge of RS1 Branch of the Road Safety Division takes the leading interest in alcohol, road safety and related legislation. The Home Office is also represented on an Interdepartmental Advisory Committee formed in 1984 to examine a number of road safety issues. The Committee is chaired by the

Under Secretary from the Road and Vehicle Safety Division in the Department of Transport and other members are drawn from the DoH and the DES. The Principal in charge of the Road Traffic Section of the Home Office is a member of the Road Traffic Law Review.

As with liquor licensing issues, the Home Office's law enforcement responsibilities bring the police into the policy network as the major non-departmental interest on road safety. Again, ACPO is the principal medium through which the views of the police are made known to the Home Office and vice versa. ACPO's strongest links are with the Home Office Police Department. The Committees of the Central Conference established to maintain day-to-day contact between ACPO and the Home Office include the Traffic Committee which often considers alcohol-related topics. ACPO does not adopt a stance on the level of blood or breath/alcohol concentration. They argue that it should be the decisions of politicians that determine public policy, under the guidance of scientific evidence on the effects of alcohol on driving ability. ACPO merely observes that, if asked, its own experience leads it to advise all motorists 'not to drink and drive'.

The drink-driving policy network involves a comprehensive range of participants with a concern for many aspects of road safety, which highlights the deficiencies in certain related policy areas, such as marine and rail safety. Of the many groups involved, some have a more 'central' interest than others and most importantly, the kinds of interest vary considerably. Organisations such as the Institute of Public Lighting Engineers or the Convention of Scottish Local Authorities represented on RoSPA's Road Safety Committee have an interest in environmental safety, but do not have a 'view' about drink-driving issues. Of those bodies that do hold a 'view', there are disagreements over policy options. Despite the many links, it becomes difficult to distinguish between peripheral member organisations and those who may be drawn into the network for consultation as the need arises.

But there is little doubt that some organisations, such as ACPO, exert considerable influence over policy, by virtue of their proximity to government. Ministers have frequently referred to the fact that the police appeared to be satisfied with the existing drink-driving law, in refusing to introduce random breath-testing.

ACPO operates on a consensus basis, and while several Chief Constables were calling for greater police powers, others remained to be convinced. As a result, ACPO could not support a change in the law. In effect, they exerted a veto power, as no campaign to introduce random breath-testing would succeed without their backing.

This internal debate appears to have been resolved in 1988, when ACPO called for the police to have 'unfettered discretion' in the administration of breath tests. While not technically the same as random testing, permitting the police greater discretion in the use of breath tests would open the way to a more stringent application of the law. ACPO's change of policy will not ensure government action, but it does remove the most important institutional impediments to legislative change.

CONCLUSION

The mapping of policy networks clearly shows that where legislation is used to regulate policies for manipulating consumption, there exists a diversity of interests and structures which must be considered, or changed, if appropriate legislation is to be effectively implemented. Public health campaigns which look to legislation to provide a more rigorous defence of the public interest must consider the implications of the policy networks through which the policy instrument is operationalised. Liquor licensing is one issue where 'the law' as a policy instrument is not necessarily the product of interest-free decisions about public welfare. Chapter 6 goes on to discuss a range of policy options in the liquor licensing debate and the implications, given the policy networks described above. Drink-driving is an issue where 'the law' as a policy instrument also provides policy makers with a monitoring and development tool. Again however, the process is not 'interest-free'. Chapter 7 looks at drink-driving issues in greater detail.

References

Action on Alcohol Abuse, (1985), *Triple A Review*, 2, (5), 37.
Advisory Committee on Alcoholism (ACA), (1977), *Prevention*, DHSS, London.
Alcohol Concern, (1986), *Pub Opening Hours: The Case Against Change*, (Leaflet), Alcohol Concern, London.
Brewing Sector Working Group, (1983), *The Outlook for the Brewing Industry*, National Economic Development Office, London.
Conservative Central Office, (1987), *The Next Moves Forward*, Conservative Central Office, London.
Department of the Environment, (1976), *Drinking and Driving*, a report of the Departmental (Blennerhassett) Committee, HMSO, London.
Department of Transport and Home Office, (1988), *Road Traffic Law Review Report*, HMSO, London.
Goddard, E., (1986), *Drinking and Attitudes to Licensing in Scotland*, HMSO, London.
Home Office, (1985a), *The Prevention of Violence Associated with Licensed Premises*, Report of a Standing Conference on Crime Prevention (SCCP) Working Group, HMSO, London.
Home Office, (1985b), *Implementing Crime Prevention Measures*, Research Study No. 86, HMSO, London.
Justices' Clerks' Society, (1983), *Licensing Law in the Eighties*, Justices' Clerks' Society, London.
Maynard, A. and Tether, P. (eds.), (1989), *The Addiction Market: consumption, production and policy development*, Avebury/Gower, Aldershot.

6 Liquor licensing

PHILIP TETHER AND CHRISTINE GODFREY

Some form of licensing designed to regulate the public sale of intoxicating liquor is a feature of control policies in most countries (Davies and Walsh, 1983). In the UK, licensing law has a long history. Some of the difficulties in using legislation to attempt to control consumption, as discussed in Chapter 1, are illustrated in the following examination of liquor licensing.

Most accounts of the British system of liquor licensing have traced its origins to a 1494 Act 'For Punishment of Vagabonds and Beggars, and touching Ale houses' (Williams and Brake, 1980, p.1; Dorn, 1983, p.32). The Act authorised a quorum of two Justices of the Peace to 'reject common selling of Ale' at their discretion and to take sureties from the keepers of ale houses against their good behaviour. This Act and other licensing controls introduced in the sixteenth century embodied two important principles; that alcohol is a special commodity and, that licensing justices have absolute discretion. These central principles have endured despite many subsequent changes in the general power and role of the magistracy.

The history of liquor licensing is characterised by periods of relaxation followed by a tightening of controls. According to tradition, gin was introduced into England by William III in 1688. The government of the day, convinced of the economic potential of this new beverage, removed all restrictions on its manufacture and sale in an effort to provide a market for low-grade domestic corn. The results are well known and led to the Gin Act of 1736. This was the first measure to attempt macro-social control in the interests of public health as well as public order. It prohibited the sale of spirits in quantities of less than two gallons without an annual licence which

116

cost £50.00 and it introduced duty at £20.00 a gallon. These events provide an early example of potential conflicts between economic and public health policies.

The next relaxation over availability concerned not gin but beer. Public drunkenness and all the associated problems of widespread and heavy alcohol consumption among the labouring classes were issues of great concern for anxious and respectable Victorians. Hogarth, who documented the miseries of Gin Lane, depicted Beer Street with the intention of contrasting gin-sodden vice and depravity with the wholesome pleasures of beer. This distinction between the pernicious nature of spirits—distilled by men's artifice, and benign beer—produced from nature's ingredients by natural processes, has a long history and still endures in attenuated form to colour popular misconceptions about drink and drinking.

The first determined nineteenth century effort to restore order and discipline was the Beer Act of 1830 which, drawing on the myths of the previous century, amended the licensing law in a way which sought to distinguish between harmful and harmless liquor. The Beer Act allowed any householder assessed to the poor rate to sell beer for consumption on or off the premises on payment of a two-guinea fee to the Excise, without reference to the Justices. A fortnight after this radical relaxation of the licensing law, the Reverend Sydney Smith described the consequences in a few memorable lines: 'The Sovereign People are in a beastly state. Everybody is drunk. Those who are not singing are sprawling' (Harrison, 1971). A variety of Acts was introduced over the next forty years in an attempt to bring the situation under control and re-establish the authority of licensing Justices. But the drink question remained a major issue throughout the whole of the Victorian era and it played a prominent role in the emergence of modern party politics—in marked contrast to the twentieth century in which drink questions in general, and liquor licensing issues in particular, have remained for the most part matters of cross-party concern.

The last major reform of the UK's licensing controls was implemented during World War I. Because of drunkenness among munition and shipyard workers, Lloyd George set up a Liquor Control Board endowed with sweeping powers which it did not hesitate to exercise. These included imposing a ban on the sale of spirits, ensuring the provision of food in public houses, regulating opening hours, improving the standard of the premises, closing down unwanted premises or running them itself. After the war, the most severe controls were lifted, although their main provisions concerning 'permitted hours' were embodied in the Licensing Act 1921. This Act laid down maximum daily opening hours for public houses in a specified period within which some discretion could be exercised. There was a mandatory afternoon break. Clubs were also required to observe the regulations concerning permitted hours. Although variations have subsequently been introduced, the basic principle of permitted hours still holds. Their number and disposition have, however, been the subject of intense debate which is considered in this chapter.

During the first part of the twentieth century, per capita alcohol consumption in the UK remained low and only began to rise sharply in the 1950s. However, consumption has doubled since this date and the rise is 'accounted for by a 60 per cent increase in consumption of beer, a 350 per cent increase in spirits and a 600 per cent increase in the consumption of wine' (Tether and Robinson, 1986, p.4). As consumption has risen so have the various indicators of harm:

> 'The recent sharp increase in misuse, as measured by a variety of indicators, seems clearly to be linked with the equally marked rise in overall consumption of alcohol that has occurred in the United Kingdom in recent years and the changes in people's drinking habits which underline it.' (DHSS, 1981, p.64)

During this period of increasing consumption and misuse, economic pressures resulting from changes in the alcohol market have led to demands for the relaxation of some aspects of the licensing laws. The 1988 Licensing Act which increased the number of permitted hours during which licensed premises can open has, however, generated considerable controversy. The purpose of this chapter is to review present licensing policy, the factors which have determined the trend towards liberalisation of licensing controls, and the available evidence concerning the impact of licensing controls on consumption and alcohol-related problems. This analysis is used to determine the impediments to alternative licensing policies designed to reduce alcohol-related problems. In the first section of the paper, the different aspects of present licensing law are outlined.

PRESENT LICENSING LAW IN ENGLAND AND WALES

The two major kinds of licence are on-licences which permit the sale of alcohol for consumption either on or off the premises—unless a condition is attached to the licence prohibiting off sales—and off-licences where alcohol is sold only for consumption off the premises. In addition, the Licensing Act 1961 created what are often described as three new types of licence—restaurant licences, residential licenses and combined restaurant and residential licenses. However, this description is not strictly accurate since these are, in effect, ordinary on-licences with specific conditions attached under a power conferred in 1904. Thus, what was new about them was the fact that the discretion of licensing Justices to refuse a grant was restricted. A restaurant licence is granted on the condition that the sale or supply of intoxicating liquor is confined to those taking table meals and is consumed as an ancillary to those meals. A residential licence is granted to enable residents to drink on the premises of guest houses or hotels. These three new licences are collectively known as Part IV Licences after the section in the Licensing Act, 1964 which controls their issue. The 1961 Act also introduced the ten-minute drinking-up period. Provision was made for the removal, by local option, of the ban on Sunday drinking in licensed premises in Wales and Monmouthshire which had been in existence since 1881. The hours for off-licences in England and Wales were also extended from 9.5 to 15 hours. The 1961 Act enshrined the right of appeal by an applicant against a refusal to grant a licence.

Licensing Justices are responsible for granting all kinds of liquor licences and they are appointed annually from among the magistrates of the local bench. Subject to the suitability of both the premises and the applicant, Justices have absolute discretion over the granting of on- and off-licences except where Part IV Licences are concerned. Once a licence is granted, licensing law specifies not only the maximum permitted hours during which premises may retail alcohol, but also who may purchase and/or consume intoxicating liquor. 'Drunks' may not be served nor 'young people'. The Licensing Act 1872 had forbidden the sale of spirits for consumption on the premises to any person apparently under the age of 16 and this prohibition was extended in 1901 with the passing of the Intoxicating Liquor (Sale to Children) Act known as the anti-sipping Act. This Act made it illegal to sell drink for off-consumption to any child under 14 except in sealed containers. The current law on under-age drinking dates from the Intoxicating Liquor (Sale to Persons under 18) Act 1923, which prohibited the sale or purchase of intoxicants to persons under the age of 18 years. This Act was the final stage in a series of measures designed to protect the young—and hence vulnerable—from drink and the public house ambience.

Present licensing law, therefore, controls availability in a number of ways. A source of confusion in the liquor licensing debate is the frequent failure to distinguish these dimensions of licensing law and their separate effects on alcohol availability. The law provides controls over the *number* of outlets in a locality, the *persons* permitted to purchase alcohol and the *hours* during which outlets are allowed to remain open. Control over the number of outlets lies in the hands of the licensing justices whilst persons and permitted hours are enshrined in legislation, though some minor local discretion exists. Various combinations of controls over the number of outlets and permitted hours are possible, as illustrated in Table 6.1.

Table 6.1

Control over availability

	Control by number of outlets	Control by permitted hours
Reduce	Option 1	Option 2
Increase	Option 3	Option 4

Different combinations of these options may increase or decrease alcohol-related problems. For example, fewer outlets but increases in permitted hours, particularly if hours are not uniform, may result in fewer public order offences. Also the economic benefits to the trade from changes in policy may vary. Existing licence holders may oppose increases in the number of outlets but depending on market conditions may welcome an increase in permitted hours.

The separate effects of the numbers of outlets and permitted hours on alcohol availability are considered in the following sections. Developments in licensing policy since the 1961 Act are described and evidence on the links between availability, alcohol consumption and alcohol-related problems is examined. The trade and health arguments which have formed the background to the present debate and movement towards liberalising licensing laws are also reviewed.

OUTLETS, ALCOHOL CONSUMPTION AND LICENSING POLICY

Recent reform debates in the UK have concentrated on relaxing controls over permitted hours. However, control by Justices over the numbers of outlets in their localities has been eroded since the 1961 Act. Part IV Licences significantly reduced their absolute discretion to grant or withhold permission to retail alcohol. Secondly, they are defeated by the concept of need. Case law enshrined in Sharp-V-Wakefield (1891) 55 JP 197 confers on Justices 'the power and even the duty ... to consider the wants of a neighbourhood with references both to its population, means of inspection by proper authorities and so forth'. However, a locality's need for outlets can be expressed in many different ways including total number, density, quality, the range of types, and any combination of these features. It is difficult to quantify and specify need with any degree of precision, and applicants who

120

are turned down by licensing Justices can usually confidently appeal to the Crown Court against the decision, and challenge the Justices' assessment of need. The likelihood of success is increased by the fact that all licensing decisions must be exercised judicially, 'that is to say according to the rules of reason and justice and not a private opinion. It must not be arbitrary, vague or fanciful but legal and regular' (Justices' Clerks' Society 1983, p.27). The result is a case by case approach by licensing committees to each application for the grant of a licence which, as we have underlined before, means that:

> 'appeals are often upheld if there is any suggestion that the Justices are making their decisions in terms of some broad policy about the 'needs' of a locality rather than in relation to the merits of the particular case under consideration'. (Tether and Robinson, 1986, p.121)

The numbers of licences of all kinds have increased since the early 1960s. In 1960 there were 116,627 licensed premises, including clubs, in England and Wales. By 1986, this number had risen to 172,051, an increase of 68 per cent in twenty-six years. Table 6.2 shows the growth in various categories of licence during this period.

Table 6.2

Number of licensed premises in England and Wales, 1960–1986

	Full on licences	Part IV licences	Licensed and reg. clubs	Off licences
1960	69184	–	23773	23670
1965	66570	2810	23598	26352
1970	64702	5989	26032	27910
1975	64614	10313	27733	31644
1980	67091	17657	29978	37252
1985	70331	20622	30277	42646
1986	71200	26503	30557	43891

Source: *The Brewers Society Statistical Handbook,* various years.

Although full on-licences have only increased in number by 2.9 per cent since 1960, the numbers of other outlets have grown considerably. Four years after their introduction in 1961, there were 2,810 Part IV Licences in England and Wales, but by 1986 this figure had grown by 943 per cent. Licensed and registered clubs have increased by 28.5 per cent and off- licences by 85.5 per cent.

Consumption of alcohol also rose substantially between 1960 and 1980 and a number of studies have attempted to examine the relationship between the number of licences and alcohol consumption. In a study of UK annual data, from 1956 to 1975, McGuinness (1980) found a significant relationship between the number of licences and consumption. His model related per capita alcohol consumption to the price of alcohol, income, advertising expenditure, a time trend and the number of licensed premises. Two reasons were put forward for including the number of licences as an explanatory variable. One argument was that consumption of alcohol may be affected by the ease of access to the product. Another way of regarding this argument is that more outlets lower the transaction costs involved in obtaining the product, such as the cost of travelling and time involved in locating and arriving at an outlet. The second argument is that the number of licences may be a proxy for an advertising effect. Off-licences may have considerable amount of point of sale promotion and public houses can have, for example, large illuminated signs which may stimulate demand. McGuinness's results imply that a 1 per cent fall in the number of licensed premises would result in a 2.15 per cent fall in consumption.

McGuinness's original work has been criticised on the grounds that he grouped all alcohol consumption together. Both McGuinness (1983) and Walsh (1982) provided estimates of demand for beer, spirits and wine separately, but still included a licensing variable. McGuinness's results suggested that the number of licences has a sizeable effect on the demand for beer, a 10 per cent drop in licences would result in a 7.8 per cent drop in beer consumption, all other things being equal. Walsh found larger effects for all drinks.

Another criticism of these studies concerns the statistical problems of detecting the direction of causality between consumption and licensing. It might be argued that if profits increased along with alcohol consumption, so, as a result, would the number of licence applications. McGuinness argued that the length of gestation period for the opening of new licensed premises, including for example planning permission and licensing application, seemed long enough to break the impact of current sales on the current number of licences. This argument, however, suggests a long gestation period of a year. Duffy (1983), on the other hand, did not include a licensing variable when modelling alcohol consumption because he felt the number of licences was dependent upon consumption levels, rather than being a determining factor of consumption. McGuinness and Duffy, therefore, took opposite views, with McGuinness assuming that the causal flow was only from increases in licences to increases in consumption, while Duffy maintained that increases in consumption resulted in a growth of licensed premises.

These studies vary in a number of respects and therefore the differences in results cannot be solely attributed to the inclusion or exclusion of a variable for licences. The differences were sometimes substantial. For example, McGuinness's estimates for price elasticity for spirits and wine were -0.4 and -0.2 respectively, compared to Duffy's estimates of between -0.8 and -0.1 for spirits and -0.7 and 1.0 for wine.

The differences in these estimates of the coefficients suggest that further empirical investigation is required to assess the impact of the number of licences on consumption. Versions of the McGuinness and Duffy models were re-estimated using a common data set to evaluate the role of licensing in the demand for alcohol in the UK (Godfrey, 1988). The two models were estimated including three separate licensing variables for on, off and registered and other clubs, in order to test whether the different types of licences had different effects on consumption. The empirical analyses carried out were structured to test several hypotheses about the role of licensing. The first step involved testing for feedback effects between the number of licences and consumption. If feedback effects are present, such that the number of licences affects consumption and also the level of consumption influences the number of licences, a special technique is required to estimate the size and significance of the effect of the number of licences on consumption. The general validity of the demand models was also tested along with the need to disaggregate the licensing variables into their separate types. If the aggregate licensing variable was found to be sufficient, the significance of its effect was also tested.

The major conclusion from this research was that different alcoholic drinks required different assumptions about the relationship between consumption and licensing. For wines and spirits consumption, there was no evidence of feedback effects in the relationship between consumption and the number of licences. Further, for spirits consumption the number of licences was insignificant in most forms of the tested models. Significant licensing effects were found for wine consumption measures. When consumption was measured in units of alcohol, disaggregation of the total licensing variable was not necessary. Licensing elasticities evaluated using 1980 figures were in the range 1.39 to 4.94. The higher estimate suggests that a 1 per cent fall in the number of licensed outlets would result in nearly 5 per cent fall in wine consumption, other things being equal. The results for the expenditure measure were not, however, so clear cut.

For beer consumption, significant feedback effects between licensing and consumption were found. The presence of such feedback effects would invalidate the results reported in previous research. The models were re-estimated using an appropriate technique, but these estimates need to be interpreted with care because of the limited information content of data. Although in general coefficients were imprecisely estimated, significant licensing effects were found with, for example, 1980 elasticities for club licenses being in the range 0.96 to 2.88.

Further evidence on the differential effects by beverage of the number of licences on alcohol consumption is available from studies in North America. Ornstein and Hanssens (1985) found the coefficient of on-licensed premises per head consistently positive and significant in US beer and spirits demand equations. Availability on Sunday, however, was found to be important for beer consumption, but not for distilled spirits. In a Canadian study, Bourgeois and Barnes (1979) found that the number of retail stores had a positive effect on wine consumption, no significant effect on spirits, and a negative and significant effect on beer consumption.

The empirical studies suggest, therefore, that one preventive policy alternative may be to control the number of licensed outlets; option 1 in Table 6.1. Options involving restrictions on the number of licenses have, however, received little attention from either the health or trade lobbies or governments. To help understand this apparent neglect, health and trade arguments surrounding reforms of licensing hours are now considered.

PERMITTED HOURS, THE ALCOHOL TRADE, HEALTH AND LICENSING REFORM

As has often been the case, the current licensing debate on increasing permitted hours has centred on the conflicts between trade and health arguments, and the resulting legislation has been a result of the complex interactions of the different interest groups described in Chapter 5. The actions of some of these interest groups and the development of health and trade arguments are now examined.

Trade and competition

The present reform debate had its roots in the 1969 Monopolies Commission report. This report concluded that 'licensed outlets are individually and collectively protected from free competition by the restrictions of the establishment of new competitors in the licensed trade' (Monopolies Commission, 1969). They were concerned with brewer ownership of retail outlets and recommended a substantial relaxation of the licensing system. The Erroll Committee was set up to review licensing law in England and Wales, and came to broadly similar conclusions (Erroll Report, 1972). For example, Justices' absolute discretion over the granting of licences should, the Committee believed, be removed. Licensing hours should be extended from 10am to midnight with no afternoon break, although the local Justices would be able to suspend sales for up to two hours at any time before 7pm if such restrictions seemed necessary in the interests of public order, safety, health or amenity. Restaurants should be allowed to sell alcohol whenever they were open and young people should be permitted to purchase and drink in on-licensed premises when they were 17 years of age.

The Erroll Committee's radical proposals were presented as a means of making drinking more relaxed and socially integrated. However, the Committee's underlying advocacy of a market place approach to drink sales generated considerable criticism, as did its failure to present research evidence on the effect its various proposals would have on drinking behaviour (Robinson, 1974). The Erroll Committee did not have any legislative consequences. The Government has, however, continued to be concerned about the relationship between licensing laws and competition, and a further report on the brewing industry from the Monopoly and Mergers Commission was published in 1989.

The 1961 Licensing Act did have a number of important features which have changed the retailing of alcohol. The alcohol trade has strengthened and united its arguments for liberalising licensing laws and, in particular, increasing the permitted hours for on-licensed premises. One of the most important features of the 1961 Act was the lengthening of permitted hours for off-licence premises. Previously off-licences had been restricted to the same hours as on-licence premises. Most alcohol for consumption at home was therefore retailed in specialist stores or from on-licence premises. The extension of opening from 9.5 to 15 hours meant that more general retailers were freed from the responsibilities of having to maintain a shop within a shop with its opening and closing times differing from those of the main store. This change, combined with the later abolition of retail price maintenance on alcoholic drink, paved the way for a considerable change in the off-licence trade.

In the 1960s the off-licence trade was only seen as a small part of the beer market. Sales to off-licences were seen by brewers as marginal but useful by making more than proportional contributions to profits (Economists Advisory Group, 1969). Changes both in demand and supply have, however, changed the significance of the trade. In Table 6.3 estimates of the proportion of beer sold from different outlets, made for the Brewing Sector Working Group, are shown. These indicate the growth of clubs and off-licensed trade. Figures on the distribution of both beer and other alcoholic expenditure derived by the Central Statistical Office are given in Table 6.4. These estimates also indicate the recent decline of the sales of beer from on-licensed premises, while off-licence sales have grown. Also, beer is a smaller proportion of total alcohol expenditure.

Table 6.3

Changes in beer sales by outlet

| Year | Bulk barrels | | | % of total | | |
	Public houses	Off-licence/ take home	Clubs	Public houses	Off-licence/ take home	Clubs
1970	26.51	2.75	5.16	77	8	15
1975	28.07	4.01	8.02	70	10	20
1980	25.32	4.80	10.01	63	12	25

Source: Brewing Sector Working Group (1983).

Table 6.4

Consumer expenditure on alcoholic drink—£m, constant 1980 prices

| Year | Off-licence expenditure | | On-licence expenditure | |
	Beer	Other alcohol	Beer	Other alcohol
1973	420	1356	4993	2525
1974	474	1484	4934	2596
1975	474	1493	5107	2357
1976	540	1670	5088	2209
1977	510	1725	4964	2322
1978	564	1891	4984	2491
1979	586	2017	5002	2777
1980	572	1908	4748	2726
1981	552	1879	4448	2733
1982	561	1855	4264	2690
1983	649	1965	4265	2851
1984	720	2045	4223	2995
1985	770	2149	4164	3141
1986	822	2164	4113	3198

Source: *UK National Accounts,* (CSO Blue Book), HMSO, London, various years.

One of the major interests of the brewers is the production of beer. As producers, therefore, it may be expected that brewers would campaign for the licensing regulation that maximised their sales or profits, and hence may

126

oppose restrictions on the retailing of alcohol. The long history of state regulation on the retailing of alcohol and other factors have, however, resulted in the brewers taking control over a large number of retail outlets. Such vertical integration cannot be wholly attributed to licensing and does bestow advantages to the brewer in economies of distribution, establishment of brands and control over the standard of amenity in public houses. Control of the product was, of course, even more important before the introduction of keg beer, since when the handling of beer has become less important in ensuring its quality.

Another important feature of the retailing of alcohol has been the tied-house system. This tied system also has a long history. Licensees found it difficult to provide capital to maintain the standard of premises, and brewers made loans and eventually purchased premises with the tie that the licensees stock their brand of beer. Similar arrangements continue to be made with private clubs. Public houses owned by brewers, but managed by self-employed tenants, are tied to the brewery to purchase wines and spirits as well as the brewers' own beer. The British licensed trade has therefore been characterised by a vertically integrated system with brewers engaged in the manufacture, wholesale and retailing of their own product, and with interests in the sales of other alcoholic and non-alcoholic beverages.

In Table 6.5, figures for the ownership by brewers of licensed premises are reported. These figures indicate that earlier in the period brewers had a considerable interest in the on- and off-licence trade. Their control over the total number of licensed premises has clearly declined.

The ownership of public houses does involve large amounts of capital. The Brewing Sector Working Group's (1983) report emphasised both this fact and that large sums that had been spent in recent years modernising these premises. They estimated that 75 per cent of capital expenditure was devoted to retailing, rather than production, and this breakdown of expenditure was likely to continue. For brewers to maintain profitability, they need to ensure that this capital attracts a reasonable rate of return. The Brewing Sector Working Group (BSWG) expressed concern over profitability and Booth, Hardman and Hartley (1986) suggest that profitability in the brewing and distilling industry is below average. The BSWG endorsed the brewers' viewpoint that licensing laws should be liberalised because 'it is clearly at a competitive disadvantage to clubs (opening hours, AWP machines, access to children) and supermarket (opening hours)'.

This argument assumes that on- and off-licences are in direct competition for alcohol sales and that the growth in off-licence sales has been at the expense of on-licence trade. There are, however, many differences between, for example, packaged beer brought from an off-licence and draught beer, especially when the amenity value of drinking in a public house is also

Table 6.5

Brewers ownership of licensed premises in the UK

	Percentage of licensed premises owned by brewers by type					
	On-licences			Off-licences	Clubs	Total
		% of which				
Year	Total	Managed	Tenants			
1967	78.0	23.6	76.4	29.9	–	48.3
1973	73.0	27.8	72.1	18.1	0.7	39.3
1976	69.0	28.9	71.0	14.5	0.7	35.7
1977	68.1	28.4	71.6	12.5	–	34.3
1978	66.6	28.3	71.7	12.3	0.7	33.2
1979	65.3	28.4	71.6	12.1	0.7	32.2
1980	64.1	28.6	71.4	11.8	0.9	31.2
1981	62.9	28.4	71.6	10.9	0.8	30.2
1982	61.4	27.8	72.2	10.2	0.8	29.2
1983	60.1	27.4	72.6	9.1	0.8	28.1
1984	58.7	27.4	72.6	9.5	1.1	27.6
1985	57.9	27.7	72.3	8.9	1.1	27.0
1986	56.9	28.9	71.1	8.4	0.9	26.3

Source: *The Brewers Society Statistical Handbook*, various years.

considered. Consequently it is not clear whether liberalising the hours for on-licences will increase total alcohol consumption or redistribute consumption between on- and off-licences.

It can also be seen from Table 6.5 and Table 6.6 that the brewers' interest in the off-licence trade has declined. The off-licence trade also began to be dominated by large retail companies which have the ability to negotiate large discounts from brewers, resulting in a lowering of the brewers' margins in the take-home trade. Undoubtedly this domination also has resulted, along with other factors such as new packaging, in lower price differentials between public houses, where traditionally beer had been cheaper, and the take-home trade. During the last decade, public houses have changed in a number of other ways with a large increase in the retailing of food as well as drink. Clearly public houses are in competition with a wider range of leisure activities. Restrictive licensing laws may also put public houses at a disadvantage in competing in these markets.

The interest of other producers in licensing reform will depend on the forecasts they make of how such changes will affect the consumption of their good. If liberalising the licensing hours, for example, is expected to increase beer sales at the expense of alcohol, then these other producers may not

Table 6.6
Sales of alcohol from retail stores by outlet type

Year	Grocers + General food retailers	Type of outlet (% of sales) Off-licences	Confectioners Newsagents Tobacconists	Mixed retail business
1961	25.9	70.0	0.4	1.5
1966	23.7	66.6	0.4	2.9
1971	33.2	63.3	0.2	2.4
1976	25.9[a]	58.2	1.8	13.8[a]
1977	25.4[a]	55.2	2.8	16.0[a]
1978	30.7[a]	51.8	3.4	13.6[a]
1979	30.8[a]	52.2	3.2	13.6[a]
1980	41.9	48.4	5.3	4.1
1982	44.3	45.9	5.7	4.1
1984	45.0	44.1	6.7	3.9

a. Definitional changes

Source: Census of Distribution, *Retailing* for 1980, 1982, 1984, Business Statistics Office, HMSO.

welcome the change. Similarly they may have strong views on any attempt to control the number of off-licence outlets if this is believed to adversely affect their trade. On the other hand, a general liberalisation of the law may be expected to increase all alcohol sales. These other producers are less closely involved with the retailing of alcohol and therefore have not taken a large part in the debates about legislation.

Demands to change permitted hours did, however, grow over the period. The precise nature of these demands varied over time and from group to group, but they contained two features, some increase in the daily opening hours and/or flexibility in the disposition of permitted hours. Some cohesion in the alcohol trade lobby was achieved in 1984 by the creation of the Flexi Law Action Group (FLAG) which included the Brewers Society, the British Hotel Restaurants and Caterers Association and the Restaurants Association of Great Britain as well as the Campaign for Real Ale (CAMRA). FLAG explained that it sought an amendment to licensing law in England and Wales that would retain permitted hours as at present but a provision would be added to allow individual licensees to select the hours most suited to their trade and to apply to the licensing Justices for a variation to cover such hours. It was proposed that the maximum should be 12 hours between 10am and 12 midnight (14 hours in special circumstances). Licensing Justices would consider each variation application, hear objections and decide to grant, or to refuse the application on its merits, using their local knowledge. FLAG emphasised that tourism would benefit from this kind of change and that reform would lead to more employment, although trade estimates of the employment benefits that might accrue varied widely. These demands were supported by sections of the government, principally the Department of Employment and the Department of Trade and Industry.

During the first part of the twentieth century, per capita alcohol consumption in the UK remained low and only began to rise sharply in the 1950s. However, consumption has doubled since this date. Given this background of increasing consumption and the associated indicators of harm, the 1988 liberalisation of the licensing law, which increased the number of permitted opening hours, generated heated controversy. Opponents claimed that the reform would usher in a new cycle of harms and was 'a reckless gamble with the nation's future health and well-being' (Alcohol Concern, 1986). The pressure for relaxation of different aspects of the licensing laws had not come directly from public demand, and public opinion data have not generally suggested dissatisfaction with existing legislation. There was, for example, little evidence of public demand for an increase in the number of retail outlets for alcohol (Leedham, 1987), and a majority of respondents to polls, including under 18s, favoured keeping the legal drinking age at 18 (Gallup, 1976; Bradley and Fenwick, 1974; Hawker, 1978).

Surveys showed that public opinion tended to favour a maintenance of the status quo when it came to the number of permitted hours (Gallup, 1976; Blackburn Report, 1979; NOP, 1977, 1984; Leedham, 1987). A review of the beer, wine and pub and club market produced a figure of only 15 per cent of respondents who thought that longer hours would lead them to drink more (Public Attitude Surveys, 1985). The evidence from Scotland, however, suggests that once a relaxation of permitted hours is introduced, then the public tend to find longer hours more favourable (Knight and Wilson, 1980; Goddard, 1986). What may be a more significant feature of the development of licensing law than public attitudes to alcohol consumption are changing attitudes to regulation itself. Since 1979, the Conservative administration has advocated economic and legislative deregulation in the interest of freedom of choice, gradually changing the climate of opinion on many aspects of regulation. For example, until 1977, public opinion favoured the law, rather than licensees, deciding pub opening hours (Erroll Report, 1972; Bradley and Fenwick, 1974; NOP, 1977). A survey by NOP in 1984 showed that 15 per cent would prefer more freedom for licensees to decide their own hours.

Health arguments and evaluation of Scottish law changes

While there has been support for liberalisation of licensing laws from some departments, the Home Office has taken a more cautious approach and has been concerned with the effects which any changes in the law might have on alcohol-related problems and, in particular, public order offences. The evaluation of Scottish licensing law changes have played an important part in shaping health arguments.

The reforms in Scotland arose from the Clayson (1973) report into the licensing laws in Scotland, and a number of its proposals were embodied in the Licensing (Scotland) Act, 1976. Like Erroll, Clayson argued that some relaxation over availability was desirable in the interests of de-mystifying alcohol consumption and promoting sensible drinking. However, this approach was not tied to a market place philosophy and, in fact, the proposals for liberalisation were balanced by changes to the system of granting licences which appeared to provide an assurance of overall control. Moreover, the effect of the changes proposed regarding availability could be seen broadly as bringing Scotland's system into line with that of England and Wales and could therefore be justified on grounds of consistency and equity.

Under the 1976 Act, public houses in Scotland were permitted to open on Sundays. Previously, Sunday opening had only been possible for bars situated in hotels and for licensed clubs. Prior to 1976, closing time in Scotland had been 10pm and the Act allowed public bars to remain open, if they wished, for a further hour until 11pm. Sunday opening and the extension to 11pm brought Scotland into line with England and Wales. However, the Scottish legislation also permitted licensees to obtain permanent extensions to their normal permitted hours, thus allowing them, if they wished, to remain open during the afternoon break and after 11pm. These extensions were soon being routinely granted.

The so-called Scottish experiment occupied an important place in the debate leading up to the introduction of the 1988 licensing changes. Supporters of change to the English and Welsh licensing laws claimed that the measures introduced in Scotland in 1976 showed that increased availability does not have harmful effects. Clayson himself reviewed the impact of his Committee's changes by comparing drunkenness convictions, drink-driving convictions, alcohol-related violent crime and liver cirrhosis mortality in both England and Wales and Scotland for the six years prior to and after the implementation of the Act (Clayson, 1984). His handling of the data suggests that drunkenness, drink-driving and alcohol-related violent crime all declined in Scotland following the introduction of the 1976 Act. Only liver cirrhosis mortality showed a rise in the post-1976 period and any relationship to changes in the licensing law was discounted because of the considerable time lag needed for problems to develop.

Clayson's methodology was criticised by Saunders (1985) who argued that collapsing data into six year blocks obscured important trends in the movement of harm indicators in England, Wales and Scotland. If the trends are followed on a year-to-year basis, the decline in Scottish harm indicators appears much later than 1976. This suggests the influence of non-licensing factors such as the markedly higher Scottish unemployment rate and also the Criminal Justice Act 1980, which banned the consumption of alcohol on the way to or during sporting fixtures and decriminalised the drunkenness offence. Saunders argued that the upward cirrhosis mortality trend in Scotland was significant and he rejected Clayson's claim that this cannot be associated with the 1976 licensing changes. Saunders argued that the condition can manifest itself rapidly when changes in availability lead to increased consumption since there will be a pool of already damaged heavy drinkers whose condition will be rapidly accelerated by increased access.

More data on the Scottish changes were contained in a report by the Social Survey Division of the Office of Population Censuses and Surveys *Drinking and Attitudes to Licensing in Scotland* (Goddard, 1986). The Report showed that the measures designed to bring Scotland into line with the situation in England and Wales were generally popular, and that 77 per cent of those surveyed approved of the extra hour and 55 per cent agreed that Sunday opening was desirable. However, support for extensions was much more mixed. Post-1976 consumption among males had only increased fractionally, whereas among women there had been a statistically significant increase, from 2.8 units in 1976 to 3.8 units in 1984. The increase had occurred across all age groups. These results have been used to suggest that liberalising licensing laws led to more sensible drinking, rather than to people drinking more. Such analysis does not, however, take account of the many other factors which may have resulted in consumption levels being at a similar level in 1984 and 1976, such as price and income changes.

Eagles and Besson (1985) considered trends in both general hospital admissions and psychiatric referrals in North East Scotland between 1974 and 1982. They concluded that the fall in male general admissions might reflect a beneficial effect of the liberalisation of licensing laws, but noted that other factors had also changed over the period, such as prices, income and unemployment levels.

In an analysis of changes in alcohol-related problems, Duffy and Plant (1986) compared trends in England and Wales, and Scotland, and concluded that: 'in relation to health, the new Scottish licensing arrangements may be viewed neither as a cause of harm nor a source of benefit'. They were encouraged by the reduction of public order offences, but noted changes in police practices. This study was criticised by Eagles and Besson (1986) for the quality of the data used. Liver cirrhosis, for example, develops over a number of years and may be an unsuitable indicator for the short time period considered. Also the changes in police practices were considered to invalidate the use of drunkenness offences and the frequency of breathalyser tests as indicators. In a separate study, Northridge, McMurray and Lawson (1986) suggested that after the liberalisation of Scotland's law, admissions for self-poisonings rose in West Fife. These findings were, however, also criticised for the lack of control data (Platt, 1987).

A number of non-UK studies have also indicated that there are some problems with some studies of this kind. In particular, there are difficulties in interpreting the results of studies linking availability to measures of alcohol-related problems when other factors which may affect the levels of alcohol-related problems (or consumption) are not controlled for (Holder and Blose, 1987; Smith, 1987). Also Popham, Schmidt and de Lint (1976) examined two conflicting examples of the influence of hours of sale and indicate some of the problems of interpreting such studies from different time periods and for different geographical areas. The different effects of different types of regulatory controls was also indicated in a study by Hoadley, Fuchs and Holder (1984). They found some small impact on consumption for the density of outlets, but earlier closing laws in bars seemed to be associated with higher sales.

A number of points can be drawn from the review of these studies. Evaluation of the changes in Scotland has obviously been severely hampered by a lack of appropriate and rigorously collected data and validated models of the links between consumption and indicators of harm. Many studies have been unable to control for other factors which may have influenced consumption and harm, and certainly there were changes during the period. The economic recession in Scotland and large rises in beer prices are the most notable features which may have influenced consumption, while changing medical and police practices may have had an important impact on the statistics related to alcohol problems.

There are also dangers in using the evidence from such studies to make forecasts of the effects of a liberalisation of licensing hours in England and Wales on alcohol-related problems and consumption. No distinction has been made between a change in the Scottish law which extended the closing hour from 10pm to 11pm and the ability to obtain extensions over the afternoon period. The more 'civilised' drinking habits referred to may stem from the change in evening hours, rather than the extension covering afternoon opening.

The empirical evidence on the link between increasing permitted hours and alcohol-related problems is therefore unclear. However, balance of the evidence and potential trade gains as judged by the present Government is indicated by the arguments contained in the Conservative Party's Campaign Guide for its candidates in the June 1987 General Election.

> 'The success of the licensing law change in Scotland was confirmed in the OPCS study.... Between 1979 and 1984, drunkenness convictions fell by 51 per cent; during the same period convictions fell by 23 per cent in England and Wales. A report published in the *British Medical Journal* in January 1986 concluded that no health or related harm had resulted from relaxation. As a result of the change of the law in Scotland, employment prospects have improved—nearly a third of the pubs opening longer hours since 1977 reported taking on more staff. It is clear, therefore, that some relaxation of the existing controls would assist tourism and small businesses as well as increasing personal freedom. Nevertheless, the Government is determined to ensure that whatever new arrangements may be made, adequate control on licensed premises will be retained in view of the real concern that exists about alcohol and its use, particularly among the young; its link with crime; and the need to provide protection for the public against any possible added noise and nuisance.' (Conservative Central Office, 1987a, p.394)

The promise of licensing law reform appeared in the Conservative's 1987 General Election Manifesto under, significantly, the section headed 'Freedom, Law and Responsibility':

> 'And we will liberalise the laws on liquor licensing hours so as to increase consumer choice, but we will also keep a sensible limit on late-night opening.' (Conservative Central Office, 1987b, p.60)

Following their re-election, the Government announced in the Queen's Speech that it would introduce a Bill later in the year to provide unrestricted opening of public houses between 11am and 11pm thus rejecting the Brewers Society's proposal for variation orders, presumably to avoid the obvious problem of drinkers moving from one open public house to another. The proposal completed a set of liberalisation measures including the Licensing (Restaurant Meals) Act introduced in the preceding Parliament and changes in Northern Ireland brought about by an Order in Council.

CONCLUSION

Licensing policy has been characterised over a long period by cycles of relaxation followed by a tightening of controls. During the 1960s and 1970s, all the demands were for a relaxation of licensing controls. As described in Chapter 5, the introduction of legislation involves the Home Office. It is this department which has restrained the calls for deregulation from other departments until it was convinced that there would be no adverse consequences from changes in the law. The analysis in this chapter outlines the uncertainty involved in estimating the effects of any changes in licensing regulations and the complexity of current licensing law.

The present reform of licensing laws would seem to have been undertaken on the basis of expected benefits to the trade with no adverse public order effects. Hence the 1988 reforms have increased the number of permitted hours for on-licensed premises, but retained controls on evening closing times. However, a careful examination of available evidence suggests that it is difficult to sustain the claim that trade and consumers will benefit from increased competition, and that there will be no increase in alcohol-related problems.

The issue of increased on-licence hours has succeeded in uniting a number of trade groups. As in the past, other reforms may divide these interest groups as Weir (1984) has suggested. The major brewers, for example, have large amounts of capital involved in on-licensed properties and they will continue to apply pressure for reforms to licence laws which will increase the profitability from such properties. These brewers and their tenants may, therefore, welcome some control on the number of licensed outlets. Other producers and retailers may resist pressure to control the off-licence trade by, for example, restrictions on the number of off-licence premises or stricter restrictions on persons through higher minimum drinking ages or restrictions on public drinking. An appreciation of the economic interests of the industry, consumers and the Government is a necessary input into the process of understanding decisions on licensing policy.

One of the difficulties of evaluating any future weakening or strengthening of licensing laws is the complex nature of the relationship between licensing laws and alcohol-related problems (Rabow and Watts, 1983). As suggested earlier, licensing laws have a number of different dimensions and various policy options are available. Present evidence suggests that the overall availability of alcohol may well affect consumption levels and policies of general deregulation may lead to an increase in health-related problems. On the other hand, change in more specific aspects of regulation may lead to a decrease in some problems. Thus studies have tended to suggest that extending the closing hours may result in fewer public order offences by preventing excessive speed of drinking. Although there may be a potential gain from a drop in such offences, other indicators of harm may increase if alcohol consumption rises.

Finally, changes in licensing laws may be combined with other measures in a package that attempts to control problems arising from alcohol consumption. For example, greater control of the number and conditions of off-licences could be combined with bans on drinking in public places similar to those imposed in recent experiments in Coventry and other towns. Further research on the complex relationship between the availability of alcohol, licensing laws, and alcohol-related problems is required if policies are to be designed to meet the potential conflicts between the government and industries, and to minimise impediments to preventative health measures.

References

Alcohol Concern, (1986), *Pub Opening Hours: The Case Against Change*, Alcohol Concern, London.

Blackburn Report, (1979), H.M. Government, *Report of the Inter-Departmental Review Body on Intoxicating Liquor Licensing in Northern Ireland*, HMSO, Belfast.

Booth, M., Hardman, G. and Hartley, K., (1986), 'Data Note 6, The UK alcohol and tobacco industries', *British Journal of Addiction*, 81, 825-830.

Bourgeois, J.C. and Barnes, J.G., (1979), 'Does advertising increase alcohol consumption?', *Journal of Advertising Research*, 19, (4), 19-29.

Bradley, M. and Fenwick, D., (1974), *Public Attitudes to Liquor Licensing Laws in Great Britain*, HMSO, London.

Brewing Sector Working Group, (1983), *The Outlook for the Brewing Industry*, National Economic Development Office, London.

Clayson, C., (1973), *Report of the Departmental Committee on Scottish Licensing Laws*, Cmnd. 5354, HMSO, Edinburgh.

Clayson, C., (1984), 'Licensing law and health: the Scottish experience in Action on Alcohol Abuse', *Policy Forum-Licensing Law and Health*, Action on Alcohol Abuse, London.

Conservative Central Office, (1987a), *Campaign Guide*, Conservative Central Office, London.

Conservative Central Office, (1987b), *The Way Forward*, Conservative Central Office, London.

Davies, P. and Walsh, D., (1983), *Alcohol Problems and Alcohol Control in Europe*, Croom Helm, London.

Department of Health and Social Security (DHSS), (1981), *Drinking Sensibly*, HMSO, London.

Dorn, N., (1983), *Alcohol, Youth and the State*, Social Analysis. A series in the social sciences, Croom Helm, London.

Duffy, M., (1983), 'The demand for alcoholic drink in the United Kingdom, 1963-1978', *Applied Economics*, 15, 125-140.

Duffy, J.C. and Plant, M.A., (1986), 'Scotland's liquor licensing changes: an assessment', *British Medical Journal*, 292, 4 January, 36-39.

Eagles, J.M. and Besson, J.A.O., (1985), 'Changes in the incidence of alcohol-related problems in North East Scotland, 1974-1982', *British Medical Journal*, 292, 39-43.

Eagles, J.M. and Besson, J.A.O., (1986), 'Scotland's liquor licensing changes', *British Medical Journal*, 292, 15th February, 486.

Economists Advisory Group, (1969), *The Economics of Brewing* Economist Advisory Group, London.

Erroll Report, (1972), *Report of the Departmental Committee on Liquor Licensing*, Home Office, HMSO, London.

Gallup, G.H., (1976), *The Gallup International Public Opinion Polls, Great Britain 1937-1975*, Random House, New York.

Goddard, E., (1986), *Drinking and Attitudes to Licensing in Scotland*, HMSO, London.

Godfrey, C., (1988), 'Licensing and the demand for alcohol', *Applied Economics*, 20, 1541-1558.

Harrison, B., (1971), *Drink and the Victorians: The Temperance Question in England, 1815-1872*, Faber and Faber, London.

Hawker, A., (1978), *Adolescents and Alcohol*, Edsall, London.

Hoadley, J.F., Fuchs, B.C. and Holder, H.D., (1984), 'The effect of alcohol beverage restrictions on consumption: a 25 year longitudinal analysis', *American Journal Drug Alcohol Abuse*, 10, (3), 375-401.

Holder, H.D. and Blose, J.D., (1987), 'Impact of changes in distilled spirits availability on apparent consumption: a time series analysis of liquor-by-the-drink', *British Journal of Addiction*, 82, 623-631.

Justices' Clerks' Society, (1983), *Licensing Law in the Eighties*, Justices' Clerks' Society, Bristol.

Knight, I. and Wilson, P., (1981), *Scottish Licensing Laws*, HMSO, London.

Leedham, W., (1987), 'Data Note 10, Alcohol, tobacco and public opinion', *British Journal of Addiction*, 82, 935-40.

McGuinness, T., (1980), 'An econometric analysis of total demand for alcoholic beverages in the UK, 1956-1975', *Journal of Industrial Economics*, September, 85-109.

McGuinness, T., (1983), 'The demand for beer, spirits and wine in the UK, 1956-1979', in Grant, M., Plant, M. and Williams, A. (eds.), *Economic and Alcohol*, Croom Helm, London.

Monopolies Commission, (1969), *Beer—A Report on the Supply of Beer*, Monopolies Commission, London.

National Opinion Polls (NOP), (1977, 1984).

Northridge, D.B., McMurray, J. and Lawson, A.A.H., (1986), 'Association between liberalisation of Scotland's liquor licensing laws and admissions for self poisoning in West Fife', *British Medical Journal*, 293, 1466-1468.

Ornstein, S.I. and Hanssens, D.M., (1985), 'Alcohol control laws and the consumption of distilled spirits and beer', *Journal of Consumer Research*, 12, 200-213.

Platt, S., (1987), 'Association between liberalisation of Scotland's liquor licensing laws and admissions for self poisoning', *British Medical Journal*, 294, 116-117.

Popham, R.E., Schmidt, W. and de Lint, J., (1975), 'The prevention of alcoholism: epidemiological studies of the effects of Government control measures', *British Journal of Addiction*, 70, 125-144.

Public Attitude Surveys Research, (1985), *Drinkers Views*, Press Release, 9 October 1985.

Rabow, J. and Watts, R.K., (1983), 'The role of alcohol availability in alcohol consumption and alcohol problems', *Social Mediators and Prevention*, 285-302.

Robinson, D., (1974), 'The Erroll Report: key proposals and public reactions', *British Journal of Addiction*, 69, 99.

Saunders, W., (1985), 'A reply to Clayson', *Action on Alcohol Abuse (Triple A) Review*, 2, 3-10.

Scottish Home and Health Department, (1987), *Licensing (Scotland) Act 1976: A Consultation Paper*, JAB23405, SHHD, Scotland.

137

Smith, D.I., (1987), 'Australian studies of the effects of increasing the availability of alcoholic beverages', Paper presented at Research Conference: Statistical Recording Systems of Alcohol Problems, September 14-18, Helsinki, Finland.

Tether, P. and Robinson, D., (1986), *Preventing Alcohol Problems: A Guide to Local Action*, Tavistock, London.

Walsh, B.M., (1982), 'The demand for alcohol in the UK: a comment', *Journal of Industrial Economics,* 30, (4), 439-446.

Weir, R.B., (1984), 'Obsessed with moderation: the drinks trade and the drinks question (1879-1930)', *British Journal of Addiction*, 79, 93-107.

Williams, G.P. and Brake, G.T., (1980), *Drink in Great Britain, 1900-1979*, Edsall, London.

7 Drinking and driving

PHILIP TETHER AND CHRISTINE GODREY

The drinking and driving issue provides a further opportunity to consider the role of legislation in prevention strategy. Drunken driving is one of the most visible and costly alcohol-related problems. The Department of Transport estimates that one in four of all accident fatalities is alcohol-related (Harrison, 1987) and this is confirmed by a Tayside study which found that 23 per cent of a sample of road accident deaths were wholly or partly attributable to alcohol (Foster et al., 1988). The scale of the problem can be illustrated by the figures for 1986 in which there were 248,000 road accidents which resulted in 5,382 fatalities (Department of Transport, 1986). The material costs of such accidents are high. Using a low estimate for the number of alcohol-related accidents, McDonnell and Maynard (1985) suggested that 10 per cent of the total calculated costs from all alcohol-related problems could be attributed to drink-driving fatalities and the policies necessary to deter offences. These costs, amounting to approximately £200 million in 1987, exclude any allowance for pain, grief or suffering by accident victims or their relatives (Maynard, 1989).

Successful prosecutions for drink-driving offences in Great Britain per 100,000 vehicles licensed and per capita consumption levels have, broadly, moved in tandem since the early 1970s (Harrison, 1987) and not surprisingly, drinking and driving emerged as an area of policy concern when consumption levels began to increase markedly in the 1960s. The result was the Road Safety Act 1967, which introduced both the roadside 'breathalyser' and the drink-driving limit of 80 mg/100 ml of blood. The 1967 Act became the foundation of current drink-driving policy in Great Britain although there has long been a legal proscription on driving whilst under the influence of drink, dating from the Criminal Justice Act 1925.

However, current drink-driving policy in Great Britain has many critics who claim that it lags behind that of most other western countries where much larger reductions in alcohol-related accidents have been achieved, largely thanks to the use of random breath tests. This central issue first surfaced in the debates surrounding the Road Safety Act 1967 and has continued to dominate discussions on the possible development of drink-driving policy. This chapter traces the development of drink-driving policy over the last two decades and examines the various options facing policy makers. In the first part, the content of current policy and the development of various policy debates are outlined. The second part builds on this material to present a review of the available econometric evidence on the impact of possible alternative policies in the drink-driving policy area and of the likely costs and benefits they entail.

CURRENT POLICY

The 1967 Road Safety Act

In 1965, a Government White Paper (Department of Transport, 1965) proposed the introduction of a drink-driving limit of 80 mgs/100 ml of blood. This limit was recommended by the British Medical Association during extensive consultations with both the Ministry of Transport and the Home Office which preceded the publication of the White Paper. It was selected because it was the one at which most experienced drivers are exposed to an increased risk of an accident and young and inexperienced drivers, or those who drink infrequently, are seriously impaired. Drivers of this kind will experience a five-fold increased risk of an accident with a blood/alcohol concentration of 80 mgs/100 ml (Transport and Road Research Laboratory (TRRL), 1983).

However, at the time of the White Paper the limit was not the most important issue. Rather, controversy centred around the proposed powers of the police to test the blood/alcohol levels of motorists. The enforcement issue, then as now, was a central feature of the drink-driving policy debate. The Government's position, as outlined in the White Paper, was unambiguous—it recommended that the police should have the power to require a breath test of any person driving or attempting to drive a motor vehicle or who had been involved in an accident. The unfettered discretion to test without, necessarily, any suspicion of impairment, created fierce opposition and charges that the police would engage in random testing, thus harrying an innocent motoring majority. Considerable confusion surrounded this debate and the term random testing continues to be used in unhelpful ways.

The term random testing as used in policy debates is more than simple, unfettered discretion. Random breath testing seeks to exploit the deterrent potential of unfettered discretion by testing *all* drivers passing static check-points. The place and time of the check-point may be random, but there is nothing random about who gets tested. Random testing is the methodical and highly visible application of unfettered discretion. Its aim is to make it clear that even drivers who believe they can have a drink and drive home unmolested if they avoid committing a moving traffic offence or accident will be caught.

Random breath tests (RBTs) administered at static check-points are said to have a number of distinct advantages. They are seen to be fair since all drivers are tested, whereas the more truly random application of unfettered discretion conveys the impression that the police are 'picking on people'. Check-points can be set up at particular times and in particular places where alcohol associated accidents occur. The high probability of being breath tested deters those drivers who are ready to drink and drive when they believe they can evade detection. Finally, and most importantly, it identifies those drivers, such as the middle-aged problem drinker, who are most likely to have an accident (Valverius, 1982) but whom the police are least likely to stop and test if they cannot administer RBTs.

The most vociferous opposition in 1967 to conferring unfettered discretion on the police came from the motoring organisations which had reluctantly accepted the need for a legal limit. It was argued that testing without evidence of impairment was an unacceptable infringement of civil liberties, a claim that found support in the Conservative Party principally among members of its Transport Backbench Committee. The 'civil liberties' issue introduced an ideological, party political element into what had been hitherto an essentially cross-party consensus that 'something must be done'. In addition to the motorists' defence organisations, the police too then had their doubts, although they were later to change their views. Their objections arose out of a concern for the resource implications of unfettered discretion and their attitude was particularly important since they had been, until then, an important group in the coalition pressing for legislative action. The final group to throw its weight against the Government's proposals was the licensed trade itself. The National Union of Licensing Victuallers (NULV) and the Wine Trade Defence Committee feared that the possibility of being tested would frighten away customers and consequently damage their businesses. However, the objections of the licensed trade were muted. It was difficult for them to adopt a 'high profile' position on the issue without appearing to be a self-interested group prepared to put up with 'death on the roads in the interest of profits'.

After a short consultative period, a bill was introduced in January 1965 and it received its second reading in February. The issue of unfettered discretion was the one which dominated the debates in the House. However, the bill fell when Harold Wilson called a general election in an effort to augment the tiny majority which the Labour Party had obtained in 1964. After the re-election of the Labour Government with a healthy majority, the bill was reintroduced, although the Prime Minister's support was needed before Barbara Castle, the Secretary of State for Transport, could overcome Cabinet opposition (Castle, 1984). However, the bill, as introduced, omitted the contentious proposals that the police should have unfettered powers to test motorists. Vociferous group opposition and the doubts of Cabinet colleagues were responsible for this important change. Instead, it was proposed that police officers should have the power to breath test a motorist who commits a moving traffic offence, is involved in an accident, or if they have 'reasonable cause' to believe that the motorist has alcohol in their body. In the case of the first and last grounds, the suspected motorist had to have been 'driving or attempting to drive'. The Secretary of State attributed this change of policy to public opinion:

'Though the opposition to this proposal totally failed to convince me that our plans were wrong it did convince me that enough people thought that we would in some sense unjustly persecute completely innocent motorists to make me think again.' (House of Commons, 1966)

The stop and test formula which was adopted in the Road Safety Act 1967 was an attempt to ensure that police powers were circumscribed and applicable only in certain defined 'prima facie' suspicious and 'high risk' situations. By specifying the categories within which the police had stop and test powers, the Road Safety Act 1967 conceded victory to the opponents of random breath testing.

The Road Traffic Act 1967 was a major legislative landmark. Once on the Statute Book it became, and remains, an automatic offence to drive, attempt to drive, or be in charge of a motor vehicle in a public place if blood/alcohol content exceeds 80 mgs/100 mls of blood. The Act introduced the breathalyser as a screening test which, if positive, was followed by an evidential blood or urine test taken at a police station and then sent away for analysis. The Act had been preceded by eight years of debate which first established agreement on the desirability of a blood/alcohol limit, but which included determined opposition to the law enforcement measures which the government of the day believed were necessary to make the proposed law work effectively. The Act promoted the development of a policy network consisting of departments and their associated groups which have played a part in subsequent drink-driving debates and is still very much in existence today. Hitherto, the Ministry of Transport had been the governmental focus of the policy debate but, as the emphasis swung to the implications for law enforcement, the Home Office became increasingly involved. With this change, the current drink-driving policy network, as described in Chapter 5, began to take shape with the Ministry of Transport under pressure from road safety and medical interests and the Home Office becoming the focus for law-enforcement agencies such as the Police Federation, the Association of Chief Police Officers (ACPO) and the Magistrates' Association.

The Blennerhassett Committee

The main issue of contention in the debate surrounding the Road Safety Act 1967 had been one of law enforcement. This issue re-emerged in the 1970s with the failure of the Road Safety Act to live up to its early promise. Initially, there was an 11 per cent reduction in the national casualty toll, but the impact then appeared to decline. Nevertheless, between 1967 and 1974, 5,000 deaths and 200,000 casualties were judged to have been saved as a result of the new law. In the first year of that legislation, 1968, the total number of offences was 27,500. The number then increased steadily to a peak of 77,000 in 1975 and has increased since. The increasing number of arrests was paralleled by the increasing proportion of traffic deaths found to have alcohol in the blood (Sabey and Staughton, 1980).

In other words, after initial and substantial success, the impact of the Act faded and levels of alcohol-related death and injury on the roads climbed to new levels. As a consequence, a Departmental Committee was set up in 1974 to review the operation of the drink-driving law. The subsequent Blennerhassett Report (Department of Environment, 1976) recommended the removal of limitations on the power of the police to stop and test drivers. In addition, the committee made a number of other important proposals including: the introduction of evidential breath testing in police stations instead of taking blood and urine samples; the development of procedures by which problem drinkers, labelled high risk offenders, could be removed from the roads and not have their licences restored until the Courts were satisfied that they no longer constituted a major risk to other road users; the promotion of a continuing programme of publicity aimed particularly at young drivers; and the closing of certain procedural loop holes. The Committee also recommended that the 80 mgs/100 ml limit be retained.

The stop and test formula adopted in 1967 was criticised on a number of grounds. The Committee pointed out that drivers had been acquitted despite the results of blood analysis, on the grounds that the initial breath test was not validly acquired and that the formula set constraints on enforcement policy which were not related to actual patterns of drinking and driving behaviour. It also emphasised that the formula fostered the illusion that it was safe to drink and drive as long as one avoided an accident or moving traffic offences. The Blennerhassett Committee pointed out that unfettered discretion was needed to relate enforcement effort to actual patterns of drink-driving behaviour and emphasised that the fears expressed in 1967 were:

> 'largely misplaced (since) any law which went beyond the power to test the obviously incapable driver must give the police some discretion and that discretion could be used in a random way'. (Department of the Environment, 1976, p. 20)

This claim is borne out by enforcement initiatives which have deliberately stretched existing police powers to their limit. In the so-called 'Cheshire Blitz', the police administered ten times the usual number of tests. The result was a doubling of convictions and a reduction in the number of accidents by 60 per cent (Ross, 1984).

However, the recommendations of the Blennerhassett Committee concerning police discretion did not meet with success. No reference to the issue was made in the Government's statement on Blennerhassett on the 4 August 1976 (House of Commons, 1976). The Government was unwilling to reopen the controversy. However, it did accept Blennerhassett's recommendations on the legal limit, evidential breath testing, loopholes in the law and education. Judgement on the proposals concerning high risk offenders (HROs) was left open pending further consultations. Blennerhassett's proposals that HROs should be singled out for special attention were firmly supported by medical groups and voluntary organisations. Their stand was buttressed by several non-medical and non-alcohol organisations. For example, in 1974 the Royal Society for the Prevention of Accidents (RoSPA) and the AA had called for more restrictions on drivers who were proven problem drinkers. Two groups which gave evidence to Blennerhassett on the urgent need to ensure that drinking drivers should not receive their licences back automatically at the end of their period of disqualification were the BMA and the Medical Committee on Accident Prevention. As a result of their efforts, the Committee suggested in its report that HROs should be defined as: drivers with two convictions within ten years for drinking and driving; and drivers with blood/alcohol levels of 150 mgs/100 ml. The Committee's HRO recommendations recognised that 'problem drinking, as distinct from driving under the influence of alcohol, is ... an important factor in traffic safety' (Dunbar et al., 1985, p.827).

The Committee had identified an important issue which has been clarified in subsequent research. One of the most reliable methods of identifying problem drinkers is by a blood test for raised Gammaglutamyl Transferase (GGT) levels (Whitehead et al., 1978; Rosalki and Rau, 1972). The Tayside Safe Driving Project, funded by a grant from the Association of Police Surgeons, carried out GGT tests on 440 motorists arrested for drinking and driving in the Tayside Region. Overall, 91 drivers were found to have raised GGT levels. The proportions in different age groups varied considerably, amounting to 10 per cent of drivers aged under thirty, 31 per cent of drivers aged between thirty and forty-four, and 29 per cent of drivers aged forty-five and over. Moreover, although no link was found between blood alcohol concentrations and accidents among drivers aged over thirty, there was a strong association between raised GGT levels and accidents in this age group. This suggests that whilst the acute effects of alcohol are the main cause of accident risk among young drivers, accidents among older drinking drivers are due to a combination of effects including chronic alcohol-induced deterioration (Dunbar, 1985). One of the most interesting features of the study was the significantly high GGT levels in drivers aged over thirty who drove for a living, including drivers of heavy goods and public service vehicles. Overall, one third of all offenders aged over thirty show evidence of alcohol problems; the highest proportion is found among professional and managerial groups and the lowest among semi-skilled and unskilled manual workers (Dunbar, 1985). These are precisely the groups least likely to be arrested for drinking and driving, but which would be detected by RBTs.

Evidential breath testing and developments in drink-driving policy, 1979-83

Blennerhassett's high risk offender proposals were the subject of protracted consultations. The Medical Advisory Branch of the Driver Vehicle Licensing Centre (DVCL) was deeply involved in these consultations and was especially concerned about the resource implications of adopting Blennerhassett's HRO criteria. Delay was also caused by the need to test the evidential breath machines which, it was proposed, would largely replace blood and urine tests. However, underpinning these delays was the generally low priority given to the drink-driving issue by the weak Lib/Lab coalition in the two years before 1979. Negotiations over the HRO issue continued under the incoming Conservative Government which reaffirmed its opposition to unfettered discretion. The refusal to endorse, once and for all, a HRO procedure reflected the continuing opposition of civil servants. In contrast, the Government's principal reason for continuing to reject discretionary testing was not the attitude of civil servants but the views of its own backbenchers and constituency workers. Both the Transport and Home Affairs Backbench Committees were hostile and opposition to discretionary testing was embodied in a number of resolutions at the Conservative Party Conference in 1980.

This internal Party dissent was sufficient to counter the drift in opinion over discretionary testing which had been evident in the post-Blennerhassett years. As the toll of death and injury had mounted, it had become increasingly difficult to deny that the most effective deterrent to drinking and driving was the high risk of apprehension and that, conversely, the main reason for the UK's relatively high levels of drinking and driving was attributable to motorists' realistic perception of this risk (Ross, 1984). As a consequence, several organisations were now prepared to endorse, with varying degrees of caution, the introduction of discretionary testing and these included the Police Superintendents Association, the Police Federation, the Association of Chief Police Officers, the Justices' Clerks' Society, the National Council on Alcoholism and the BMA. Moreover, both general public opinion and informed opinion were moving in the same direction.

The Blennerhassett Committee had established that a majority of motorists approved of random testing and this led to their statement that: 'a growing proportion of drivers would accept a wider liability to be tested in the interests of road safety' (Department of the Environment, 1976). This assertion was confirmed by an opinion poll in 1980, which indicated that the proportion of motorists favouring greater police powers to test had risen to 57 per cent (*Sunday Times*, 1980). A 1979 Minute of the Public Affairs Committee of the Automobile Association recorded that their members favoured random breath testing but this was never published. More recently, the motoring organisations appear to have changed their attitudes and, perhaps reluctantly, dropped covert opposition to RBTs. If pressed they still claim that existing legislation is perfectly adequate if it is properly enforced and that the police do not have the necessary resources of money or man power to carry out RBTs.

Evidential breath testing was finally introduced by the Transport Act 1981, which gave the Secretary of State for Transport powers to introduce testing at a later date by statutory instrument. The new evidential breath testing machines finally became operative throughout the UK on 6 May 1983. After a roadside screening test, suspected motorists are required to give an evidential breath test which is conducted at a police station. The legal breath/alcohol limit is 35 micrograms per 100 millilitres of breath (35 mg/100 ml). The Transport Act 1981 requires a motorist to provide two samples and court proceedings are taken on the lower of the two readings.

A number of safeguards are built into the Act. When blood/alcohol or urine/alcohol measurements were the evidential test, the Forensic Science

Laboratories deducted six per cent from the mean result of the blood/urine analysis when reporting their findings. A similar allowance is now made for breath tests. Thus, in practice, readings between 36 mg and 40 mg/100 ml breath do not lead to prosecution. In other words, the legal limit is not what it is commonly supposed to be. In addition, drivers in England and Wales (though not in Scotland) are entitled to a blood test at any breath level. This entitlement was introduced following a campaign by the *The Daily Express*, mounted when the alcometers used for evidential breath testing came under suspicion. It is alleged that the Home Office would like to end this facility but fears adverse publicity.

Development of a policy for high risk offenders

Procedures for identifying HROs and ensuring that they do not get their licences back automatically after a period of disqualification, also came into effect in May 1983. The system is based on the Road Traffic Act 1972 which obliges applicants for and holders of a motor vehicle licence to notify the Secretary of State of any 'relevant or prospective disability' which may effect their competence to drive. The current HRO definition is considerably at variance with that recommended by the Blennerhassett Committee. The Committee had suggested that such offenders should be distinguished by two convictions within ten years for drinking and driving (at any level) and by a single offence at 200 mg/100 ml, although the BMA favoured 150 mg/100 ml. In the event, opposition within the Government led to the amalgamation of these two criteria, that is, two offences within ten years at 200 mg/100 ml (or more). A second drink-driving conviction at any level automatically carries a three year disqualification.

At the start of this disqualification period, all HROs receive a letter from the DVCL advising them that they may have a problem, where to receive help and informing them that they may be required to undergo an examination at the end of the disqualification period in order to establish their competence to drive. It is made clear to offenders that, if this test is 'positive', they will not get their licence back at the end of the disqualification period. The examinations are carried out at ten centres in the UK and are based on blood tests designed to identify GGT levels. However, as the Tayside Safe Driving Project found, many problem drinkers cannot be identified on the basis of alcohol levels at the time of arrest or previous convictions. In the circumstances, it is difficult to see why the Government proceeded with this measure unless it was to satisfy the need to be seen to be 'doing something'. A general screening programme of all arrested drivers aged over thirty would be much more appropriate, given the research findings on problem drinkers.

The existing system suffers from a major weakness. It is alleged that the DVCL are unwilling to go into court and assert that a driver has an alcohol problem because of their uncertainty over diagnostic methods and unfamiliarity with the court environment. The BMA's original suggestion to the Blennerhassett Committee was that this work should be handled by police surgeons operating at regional levels on behalf of their Chief Constables. This suggestion seems to have much to recommend it.

Transport Select Committee Review, 1984-85

HRO policy. Shortly after the introduction of the HRO procedure, it and other drink-driving issues were investigated by the Transport Select Committee in a wide ranging review of road safety measures (House of Commons, 1985). A number of witnesses, including the BMA, indicated that they felt that the HRO definition was too restrictive. The Medical Committee on Accident Prevention and the Parliamentary Advisory Committee on Transport Safety (PACTS) both advocated that the level should be reduced to 150 mg/100 ml. The Department of Transport frankly admitted to the Select Committee that the resource implications of the HRO procedure had been the guiding consideration behind the formula. The Department did, however, indicate its willingness to consider lowering this threshold in the light of experience.

Informed opinion favours adjustment of the HRO formula but this is currently blocked by resource considerations. As with discretionary testing, the argument about resources focuses only on the initial costs to policy makers and not on the savings which they could achieve. An important dimension of the resource argument concerns the availability of treatment services around the country which, it is said, would not be able to cope with the influx if the HRO procedure were amended. However, as Dunbar (1985) points out, most offenders who are problem drinkers fall into the 'mildly dependent' category and are amenable to minimum intervention in which a self-help component is prominent. Moreover, resource problems could be overcome if, as in many other countries, drinking drivers were made to pay for any enhanced HRO scheme. A promising minimal intervention approach to the drinking driver is being promoted by a number of probation services around the country. Hampshire Probation Service has pioneered an alcohol education group specifically for drinking drivers. The Department of Transport has ruled that the course can help HRO offenders to get their licenses back if the probation officer in charge gives a favourable report on offenders' progress on the course. The course currently lasts for eight two-hour sessions one evening a week. This pioneering course, whilst attracting much praise, was criticised by several for being too short for some

148

types of drinking drivers. In particular, it was alleged that for those with severe problems, a forty-week course with one, two-hourly session a week, would be more appropriate.

Random breath tests. The Select Committee received unequivocal representations from the Association of Chief Police Officers (ACPO) on the need for unfettered police discretion to administer breath tests, thus exposing as false the oft-repeated claim by the motoring organisations that the police do not want this power. ACPO was clear that the only way drinking drivers can be dissuaded from their behaviour is to increase the likelihood of apprehension. However, the Secretary of State for Transport gave evidence to the Committee claiming that it would be 'intolerable' to confer on the police powers to breath tests motorists who were under no suspicion. ACPO's representations did not persuade the Committee. It pointed out that the police have unfettered powers to stop motorists and take a breath test if they have any reason whatsoever to believe that the motorist has alcohol in his or her body. Consequently, the Committee preferred to emphasise the need for more and better enforcement of the existing law rather than any enhancement of police powers.

The argument that police powers are already extensive and that better enforcement would pay dividends is not without merit. Current police powers are indeed wide and give considerable scope to officers determined to stop and test. A 'moving traffic offence' can cover everything, including the slightest infringement of the traffic law. Having 'reasonable cause' to believe that motorists have alcohol in their bodies is similarly open to interpretation. Driving too slowly and with excessive care can provide an officer with justification for administering a test. In other words, the form of words in the drinking and driving legislation which confers upon police officers the right to require a breath test is elastic and open to interpretation.

This elasticity goes some way toward explaining the very wide variations in the numbers of breath tests administered by different forces (Christian Economic and Social Research Foundation, 1986). Moreover, the introduction of unfettered discretion would not necessarily alter this situation since individual forces would still be free to decide how much priority they should give to apprehending drinking drivers. Passing a law which would allow the police to carry out RBTs may leave implementation patterns unaltered, especially if the Home Office does not provide the resources needed to carry out breath tests at a level that produces deterrence. The experience of other countries suggests that this means testing one in three drivers per year. Indeed one reason why the police are now asking for unfettered powers to test is to avoid the possibility of a law which not only removes the limitations on the powers of the police to test, but which also determines how RBTs are carried out. Such a law would be a constitutional departure in that it would curtail the operational autonomy of Chief Constables. In the absence of such a law, the introduction of RBTs might create conflict with any Chief Constables in England and Wales who give low priority to the policing of drinking and driving.

The Road Traffic Law Review

The Transport Select Committee led to the establishment of the Road Traffic Law Review in January 1985 by the Secretaries of State for Transport and the Home Office with the agreement of the Secretary of State for Scotland. Its brief was to consider what improvements might be made to traffic law in respect of simplification, effectiveness and acceptability. This involved addressing a number of drink-driving issues and the Review contained the observation that 'our concern over the bad driver who has been drinking above the legal limit for driving will be evident throughout this report' (Department of Transport and Home Office, 1988, p.93). RBTs, breath/alcohol levels and the HRO scheme fell outside the Review's remit, but it did address a number of other important questions forming part of the complex cluster of drink-driving and related policy issues. Thus growing public concern over the level of penalties typically imposed on the drinking driver who kills, led the Review to recommend that there should be a specific offence of bad driving causing death when the driver was unfit to drive through drink or drugs.

A number of probation services run drink-driver retraining courses largely modelled on the pioneering example of the Hampshire Probation Service. This development was enthusiastically endorsed by the Review which urged a national experiment to develop such initiatives which would be reinforced by a requirement that all drivers disqualified from driving for twelve months or more, which includes all convicted drink-drivers, should have to resit an extended driving test before being allowed back on the road. Concern over delay in bringing drink-driving offenders to court which allows them to remain on the road for an average of 83 days, led the Review to recommend that bail conditions should be used to prevent drivers from driving during this period when there is a substantial risk that they will re-offend. Other imaginative, clear and highly pertinent proposals were, *inter alia*, that insurance policies protecting against the consequences of disqualification should be declared unenforceable and void, that courts should be able to order the forfeiture of a vehicle used in an imprisonable road traffic offence, and that licensing Justices should be able to take into account, when considering licensing renewals, whether applicants regularly or persistently served alcohol to customers committing drink-driving offences.

The review has, therefore, introduced a wide range of policy alternatives into the debate about deterring drunken drivers and many have been incorporated into the recent White Paper *The Road User and the Law* (Department of Transport, 1989). Further, the Ministerial Group on Alcohol Misuse asked the Department of Transport to review the HRO scheme. This scheme has now been extended to cover any driver convicted just once at two and a half times the limit or for refusing a breath test. It is estimated that the extended scheme will cover up to 40,000 offenders each year (Ministerial Group on Alcohol Misuse, 1989). The evidence available to assess alternative drink-driving policies is now considered.

ALTERNATIVE DRINK-DRIVING POLICIES

It is difficult to assess the impact of the current law. Convictions have risen steadily from 58,000 in 1976 to 107,000 in 1986 and positive breath tests have increased from 58,000 to 85,000 during the same period (Department of Transport, 1986). However, these data reflect police activity and not the trends in the size of the underlying problem which is being exposed. One significant indicator does show a downward trend. The number of fatalities with excess blood/alcohol levels has fallen from 33 per cent of all deaths in 1978 to 27 per cent of all deaths in 1986, though these figures need to be treated with some caution since they are based on a very small sample size and fluctuate widely from year to year. Although the general trend is downward, there have been quite marked variations in the period.

The development of current drink-driving policy and the enactment of legislation described above has been accompanied by considerable controversy. After the 1967 Road Traffic Act, there was considerable public debate concerning the civil liberty aspects of the law. However, more recently there has been a concerted campaign to change current policy by introducing random breath testing. One of the major obstacles to policy change identified in the analyses has been the potential resource costs of alternative policies. There are considerable difficulties in evaluating the costs and benefits of alternative policies compared to the current situation. The purpose of this section is to examine the costs and benefits and the empirical evidence available on the effectiveness of alternative policies.

A number of policies may affect drink-driving behaviour which results from two activities, namely drinking and driving. The level of problems associated with drink-driving may be affected not only by the interaction of drinking and driving, but also the two separate component activities. Most studies of the effectiveness of policy have considered the relationship between drink-driving and measures designed to effect the problem, such as random breath tests or minimum drinking age laws. Some authors, such as Mosher (1985) and Coate and Grossman (1987), compare the effectiveness of drink-driving policies with alternatives such as taxation, which help determine the level of alcohol consumption. Further, there is a need to consider the driving environment and how general safety measures may affect the likelihood and severity of accidents (Ross, 1988).

If these three groups of policy are considered, a wide range of alternative legislative and information-based policy instruments can be identified. A number of these alternative policies and the empirical evidence on their effectiveness in reducing the level of drink-driving problems and their associated costs to society are considered below.

Drink-driving behaviour and alternative policies

Most drink-driving legislation has been designed to raise the cost to individuals of their behaviour. If we assume that the drunken driver acts rationally, then the expected cost to the individual will be based on the interaction of a number of different probabilities and their associated costs. These are: the probability of having an accident of different severities; the probability of being stopped and breathalysed; the probability, if caught, of being prosecuted; and finally the probability of being convicted. The expected costs will also depend on the severity of punishment if convicted. It is also important to note that individuals are likely to base decisions on perceived probabilities, not the actual probabilities of events occurring. The perceived risk depends not only on the legislation as planned by policy makers but also, as was stressed in Chapter 1, on the implementation of the law. The present drink-driving-policy, as described in the previous section, has developed from a series of Acts which have attempted to alter different aspects of these expected costs. Many commentators on the 1967 Road Traffic Act suggest that the perceived probability of being stopped and breathalysed, which was high at the introduction of the law, fell as drivers became more aware of the actual probability of being stopped after drinking (Ross, 1988). Disputes about the working of the law in the 1970s may have raised the perceived probability of the ability to evade punishment, even when stopped by the police.

The severity of punishment has increased and the costs of being convicted are at present high. As well as the judicial sentence of a fine of up to £2,000 and the loss of a driving licence for a minimum of a year, insurance premiums on regaining a licence will be high. Denny (1986) suggests, however, that there may be some lack of information of the severity of penalties. One policy option for governments is to increase the flow of information about the severity of punishment to aid consumers to make rational choices. Other changes in the legal and insurance markets may also change the balance of costs of drink-driving behaviour. A recent study in the US, for example, examined the possibility that drink-drivers by their action invalidated accidental death insurance (Medico-Legal Bulletin, 1986).

Most recent attention has, however, focused on the probability of being caught. Home Office surveys suggest the actual risk is low. Riley (1985), using figures from the 1982 and 1984 British Crime Surveys, suggests that 22 per cent of men and 9 per cent of women admitted having recently driven when they knew they were over the legal limit. From such figures, it has been calculated that the chances of being convicted as a result of any one occasion of drinking and driving are between 1 in 250 and 1 in 1,000 (Martin, 1986).

A survey by a representative sample of 1,033 motorists conducted by Gallup revealed that a significant number of motorists repeatedly offended (General Accident, 1986). In the survey, 11 per cent admitted to having driven after consuming five units of alcohol more than 15 times in the last 12 months. Similar figures have been quoted for the US with the probability of being arrested for having high blood alcohol levels being between 1 in 500 and 1 in 2,000 (Forcier et al., 1986). This has led to suggestions that there is a need for government intervention to raise both the actual and perceived risk of arrest by random or discretionary breath testing. Such policies could require considerable resources which may have more effective alternative uses.

For individuals who drink and drive, there is a probability of accidents as well as arrest. Clearly the costs associated with accidents are potentially much higher—although with a lower probability—than for an arrest for drink-driving. Reed (1981) suggests that, given that the high potential costs of accidents do not deter the drink-driver, increasing the severity of punishment may only have a limited effect on behaviour. He also suggests that it may be more effective to increase the likelihood of arrest. Many studies have highlighted the lack of knowledge about individual behaviour and the risk-taking attitude of the drunk driver, particularly the young (Douglass, 1974). Another factor which has not been extensively examined is the effect that alcohol itself may have on the decision making process and the evaluation of risks. Waller (1986a) considered the interrelationship between smoking and drinking and road accidents. He suggests the higher rate of accidents among those who smoked as well as drank may reflect a devil-may-care attitude and that such individuals might be more risk-taking that those who just drank.

In making decisions the individual is likely to compare the expected costs and benefits, or adverted costs, from drink-driving. The adverted costs include the costs of alternative means of transport and intangible elements such as social pressures to drink. Information-based policies in the form of drink-driving campaigns have recently attempted to influence some of these intangible elements such as social attitudes to drinking and driving. Evaluating such policies is difficult. Benefits may be small but may continue over a long period. It is not surprising that there is no immediate visible effect on drink-driving fatalities or accidents. An evaluation would need to take account of the dynamic nature of the policy change. Other policies may seek to lower the costs of alternative transport. Some licensees, such as those in rural areas, may have strong incentives to provide such facilities if other government policies raise the perceived cost of drinking and driving.

Finally there is the problem of the relevance of assumptions about 'rational' behaviour. There are some conflicting opinions on the proportion of drunk drivers who are alcohol dependent. The numbers who confess to drinking and driving are much larger than the normal estimates of those alcohol dependent. Forcier et al. (1986) suggest that there is a low previous arrest rate among drink-driving offenders in the US, but that repeat offenders may well need treatment for alcoholism. He suggests the deterrent effect of policies that increase the likelihood of arrest or severity of punishment is based upon the premise that rational individuals will modify their behaviour in response to incentives and points out that alcoholics may be irrational and therefore little affected by such policies. As discussed above, Dunbar et al. (1985) suggest that a large proportion of accidents for those aged over 30 in Scotland may be alcohol-related. Denny (1986) suggests that the BAC limit applied to the procedure for HROs is too high and that alcoholics may form a sizeable proportion of the drink-driving problem.

To summarise, a number of different policy options can be outlined. These include: legal changes such as the severity of punishment and the probability of arrest; changes in individuals' incentives such as changes in insurance policies; and the role of information. To evaluate such policies it is necessary not only to have some knowledge of their effectiveness but also to consider all the costs and benefits such policies may impose on the non-drinking drivers as well as the offenders. The benefits of policy and lower fatalities, for example, would be experienced by non-drinking drivers who would face lower probabilities of being involved in drink-related accidents. Costs, however, vary between policies. Insurance changes would redistribute costs from non-drinking to drinking drivers. Random breath tests would impose costs on the 'innocent'. Some of these costs involve resources such as time and others, such as the threat to civil liberties, are part of the intangible costs and more difficult to evaluate. Parliamentary debate would seem to suggest that the legislators put a very high value on such intangible costs, but recent surveys on the acceptability of random breath tests suggest they may be overestimating their importance (Gallup, 1988). Public attitudes towards convicted drink-driving offenders do appear to have hardened in recent years, see Table 7.1. In 1980, 85 per cent of respondents approved of tougher penalties for drink-driving offenders.

Table 7.1

Views on tougher penalties for drink-driving offenders

	Approval %	Disapproval %	Don't know %
1970[a]	43	50	7
1970[a]	42	50	7
1976[b]	45	50	5
1977[c]	68	23	10
1980[d]	85	12	3

Sources: a. Gallup, G.H. (ed.), (1976), *The Gallup International Public Opinion Polls: Great Britain 1937–1975,* Random House, New York.
b. Gallup Political Index, May 1976.
c. Gallup Political Index, May 1977.
d. MORI Poll (1980).

Further, information policies may have an important role in changing the valuation of the intangible costs involved in alternative policies and the perceived benefits of alcohol consumption.

Evaluating alternative drink-driving policies—the empirical evidence

If the relationship between detection and the deterrence of the severity of penalties could be empirically determined, the estimates would provide an important input into the analysis of alternative policy options. Some important factors emerge in studies which have attempted to specify and estimate these relationships for other types of criminal activity. One is the simultaneous nature of the relationship between crime rates, probability of detection and the severity of punishment (Taylor, 1979). The criminal justice system will respond to changes in criminal activity by adjusting expenditure on police, courts and prison. Hence arrest rates, conviction rates and severity of punishment will tend to depend on crime rates. Estimates made from models which fail to take account of such simultaneity would produce biased results (Saffer and Grossman, 1987).

It is, therefore, important not only to model individual behaviour, but also the behaviour of the criminal system and other agents. Police behaviour may affect the arrest rate. Hingson et al. (1985) noted that police attitudes towards the young and the drink-driving offence may help to explain the underrepresentation of the young in drink-driving offence data compared to the numbers involved in fatal accidents, see also Voas and Williams (1986). Changes in the attitudes of the judiciary, government and public opinion may affect the probability of being convicted if prosecuted and the imposition of more severe penalties. Information policies, as well as regulation policies, may alter such attitudes. An additional feature of the drink-driving market is the role of the licensee or server of the alcoholic drink. There have been attempts in the US to make those serving alcoholic drinks partly liable for the action of drink-drivers and, therefore, open to legal action. The present Minister of Transport has suggested that there are no legal obstacles in the UK to private prosecutions of servers, either in public houses or private houses, by relatives of drink-driving accident victims. Imposing such costs on licensees may clearly change their behaviour. Mosher and Wallack (1979) describe an experiment in California in which an attempt was made to reduce the number of licensees repeatedly serving intoxicated people. They noted that drink-driving offences can occur at much lower BAC levels than obvious drunkenness. Waller (1986b) suggests that a law should be introduced in the US imposing limits on the number of drinks bartenders can serve, so as to keep BAC levels under the permitted drink-driving margin. Some of the difficulties of imposing policies on servers are also discussed by Reed (1981).

Minimal drinking age studies. Empirical studies have, in general, not attempted to estimate causal relationships. Instead, trends in policy measures such as the minimum drinking age, and outcome measures such as drink-driving offences or the number of fatal accidents, have been considered. Most of the research in the US and Canada has focused on changes in the minimum age law. During the 1970s, many US states lowered the age at which adults could legally obtain alcoholic drinks from 21 to 18. Increasing concern over the level of teenage and other fatalities associated with alcohol, and the action of groups like Mothers Against Drunken Drivers (MADD), brought about a re-evaluation of minimum age legislation. This was strengthened by the presidential mandate to make highway aid contingent upon a minimum drinking age of 21. This debate was fuelled by studies which examined the proportion of fatal accidents which involved young drivers. For example, figures from the Morbidity and Mortality Weekly Report (MMWR) Survey (1985) show that 33 per cent of drivers involved in traffic accidents were between the ages of 16 and 24, 38 per cent of the deaths in these crashes were alcohol-related compared to 26 per cent for all other ages (MMWR, 1985). Mayhew et al. (1986) review a wide variety of studies showing similar figures.

Smart and Goodstadt (1977) wrote an early critical review of the studies examining the effects of changing minimum age legislation. They drew attention to the other factors which may have influenced trends in the data during the period such as increases in alcohol consumption and driving among the young. Some of the studies reviewed compared States in which the law changed with control States where no changes occurred. One of the most careful studies was undertaken by Wagenaar (1983). He used Box-Jenkins techniques to compare data for the States of Maine and Michigan, which first reduced then raised legal ages, with two control States where no law changes occurred. He also considered younger and older youths' pattern of drinking and driving for internal validity. All crashes were considered, not just those in which there was a fatality, and he also examined non-alcohol-related crashes. Although the study was conducted shortly after the raising of drinking ages, he did find significant changes. In Michigan, the rise of the minimum age from 18 to 20 resulted in a net reduction of 20 per cent in injury producing accidents and 17 per cent reduction in property damage crashes. In Maine, there was a 20 per cent reduction in property damage crashes, but no significant reduction for injuries. Wagenaars' study also examined the limitations of his results. He notes the need to control for intervening factors such as consumption, other driving law changes and changes in police reporting.

Not all studies reveal large effects. Vingilis and Smart (1981) who considered the effects of raising the legal drinking age in Ontario found only minimal effects. They found no significant changes in driver fatalities or drink-driving statistics. Again, however, the analysis did not attempt to estimate causal relationships and simply considered trends in series over time. DuMouchel et al. (1987) investigated the long-term effects in 48 US States. They found that the change in the law could be estimated to have produced a 13 per cent reduction in night-time driver fatal crash involvements and there was no evidence of erosion of this effect three years after the age changes. Another study which used control states was conducted by MacKinnon and Woodward (1986). They found immediate effects in some, but not all, States.

Asch and Levy (1987) attempted to examine the hypothesis that it was the inexperience in drinking, independently of age, that creates traffic accidents. Hence raising the drinking age may lead initially to a diminution in fatalities among the directly affected age group, but this fall in fatalities will be offset to some extent by increased fatalities as the group attains the higher drinking age. A single year's US data (1978) were analysed and drinking age measures were used in a regression model designed to explain traffic fatality rates across different States. This model included alcohol consumption as one of the explanatory variables. The possibility of feedback between fatality rates and minimum age legislation was also investigated. The results from this analysis suggested that minimum legal drinking age was not a significant factor in determining road accident fatalities in the US in 1978. Alcohol consumption was found to be a significant factor in equations explaining single vehicle fatalities. Also a variable measuring drinking experience was found to be important, the results suggesting that those in their first year of drinking experience have a 10 to 20 per cent higher fatality risk than the rest of the population.

It is, therefore, not clear from existing empirical studies whether minimum age legislation has directly influenced drinking fatalities. There are potential costs of minimum age policies such as encouraging young people to drink in less controlled environments and increasing criminalisation of youths (Gilmore, 1984). There are also many intangible costs involved in such policies, such as the loss of the freedom of youths to determine their own behaviour. Also the relevance of existing studies, based on US data, for evaluating policies in the UK is questionable. Social attitudes in the UK may suggest that increasing the minimum drinking age would not be acceptable, although there has been some consideration of lower BAC for the young (Denny, 1986).

Other policies. Another group of studies has considered the effects of policy changes on drink-drivers' perceptions of risk. Hingson et al. (1987) considered the effect of more severe penalties in Maine and Massachusettes and a new procedure in Maine to increase conviction rates. Pre- and post-law surveys indicated that, in other States, perceptions that drunk drivers stopped by the police would be arrested, convicted and receive automatic penalties had increased. Even after the law changes, however, only about one quarter of the respondents believed that drunk drivers were very likely to be arrested. Results from the survey suggest a higher risk of accidents than arrests, with only one arrest compared to 2.5 crashes occurring per 1,000 drink-driving trips. It is also interesting to note that a decline in fatalities was observed before the law changes and the authors suggest that this may be a result of the publicity surrounding the debate. Also the effectiveness of the changes declined in one State with fewer people reporting decisions not to drive after drinking. This may suggest the importance of continuing publicity and information about the issue.

A few studies have considered the effect of random or discretionary breath testing. Christoffel (1984) considered the effectiveness of road blocks and considered they might exaggerate the public perception of probable apprehension, but this effect would diminish over time. Dunbar et al. (1987) considered the effects of random breath testing in Finland. The random testing introduced in Finland in 1977 involved road blocks where all drivers are tested. The study quotes the official sources who claim that there was no increase in police staffing, despite a 30 fold increase in the number of breath tests. As a result of this policy, there has been a 58 per cent reduction in drivers with positive BACs in Finland between 1979 and 1985.

Random breath testing has also been introduced in New South Wales, Australia. As in Finland, the public acceptability of the measure increased after the law was introduced, from 60 per cent to 90 per cent of voters. Also there was a financial evaluation of the costs. Random testing costs and advertising in television cost $A4 million per year, but the study calculated $A131 million was saved in health and welfare costs. Research suggest that road traffic fatalities have been reduced by about 30 per cent since the introduction of RBTs (Howel, 1983; Paciullo, 1983).

To summarise, a number of studies have considered the effects of specific policies on drink-driving. The studies have not generally been of the causal model type outlined in the first part of this section and have been limited to US data. Consequently, the usefulness of these studies in evaluating UK policy options is open to question. Few studies have attempted to control for changes in alcohol consumption. The relationship between alcohol consumption, policies designed to reduce alcohol consumption, and the level of drink-driving problems is considered in the next section.

Consumption of alcohol and drink-driving problems

If the level of drink-driving accidents is linked to the level of alcohol consumption, then policies which are designed to control that consumption may also affect the levels of drink-driving and associated harm. Indeed policies such as tax changes may be more effective than specific drink-driving measures. Riley (1986) studied the relationship between self-reported drink-driving and a range of characteristics including total alcohol consumption, involvement in other motoring offences and aspects of their knowledge. The prevalence of drinking and driving was most strongly related to alcohol consumption, there was a three times greater probability of being a drunk driver if consumption was above average. Also US studies have found alcohol consumption to be a significant factor in models of driving fatalities (Zlaptoper, 1987; Asch and Levy, 1987).

Cook (1981) used a quasi-experimental approach to compare changes in liquor taxes with changes in driver fatalities, and calculated an elasticity of -0.7, that is, a 10 per cent increase in price of US alcohol would be predicted to decrease fatalities by 7 per cent. One of the problems with the approach used is that the effect of other factors such as income cannot be determined. In a more conventional demand analysis of the consumption of beer by youths, Coate and Grossman (1988) found that the frequency of the consumption of beer was inversely related to price and the minimum legal age. A number of policy simulations were undertaken which indicated the usefulness of both tax and the minimum drinking age for reducing alcohol consumption of youths and they concluded that tax may be the more effective policy. In another study, Saffer and Grossman (1987) constructed a model including youth traffic fatalities. The empirical model consisted of two equations. The first was a demand for alcohol equation that was similar to those of other studies (Godfrey, 1989). In the other equation of the model, the probability of fatalities was specified as being determined by alcohol consumption and a set of variables measuring highway conditions and vehicle quality. The authors also considered the endogeneity of the drinking age laws, increases/decreases being motivated by changes in mortality rates, affecting consumption which also a determinant of fatalities. The results of the study suggest that an increase in the drinking age to 21, an 8 per cent increase, would reduce mortality in the 18 to 20 year old group by approximately 18 per cent. A 10 per cent rise in beer tax would be predicted to reduce youth mortality by 2.7 per cent for 18 to 20 year olds, 1.8 per cent for 15 to 17 year olds, and 1.9 per cent for the 21 to 24 year olds.

It is not only the absolute levels of alcohol consumption that may affect the probability of drink-driving accidents. The drinking place selected and the type of beverage may have independent effects. Berger and Snortum (1985) considered the beverage preferences of drink-driving violators in the US and found substantial differences between beer drinkers and others. Beer drinkers were more likely to drive after drinking and tended to consider drink-driving less seriously. Riley (1985) also found that beer drinkers under 25 in the UK were twice as likely to be drunk drivers compared to the whole sample. Snow and Anderson (1987) considered the reasons for selecting drinking places among drunk drivers and how such selection may interrelate with offences. Blose and Holder (1987) considered how changes in retail availability of spirits in some states affected traffic crashes. They found that after 'liquor by the drink' was introduced there was a statistically significant increase of 16 to 24 per cent in the number of reported accidents for male drivers aged over 21, while there was no change in alcohol-related accidents in the control states. In contrast, Smart and Adlaf (1986) found that the banning of 'happy hours' did not significantly alter consumption and the reduction of traffic accidents could not be attributed to the change in policy.

The driving environment

Finally, although not a central part of this analysis, the effect of the driving environment must be considered briefly. Clearly such factors may be particularly important for the young. Some studies have indicated that it is the interaction of the risks of drinking and driving which may contribute to high youth fatalities. Reed (1981) considered that general improvements to roads could bring more benefit to drink-drivers than others (see also Christoffel, 1984). In a study of the impact of drink-driving policies, Cameron (1979) considered a number of road safety measures. A cost-effectiveness ranking of 37 measures indicated that 'combined alcohol safety action countermeasures' was ranked third in terms of potential casualty savings, but only twenty first when ranked by cost-effectiveness. In reducing casualties and harm, rather than increasing the rate of detection, general safety procedures may be more cost-effective than specific alcohol policies.

To summarise, there is little available evidence to evaluate specific drink-driving measures. However, the effectiveness of any policy needs to be considered in terms of final outcomes, that is, the incidence of drink-related accidents and their associated costs, rather than in terms of intermediate processes such as the number of positive breath tests (Ross, 1988). Many factors including alcohol consumption, the level and concentration of road vehicles, road building and maintenance, and safety legislation may affect the number of drink-driving fatalities and injuries. Any legislation or information-based drink-driving policy can only be properly evaluated by controlling for such factors.

There is little information about the range of tangible and intangible costs associated with present or alternative policies. The available evidence from Finland and Australia does suggest that random breath testing has been cost-effective in these countries. The level, type and place of alcohol consumption can affect drink-driving behaviour and a number of policies which affect alcohol consumption may be considered as alternatives to drink-driving controls. American evidence suggests that careful consideration should be given to controlling alcohol consumption. Even though the UK evidence is limited, these empirical studies suggest that an examination of the different costs and benefits attached to the various policies would aid the debate and help focus future evaluative research.

CONCLUSION

In the UK, there was an early adoption of a legislative approach to controlling drink-driving problems. During the period since the 1967 Road Traffic Act, there has been considerable development of policy as described in the first section of the chapter. Penalties for drink-driving offences have been increased and loopholes in the law which reduced the certainty of convictions have been closed. Despite the incremental development of policy and legislation, there has been considerable criticism of current policy because drunken drivers have a low probability of arrest. However, policy makers, for a variety of administrative, electoral and ideological reasons, have resisted demands for the introduction of RBTs and comprehensive systems for identifying problem drinkers and removing them from the roads.

Both the Blennerhassett and Road Traffic Law Review reports have suggested a number of alternative policies. The empirical evidence of the effectiveness of different measures is mixed. The framework of identifying the costs and benefits of alternative and current policies does, however, provide useful insights into the drink-driving debate. In particular, this framework focuses attention on the outcome of drink-driving rather than the intermediate effects of policy, that is, the number and costs of drink-related accidents, rather than drink-driving arrests or the rate of positive breath tests. Previous empirical work also suggests that it is important to recognise the feedback effects between policies and public attitudes. Information policies may have an important role both before and after any change in legislation to aid its acceptance and effectiveness.

Drink-driving accidents, however, may also be affected by a number of other factors, including the level of alcohol consumption and road safety measures. Road safety measures, such as seat belts, may lower the probability of fatal accidents. Also, policies such as tax, information or licensing policy may be effective in reducing alcohol consumption and hence drink-driving accidents. In contrast, relaxation of other alcohol legislation, rising income levels or other factors may increase alcohol consumption and related problems. Such analyses suggest that drink-driving problems cannot be considered in isolation. The adoption of any single policy is unlikely to be sufficient to reduce the costs of drink-related accidents to acceptable levels for health campaigners.

One of the major impediments to further government action would seem to be that further drink-driving deterrent measures would prove electorally unpopular. This attitude may have arisen because of the reaction to the 1967 legislation. There is, however, some evidence that attitudes towards drink-driving have changed since this early legislation and present policy may be behind, rather than ahead of, current public opinion.

A second impediment would seem to be the possible resource costs of schemes that were effective in arresting drunk drivers. The evidence from Finland and Australia does indicate that RBTs were cost-effective. A major barrier to sensible and informed policy debate, on this and other issues, is, however, the lack of data on the frequency of drinking and driving in Great Britain and the determinants of this behaviour. Improved information may prove to be an effective means of educating the drink-driver and the rest of society on the extent of the problem, and allow a more general debate on policies which may alleviate its consequences.

References

Asch, P. and Levy, D.T., (1987), 'Does the minimum drinking age affect traffic fatalities', *Journal of Policy Analysis and Management*, 6, (2), 180-192.

Berger, D.E. and Snortum, J.R., (1985), 'Alcohol beverage preferences of drinking driving violators', *Journal of Studies on Alcohol*, 46, (3), 232-9.

Blose, J.O. and Holder, H.D., (1987), 'Liquor by the drink and alcohol-related traffic crashes: a natural experiment using time series analysis', *Journal of Studies on Alcohol*, 48, (1), 52-60.

Cameron, T., (1979), 'The impact of drinking-driving countermeasures: a review and evaluation', *Contemporary Drug Problems*, 8, (4), 495-565.

Castle, B., (1984), *The Castle Diaries 1964-70*, Weidenfeld and Nicholson, London.

Christian Economic and Social Research Foundation, (1986), *Annual Report on Drink Offenders: Chief Constables' Reports, England and Wales,* The Foundation, London.

Christoffel, T., (1984), 'Using roadblocks to reduce drunk drivers: public health or law and order', *American Journal of Public Health*, 74, (9), 1028-30.

Coate, D. and Grossman, M., (1987), 'Change in alcohol beverage prices and legal drinking ages', *Alcohol Health and Research World*, Fall, 22-25.

Coate, D. and Grossman, M., (1988), 'Effects on alcoholic beverage prices and legal drinking ages on youth alcohol use', *Journal of Law and Economics*, 31, 145-171.

Cook, P.J., (1981), 'The effect of liquor taxes on drinking, cirrhosis, and auto fatalities', in Moore, M.H. and Gerstein, D.R. (eds.), *Alcohol and Public Policy: Beyond the Shadow of Prohibition,* National Academy Press, Washington DC.

Denny, R.C., (1986), *Alcohol and Accidents*, Sigma, Cheshire.

Department of the Environment, (1976), *Drinking and Driving*, a report of the Departmental (Blennerhassett) Committee, HMSO, London.

Department of Transport, (1965), *Road Safety Legislation*, 1965-6, Cmnd. 2859, HMSO, London.

Department of Transport, (1986), *Road Accidents in Great Britain 1985*, The Casualty Report, HMSO, London.

Department of Transport, (1989), *The Road User and the Law*, HMSO, London.

Department of Transport and Home Office, (1988), *Road Traffic Law Review Report*, HMSO, London.

Douglass, R.L., (1974), 'Youth alcohol and traffic accidents', *Social Mediators and Prevention*, 13, 347-366.

DuMouchel, W., Williams, A.F. and Zador, P., (1987), 'Raising the alcohol purchasing age: its effects on fatal motor vehicle crashes in twenty-six States', *Journal of Legal Studies*, 16, (1), 249-266.

Dunbar, J.A., (1985), *A Quiet Massacre*, Occasional Paper No. 7, Institute of Alcohol Studies, London.

Dunbar, J.A., Ogston, S.A., Ritchie, A., Devgun, M.S., Hagart, J. and Martin, B.T., (1985), 'Are problem drinkers dangerous drivers?', *British Medical Journal*, 290, 827-830.

Dunbar, J.A., Pentula, A. and Pikkarainen, J., (1987), 'Drinking and driving: success of random breath testing in Finland', *British Medical Journal*, 295, 101-103.

Forcier, M.W., Kurtz, N.R., Parent, D.G. and Corrigan, M.D., (1986), 'Deterrence of drunk driving in Massachusettes: criminal justice system impacts', *International Journal of the Addictions*, 21, (11), 1197-1220.

Foster, G.R., Dunbar, J.A., Whittet, D. and Fernando, G.C.A., (1988), 'Contribution of alcohol to deaths in road traffic accidents in Tayside, 1982-6', *British Medical Journal*, 296, 1430-1432.

Gallup, (1988), Gallup Political Index, May.

General Accident, (1986), Press Release, 12th December.

Gilmore, A., (1984), 'Should we raise the legal drinking age?', *Canadian Medical Association Journal*, 131, 796-798.

Godfrey, C., (1989), 'Modelling demand', in Maynard, A. and Tether, P. (eds.), *The Addiction Market: consumption, production and policy development*, Avebury/Gower, Aldershot.

Harrison, L., (1987), 'Data Note 7, Drinking and driving in Great Britain', *British Journal of Addiction*, 82, 203-8.

Hingson, R., Merrigan, D. and Heeren, T., (1985), 'Effects of Massachusettes raising its legal drinking age from 18 to 20 on deaths from teenage homicide, suicide and non-traffic accidents', *Paediatric Clinics of North America*, 32 (1), 221-232.

Hingson, R., Heeren, T., Kovenock, D., Mangione, T., Meyers, A., Morelock, S., Lederman, R. and Scotch, N.A., (1987), 'Effects of Maine's 1981 and Massachusettes' 1982 driving-under-the-influence Legislation', *American Journal of Public Health*, 77 (5), 593-597.

House of Commons, (1966), *Parliamentary Debates,* 7th November, col. 985.

House of Commons, (1976), *Parliamentary Debates,* 4th August, 941, col. 271.

House of Commons, (1985), Transport Committee, Road Safety, Vols. 1, 2 and 3 with Minutes of Evidence and Appendices, HC 103.

Howel, R., (1983), 'The impact of random breath testing in New South Wales', *Medical Journal of Australia*, 1, 616-19.

McDonnell, R. and Maynard, A., (1985), 'The costs of alcohol misuse', *British Journal of Addiction*, 80, 27-35.

MacKinnon, D.P. and Woodward, J.A., (1986), 'The impact of raising the minimum drinking age on driver fatalities', *The International Journal of the Addictions*, 21, (12), 1331-1338.

Martin, J.P., (1986), 'A course for drivers convicted of drink-driving', *Justice of the Peace*, 150, 182.

Mayhew, D.R., Donelson, A.C., Beirness, D.J. and Simpson, H.M., (1986), 'Youth alcohol and relative risk of crash involvement', *Accident Analysis and Prevention*, 18, (4), 273-287.

Maynard, A., (1989), 'The costs of addiction and the costs of control', in Robinson, D., Maynard, A. and Chester, R. (eds.), *Controlling Legal Addictions*, Macmillan, London.

Medico Legal Bulletin, (1986), 'Driving under the influence and accidental death insurance', *Medico Legal Bulletin*, 35, (4), 1-5.

Ministerial Group on Alcohol Misuse, (1989), *First Annual Report 1987-1988,* HMSO, London.

Morbidity and Mortality Weekly Report (MMWR), (1985), 'Temporal patterns of motor-vehicle related fatalities associated with young drunken drivers, US 1983', *Journal of the American Medical Association*, 253, (2), 188.

Mosher, J.F., (1985), 'Alcohol policy and the presidential commission on drink-driving. The paths not taken', *Accident Analysis and Prevention*, 17, (3), 239-250.

Mosher, J.F. and Wallack, M.P.H., (1979), 'The DUI project', *Contempory Drug Problems*, Summer, 193-204.

Paciullo, G., (1983), 'Random breath testing in New South Wales', *Medical Journal of Australia*, 620-21.

Reed, D.S., (1981), 'Reducing the costs of drinking and driving', in Moore, M.H. and Gerstein, D. (eds.), *Alcohol and Public Policy: Beyond the Shadow of Prohibition*, National Academy of Sciences, Washington.

Riley, D., (1985), 'Drinking drivers: the limits to deterrence', *The Howard Journal*, 24 (4), 241-256.

Riley, D., (1986), *Drivers' Beliefs about Alcohol and the Law*, Home Office Research Bulletin, No. 6, London.

Rosalki, S.P. and Rau, D., (1972), 'Serum garmaglutoxyl tramreptiduse activity in alcoholism', *Clinica Chinica Acta*, 39, 41-47.

Ross, H.L., (1984), *Determining the Drinking Driver*, Lexington Books, Lexington, Massachusettes.

Ross, H.L., (1988), 'British drink-driving policy', *British Journal of Addiction*, 83, 863-865.

Sabey, B.E. and Staughton, G.C., (1980), *The Drinking Road User in Great Britain*, TRRL Supplementary Report 616, TRRL, Crowthorne, Berkshire.

Saffer, H. and Grossman, M., (1987), 'Drinking age laws and highway mortality rates: cause and effect', *Economic Inquiry*, 25, 403-417.

Smart, R.G. and Adlaf, E.M., (1986), 'Banning happy hours: the impact on drinking and impaired driving charges in Ontario, Canada', *Journal of Studies on Alcohol*, 47 (3), 256-258.

Smart, R.G. and Goodstadt, M.S., (1977), 'Effects of reducing the legal alcohol purchasing age on drinking and driving problems', *Journal of Studies on Alcohol*, 38 (7), 1313-1323.

Snow, R.W. and Anderson, B.J., (1987), 'Drinking place selection factors among drink-drivers', *British Journal of Addiction*, 82, 85-95.

Sunday Times, (1980), 28th December, 1.

Taylor, J.B., (1979), 'Econometric models of criminal behaviour: a review', in Heinke, J.M. (ed.), *Economic Models of Criminal Behaviour*, North Holland, Amsterdam.

Transport Road Research Laboratory (TRRL), (1983), *The Facts About Drinking and Driving*, TRRL, Growthorne, Berkshire.

Valverius, M.R., (1982), 'Roadside surveys in Northern Sweden', in Valverius, M. (ed.), Roadside Surveys: Proceedings of the Satellite Conference to the 8th International Conference on Alcohol, Drugs and Traffic Safety, Swedish Council for Information on Alcohol and Other Drugs, Stockholm.

Vingilis, E. and Smart, R.G., (1981), 'Effects of raising the legal drinking age in Ontario', *British Journal of Addition*, 76, 415-425.

Voas, R.S. and Williams, A.F., (1986), 'Age differences of arrested and crash involved drinking drivers', *Journal of Studies on Alcohol*, 47 (3), 244-246.

Wagenaar, A.C., (1983), *Alcohol, Young Drivers and Traffic Accidents,* Lexington, Massachusetts.

Waller, J.A., (1986a), 'On smoking and drinking and crashing', *New York State Journal of Medicine*, 86 (9), 459-460.

Waller, J.A., (1986b), 'State liquor laws as enablers for impaired driving and other impaired behaviours', *American Journal of Public Health*, 76 (7), 787-793.

Whitehead, T.P., Clark, C.A. and Whitefield, A.G.W., (1978), 'Biochemical and haematological makers of alcohol intake', *Lancet*, i, 978-981.

Zlatoper, T.J., (1987), 'Factors affecting motor vehicle deaths in the USA: some cross-sectional evidence', *Applied Economics*, 19, 753-761.

8 Preventing alcohol and tobacco problems

ALAN MAYNARD AND DAVID ROBINSON

A recurring theme in both this volume and its companion, *The Addiction Market: consumption, production and policy development*, (Maynard and Tether, 1989) is that the frequent calls for dramatic changes in the control of the markets for alcohol and tobacco are unlikely to be answered for a variety of political, organisational and economic reasons. Both books also stress that the use of legal addictive substances can nevertheless be curtailed within existing laws, regulations and practices.

These conclusions contrast with much of the debate about alcohol and tobacco policy over the last decade. Whilst there has been a general recognition that 'something must be done', this has largely produced little more than reports on the extent of the problem and statements of broad policy objectives from Government departments, expert committees, professional bodies and concerned individuals. All this has not lead to any significant changes in the number and range of alcohol and tobacco-related problems. Why is this so? Is it possible to develop better policies? In both volumes barriers to effective policies designed to prevent alcohol and tobacco-related problems within the UK political and economic system have been explored. A number of impediments to policy reforms emerged from the detailed analysis of policy areas, such as taxation and advertising, and the different mix of UK policy instruments, whether legislation, voluntary agreements or information. But UK national policies cannot be considered in isolation. As illustrated earlier in Chapter 3, and in the contribution on taxation policies by Christine Godfrey and Larry Harrison in the companion volume, decisions taken in the European Community have a considerable impact on the freedom of policy choice within the UK. There are, however, other broader international trends.

The prevention of alcohol and tobacco problems is increasingly being discussed within the context of the emerging worldwide concerns with the development of healthy public policy: that is, policy which, whatever its focus, makes it more rather than less likely for all citizens to be able to live a healthy life. This is discussed in the first part of this chapter and followed by an appraisal of the importance of a thorough understanding of the policy environment, without which more healthy public policies cannot be designed. The lesson to be learnt from this understanding is that much alcohol and tobacco control policy can be designed and implemented by 'taking advantage of what is there' and by mobilising existing knowledge to ensure that what is not there at the margins can be created on the basis of logic and evidence. These issues are explored in the final section.

HEALTHY PUBLIC POLICY

An increasingly important element in contemporary policy debate about health has been the recognition that health care is only one factor which influences health and that income, education, work, leisure, diet, the use of addictive substances, environmental pollution, housing, family life and other factors may influence health status far more. This shifting consensus has resulted in changes in the policy formation of international and national agencies. This shift has been based in part on efficiency arguments. For instance if, as appears probable, one of the most cost-effective ways of producing enhancements in the length of quality of life is GP advice to stop smoking (Williams, 1987), why not spend additional scarce resources on encouraging this advice giving rather than on other health care activities which produce less health for the same or more expenditure?

Such proposals are reinforced by equity arguments. The unequal distribution of health resources within and between countries is very noticeable and it may be that equity and efficiency arguments coincide and may best be met by a broad range of healthy public policies rather than health care programmes designed and implemented in isolation from other relevant activities. Much of this debate about healthy public policy has been stimulated by the World Health Organisation.

The International Conference on Primary Health Care, organised by WHO and UNICEF, reaffirmed in its *Declaration of Alma Ata* (1978) that health is a fundamental human right. It also stressed that the attainment of the highest possible level of health requires the action of many other social and economic sectors in addition to the health sector. Then, echoing the

Thirtieth World Health Assembly (WHO, 1977), it set as a target for governments, international organisations and the whole world community: 'the attainment by all the peoples of the world by the year 2000 of a level of health that will permit them to lead a socially and economically productive life'.

Primary health care, within comprehensive national health care systems, is seen by the WHO as the vehicle for achieving that target of 'health for all' by the year 2000. It was expected that each country would interpret and adapt primary health care within its own social, political and developmental context. Already, in many parts of the world, the content and organisation of primary health care is changing as more and more people come to recognise and respond to the fact that this 'front line of activity' is, in the words of Dr. Mahler, the recently-retired Director General, 'the cornerstone to ensure health for all' (Mahler, 1977).

The *Declaration of Alma Ata* emphasised that 'governments have a responsibility for the health of their people'. But just as governments must provide 'adequate health and social measures' so the people of any country have the 'right and duty to participate individually and collectively in the planning and implementation of their health care'.

As part of the movement to make more likely both that government action and that public participation, the *Ottawa Charter* was adopted in 1986 at the First International Conference on Health Promotion. The Charter recognised the increasing attention being given to what has become known as the 'new public health' and also re-emphasised the key thrust of the *Declaration of Alma Ata* by stressing the need for health promotion to put health 'on the agenda of all policy makers in all sectors and at all levels'. The Charter saw the role of health promotion as combining:

'diverse but complementary approaches including legislation, fiscal measures, taxation and organisational change. It is co-ordinated action that leads to health, income and social policies that foster greater equity. Joint action contributes to ensuring safer and healthier goods and services, healthier public services, and cleaner, more enjoyable environments.

Health promotion requires the identification of obstacles to the adoption of healthy public policies in non-health sectors, and the ways of removing them. The aim must be to make the healthier choice the easier choice for policy makers as well.' (*Ottawa Charter*, 1986)

The *Ottawa Charter* identified five key aspects of effective health promotion action:

• building healthy public policy
• creating environments that support health

- strengthening community action
- helping people to develop skills
- re-orienting health services.

The first of these concerns, 'Healthy Public Policy', was the subject of the Second International Conference on Health Promotion in 1988 from which came the *Adelaide Recommendations* which attempted to put some policy infrastructural flesh on the outline produced at Ottawa. The main aim of healthy public policy is:

> 'to create a supportive environment to enable people to lead healthy lives. Healthy choices are thereby [to be] made possible and easier for citizens. Social and physical environments are [to be] made health enhancing. In the pursuit of healthy public policy, government sectors concerned with agriculture, trade, education, industry and communications need to take account of health as an essential factor during policy formulation. These sectors should be accountable for the health consequences of their policy decisions. As much attention should be paid to health as to the economic considerations.' (*Adelaide Recommendations*, 1988)

The *Adelaide Recommendations* further stress that, since health is a fundamental right as well as a sound social investment, governments:

> 'need to invest resources in healthy public policy and health promotion in order to raise the health status of all their citizens. [and] ... New efforts must be made to link economic, social and health policies into integrated action.'

The Recommendations also underline the fact that while government plays an important role in health:

> 'health is also influenced greatly by corporate and business interests, non-governmental bodies, and community organisations. Their potential for preserving and promoting people's health should be positively encouraged. [and] ... New alliances must be forged to provide the impetus for health action.'

Thus, international agencies, with the agreement of national governments including that of the UK, are recognising the inter-relatedness of 'host, agent and environment' in the traditional epidemiological terminology—now transposed in the jargon of the healthy public policy advocates into people, products and settings. This reiteration and re-emphasis of the legitimacy and necessity of taking the broader view in health policy now means that prevention is everybody's business. It is everybody's business because everyone's behaviour affects the health of others as well as themselves. Thus, healthy public policy is:

'an integral part of policy making in every appropriate sector and sphere of activity... It is not a separate or isolated body of policy.' (WHO, 1988a, p.2)

The focus of healthy public policy is at the international, national and local levels. The WHO Healthy Cities programme, involving over one hundred cities in Europe, North America and Australasia, is concerned with developing 'health for all' through healthy public policy at the local level. This integrated approach is essential if international and national advocacy is to be translated into local action which improves the health of citizens. Changes in individual behaviour are difficult to achieve if at the local level there is ignorance of health risks and the mechanisms to reduce them. Such local action is possible only if national and international advocacy creates a favourable policy climate in which the claims of producers can be countered effectively so that legislators and politicians are not frozen into inaction for fear of the electoral consequences of adopting healthy public policies.

An example of this interaction between the local, national and international levels of policy formation can be seen from the tobacco market. The links are well known between smoking and cancer of the lung, mouth, larynx, pharynx, oesophagus and elsewhere; smoking and heart and circulatory diseases; smoking and respiratory malfunction and other disorders. It is estimated that in Western Europe four out of five premature deaths are smoking-related and that in the UK alone 100,000 people die prematurely each year as a result of their smoking. Their smoking, however, is merely the last link in a chain of international activity which is itself not always quite what it seems.

The choice offered by any local tobacconist is broad with an array of cigarettes and cigars, varying in strength and length, taste and tar level. This is the product of the forces of oligopoly: a few producers with market power across many sectors of the world economy. The structure and activities of the tobacco companies in the UK are set out by Mark Booth, Melanie Powell and Keith Hartley in the companion volume (Maynard and Tether, 1989). The world manufacture of tobacco products outside Eastern Europe is controlled by a handful of multinational companies, sometimes called transnational tobacco conglomerates or TTCs such as British American Tobacco and Imperial, with a combined annual tobacco turnover of approximately £50,000 million. But vast though this turnover is, the manufacture of cigarettes and cigars is only the tip of the iceberg of the TTC's operations. Together, in combination and cooperation, they effectively control every aspect of tobacco-related business from leaf production to the distribution of the finished product. For instance, over 90 per cent of the tobacco that enters into international trade is under the control of a small number of transnational leaf buying corporations, all of which are either TTC subsidiaries or very much more closely linked with the TTCs than with the leaf producers.

TTCs acquired shipping companies to transport their leaf tobacco and then bought oil companies to ensure fuel for those ships. They control the companies that make the machines that make the cigarettes, and the paper mills and printing companies that produce the packaging. To ensure control of outlets, the TTCs have bought leisure, food, supermarket, store, hotel and other chains that will take their products. They own the cigarette vending machine companies and, where they do not actually own the outlet, have a tight system of controlling bonuses to ensure that retailers display the correct products in the correct place in their windows at the correct non-discount price.

TTCs have now achieved a position which makes it quite difficult, if not impossible, for any new company to even contemplate entering the 'competition'. Normal market forces are almost totally irrelevant including, crucially, the pricing of the product. As a United Nations report *The Marketing and Distribution of Tobacco* (1978) revealed, a feature of the tobacco market is a seller-determined price. 'The oligopoly', it said, 'sets the price and sells at that price whatever quantity the market will take.... Price leadership (price fixing) implies that not only must pricing policies be co-ordinated, but that the price, once agreed upon, must be sustained until a further change is required by the oligopoly collectively.' From a preventive health point of view, of course, oligopoly-maintained high prices may keep consumption lower than it otherwise would be in a freer market.

The direct impact of smoking on health in developed countries is considerable, even though consumption in many is declining and smokers are becoming an ever smaller minority of the population. But at the same time, the prime targets for the TTCs have become the 'new smokers' in the developing world where the most dangerous, high tar level, products are being sold, without health warnings, to the least informed consumers and where, not surprisingly, the indicators of smoking-related diseases are rising sharply. In countries like Thailand, Zambia, Malawi and Brazil the impact on health is not merely from the smoking, but is from the working of the tobacco market itself. Many millions of acres of what could be food-growing land and thousands of millions of working days are given over to the cultivation, for barely subsistence level returns to the land worker, of something which eventually goes up in smoke at risk to health and life.

Any problems which arise in the context of an international market, whether legitimate like most tobacco and alcohol or illegitimate like most narcotics, calls for an international response. However, that international response, from for instance the WHO, has to be translated into national policies and local action. Reducing tobacco use in the developed world could be enhanced by national policies which subsidise the transition of farming from tobacco cash crops to food products. Demand and supply for addictive substances, such as tobacco and alcohol, interact in complex, sophisticated, and inter-related markets, where shifts in demand damage the interests of producers and hence create the obstacles to prevention policy.

A healthy public policy in any area, be it alcohol, tobacco, food, pharmaceuticals, illicit drugs, chemicals, water or electricity, is inevitably difficult to formulate and implement. Health enhancing policy changes, implemented with the more imaginative use of existing legislation or the enactment of new laws, have to be formulated on the basis of an awareness of economic and social relationships and with a willingness for 'gainers'—health advocates—and 'losers'—health damaging producers—to negotiate change to their mutual advantage. As Sir Robert Walpole remarked, 'every man has his price' and the development of healthy public policy requires informed exchanges of views and resources at international, national and local levels.

THE SHIFT FROM TREATMENT TO CONTROL

In all countries there is increasing recognition of the damage to health caused by the use of alcohol and tobacco. In the UK alcohol consumption has risen rapidly in recent decades, leading to perhaps 28,000 premature deaths annually (Anderson, 1988). Although tobacco consumption has fallen significantly over the same period, its use causes over 100,000 premature deaths annually (Royal College of Physicians, 1983). Recognition of the need for a control policy as well as a treatment response to the use of these products has been stimulated in large measure by WHO. In relation to alcohol, for example, the Thirty-Second World Health Assembly recognised that 'the problems related to alcohol, and particularly its excessive consumption, rank among the world's major public health problems' (WHO, 1979, Resolution 32.40). Three years later the technical discussion at the Thirty-Fifth World Health Assembly brought together participants from over a hundred countries to discuss 'the development of national policies and programmes'. In the following year a resolution at the Thirty-Sixth World Health Assembly requested the Director General to 'continue and intensify WHO's programme on alcohol-related problems as an integral part of the strategy for health for all' (WHO, 1983, Resolution 36.12).

Accompanying these and other resolutions concerning alcohol have been similar statements about tobacco and prescription drugs, while WHO has produced a series of strategic publications. Taken together, these WHO resolutions, reports and associated activities over the past decade have contributed greatly to the general shift in international concern away from the classification, identification and management of addiction problems towards prevention and the construction of national control policies in relation to alcohol and tobacco.

National alcohol and tobacco policies are increasingly being developed in the form of overall strategic objectives with in addition, in some cases, action plans to achieve these objectives and, in just a few cases, indicators of how to evaluate those actions. For example, in the draft National Health Policy on Alcohol in Australia presented in 1986 to the Ministerial Council on Drug Strategy, objectives were set in relation to availability, price and taxation, advertising and marketing, and other legal controls, together with policies in relation to education, treatment, the non-governmental sector and research. Strategies for achieving those objectives were set out and followed by evaluation indices. The indices on advertising included:

- the restriction of direct advertising of alcohol on television to those periods scheduled for adult viewing;
- the reduction of tax deductibility of expenditure on alcohol advertising to 0 per cent;
- the elimination of direct advertising of alcohol beverages, as distinct from corporate identification of sponsorship, in conjunction with sporting and cultural activities.

The good sense of such objectives, strategies for action and indices for judging progress is undeniable. But it is necessary to turn them from policy statements into policy practice. To date, however, much discussion and debate about the control of legal addiction problems has concluded with little more than a statement to the effect that the desired goals of policy will be achieved if there is sufficient 'political will'. An example of this can be found at the end of the final chapter of Don Cahalan's book *Understanding America's Drug Problem: How to Combat the Hazards of Alcohol* (1987) where he concludes:

'In relation to alcohol policy: obviously our state, local, and national governments are the agencies we should hold responsible for bringing about equitable relationships between the general consuming and tax-paying public, the sellers of the alcoholic beverages, the sufferers from alcoholism and their families, and those who treat alcoholics... Our country has solved even worse problems before. With a little *political backbone*, we should be

able to reduce drinking to a livable level without a return to prohibition.'
(Cahalan, 1988, p.196)

In the policy arena, this call for more political backbone is the equivalent of the therapeutic demand to 'pull yourself together'; namely, the last resort of those bereft of any sensible alternative course of action. The rhetoric of policy advocates has changed: in the 1960s it was a call for 'relevance', in the 1970s 'more education' was needed, and in the 1980s, the demand, in various guises, has been for 'political will'. Such advocates assert that if policy statements were only relevant/had more education/mobilised political will, then policy change, as if by magic, would be created which would put us on the right track to prevent/minimise/solve some of those awful social/ health/addiction problems which plague our organisation/locality/nation.

This is not to say that these aspects of policy are trivial. However, in relation to political will for instance, it is a matter to be considered in relation to questions such as: 'why is there insufficient political will?' And in order to begin to answer that question it is necessary to know something of the environment in which policy is formulated.

It is easy to call for national control policies and to be ignorant about the range and complexity of existing policies and activities. In fact, some advocates sometimes appear to suggest that there is no national policy at all. However, every country in which there is any alcohol or other legal drug has its *de facto* national policy. This policy may or may not be appropriate, but it nonetheless exists as the starting point for any analysis of the process of policy formation. It has been the starting point for the analyses conducted by the authors of this volume and its companion (Maynard and Tether, 1989).

A detailed map of the current policy terrain in any country reveals a wide range of statutory, commercial, voluntary, professional, service sector and other agencies, groups and organisations involved in some way with alcohol and tobacco. At government level alone, for example, there will be many ministries or departments of state that play some role in relation to some aspect of regulation, taxation and legislation, importation and exportation, production and distribution, promotion and sale, or the consequences of consumption. In the UK there are 16 different Government agencies involved in the markets for tobacco and alcohol. The laws, regulations and activities of these governmental and many other organisations constitute 'national policies'. It is these policies and their associated networks which have been analysed in earlier chapters and in the companion volume.

Disaggregating the problem and the response

Much debate about how best to combat alcohol and tobacco problems has been shown in earlier chapters to be over simple in relation to both policy issues, policy organisations and their interaction. The issues, for instance, are often no more firmly delineated in policy debate than in calls for 'something to be done' about some small combination of high profile problems or target groups such as young people, advertising, road safety, taxes, customs controls, and pregnant women. All of these are important topics and issues. But since the list could be extended endlessly it helps if they are grouped for purposes of both policy statement and policy practice. When matters are more systematically considered it is usually found that most discussion of alcohol and tobacco issues tend to be primarily concerned with:

- employment and the market
- education
- advertising and the media
- health and safety
- law and order.

Within these policy areas there are, of course, numerous specifics. For example, within 'law and order', there are among many other things matters to do with:

- illegal possession
- illicit production
- illegal sale or purchase
- product and purchase-related theft
- importation, trade and tax offences
- public drunkenness and public disorder
- liquor licensing
- drinking and driving.

However, further breakdown of these topics is possible and appropriate. For example, within the 'drinking and driving' issue which was discussed in Chapter 7, there is a multitude of policy strands such as:

- motorists' rights
- apprehension procedures
- adequacy of breath test apparatus
- police records
- court practice
- sentencing policy

together with related policy issues such as:

- highway construction
- surface markings and lighting
- car design
- learner driver education
- general public safety education.

It is obvious that any policy issue needs careful definition. The process of taking well-defined policy issues and getting organisations to determine their priorities is complex and involves dominant grouping such as:

- the Government
- the (helping) professions
- the trade
- the law
- the general public.

However, like policy issues, these organisations need to be disaggregated. There is no such thing as *a* trade or *a* professional view on alcohol or tobacco. Similarly, no 'Government' is an entity in relation to legal addictions any more than it is in relation to anything else. As has been shown earlier, governments each have many addiction relevant policies which will be more or less explicit and more or less compatible with each other.

In their analysis of alcohol policies Tether and Harrison (1988) describe the policy complexity within sixteen government departments. They outline the departmental alcohol responsibilities and then pinpoint where these responsibilities are located within departmental structures, trace out the principal intra- and inter-departmental policy making links and, finally, indicate each department's contacts with the most important non-departmental organisations which may contribute to the alcohol policy process. Their analysis has been drawn on for the 'policy network' chapters in this volume and its companion (Maynard and Tether, 1989).

The Department of Transport (DOT) will here serve as a small case example. Within the DOT various aspects of policy are divided between policy Directorates, four of which have alcohol responsibilities. These four Directorates are: Road and Vehicle Safety, Marine and Ports, Railways, and Civil Aviation. In addition, there is the Accident Investigation Branch.

In relation to alcohol the DOT has a concern with, among many other things, consumption in the Merchant Navy. This is a matter, therefore, for the Marine and Ports Directorate. The following is a extract from Tether and Harrison's account.

'The (Marine and Ports) Directorate has two sections concerned with alcohol-related problems: the Occupational Health and Safety Section, which is part of the Marine Survey Service and comes under a Deputy Surveyor; and Section B in Marine Decision 1, which is concerned with employment conditions and discipline in the Merchant Navy.

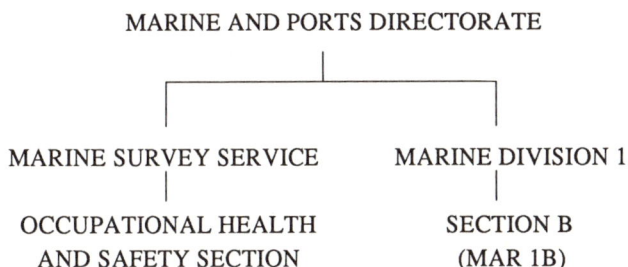

MARINE AND PORTS DIRECTORATE

```
                    |
    _____|_____
   |                                 |
MARINE SURVEY SERVICE          MARINE DIVISION 1
   |                                 |
OCCUPATIONAL HEALTH             SECTION B
AND SAFETY SECTION              (MAR 1B)
```

The Occupational Health and Safety Section has only a limited role in relation to alcohol and work policies. Guidelines on alcohol and work policies were issued in 1981 by a joint employers and trades union body, the National Maritime Board, which is now a limited company, British Maritime Technology Limited. These guidelines went to the 80 to 90 shipping companies which are members of the General Council of British Shipping (GCBS). Over half of these companies have now adopted an alcohol and work policy. The Department of Transport's Occupational Health and Safety Section distributes copies of a booklet *Don't Drink and Sink*. The Section is also concerned with environmental safety measures, such as the regulations governing the size and use of gang planks. Since most alcohol-related drownings occur in ports, when seafarers are leaving or returning to their vessels, environment safety measures are an important part of any prevention strategy. However, alcohol-related issues have been the province of the Marine Division 1 historically, and the Survey Service do not seem to have realised that many of their activities have an alcohol dimension.

In Marine Division 2, Section MAR1B deals with the discipline and medical fitness of merchant seamen. The disciplinary function is bound up with the Department's responsibility for issuing a certificate of competence to all prospective Merchant Navy Officers who pass the Nautical College examination. In cases of serious misconduct, the Department convenes an enquiry under Section 52 of the Merchant Shipping Act. This enquiry, which can take away an officer's certificate of competence, is run along legal lines, chaired by a legally qualified person. The department of Transport acts as the prosecution in such cases. The person appointed to run the enquiry adjudicates, assisted by professional assessors. There are only a few Section 52 cases each year, and of these, just under half involve alcohol-related offences.' (Tether and Harrison, 1988, p.26-27)

As has been stressed throughout the two volumes in this series, it is only after the real complexity of the policy making environment is understood that realistic proposals for preventing alcohol and tobacco problems can be made. The complexity of the policy networks, with government departments and sub-departments acting independently and each formulating policy which affects the market for alcohol and tobacco, means that it is impossible to produce what is so often called for—a simple, integrated, co-ordinated prevention strategy with a clearly defined and ranked set of targets for all policy agencies. Co-ordination may be desirable in some areas of policy but competition can also be very helpful. Indeed it may be more productive for agencies in any particular policy network to compete, since competition often throws up innovators who develop effective policy in unexpected ways. Thus some Chief Constables have sought to apply drink-driving laws more vigorously than others and in doing so, they have produced evidence about how such vigour can reduce accidents and save lives.

This competition is a manifestation of some people's priorities. All policy makers have to set targets and monitor their performance. However, activity is influenced by the sharpness of definition in target setting. What is required is the clear definition and ranking of modest targets, progress towards which can be monitored corporately and for each part of the organisation.

It is apparent from the exploration of decision making agencies at national and local levels that the quality of management control is very uneven, but equally it is obvious that managers in Government and health agencies, however well intentioned, are poorly informed about the constraints on their roles and the costs and benefits of alternative policy options. Earlier chapters have explored such policy costs and benefits in relation to alcohol advertising, tobacco advertising, liquor licensing, and drinking and driving. Until policy is better managed, its effects are likely to remain obscure, an outcome which will frustrate health advocates as much as it pleases producer interests.

EXPLOITING EXISTING POLICY

An understanding of existing policy networks, together with clearly defined policy objectives, makes it possible to exploit existing policy to produce innovations which make for healthier public policy. In the real world of policy, activity takes place in networks where the issues and the organisation interact and compete to survive and develop. In the policy networks the policy issues are the property of policy organisations and it is in policy networks that prevention policy is developed. In these two volumes, this way of understanding the policy complex has informed the broad debate, the more detailed analysis of particular policies and the organisational, political and economic barriers to prevention.

The constituents of policy networks disagree about priorities and compete and negotiate to determine priorities which shape managerial activity. The dominant actors wax and wane in their influence on these networks with policy being in a continual state of flux. To take 'alcohol and safety' in the UK as an example: in addition to the involved government departments such as Transport, Education, and Employment, there are over eighty occupational health and safety groups spread throughout the country whose membership includes health and safety at work officers, personnel officers, supervisors and managers. Most are affiliated to the Royal Society for the Prevention of Accidents and to that body's Occupational Health and Safety Group's Advisory Committee on which sit senior safety professionals from the Health and Safety Executive, the medical profession, trade unions, employers' organisations and insurance companies. Furthermore, this is only one aspect of the safety network. Add to this the Pedestrians' Association, the Guild of Experienced Motorists, the Cyclists' Touring Club, the Institution of Highway Engineers, the County Surveyors' Society, coroners with their statutory right to comment about the advise on the circumstances and conditions surrounding fatalities, local government Home Safety Committees and Road Safety Departments, the Fire Service, Accident and Emergency Departments and many, many more, and one gets some idea of the complexity of this one network area.

While sets of dominant issues may be readily identifiable, clear boundaries cannot be drawn around the policy networks. Moreover, there will be sub-networks where specific issues are focused on and fought over. Obviously, network will interact with network because the interests of particular policy organisations may overlap different policy areas. This also means that policy cultivation in one network may push an organisation or part of an organisation in one direction which may conflict with the way it is being pushed in another network. This happens most obviously with the premier policy organisation, national government, where the agriculture or trade ministry may be encouraging the further development of the tobacco or whisky industry while the health, law and transport ministries may be attempting to cope with the consequences of increased consumption.

It is in response to this state of affairs that many people are calling for a national plan of action, a national committee or even a national supremo in the belief that these conflicting activities will then disappear, and coherent and co-ordinated national policy can be cultivated. However, as has been argued throughout these two volumes, such 'co-ordinated' policy is unlikely to be achieved, not least because it would require the control of legal addiction problems to be universally agreed as the most important policy objective, that is, more important than other economic or social goals. It would have to be more important than tax and duty revenue, industrial production, the control of inflation, employment in certain localities, and international treaty obligations, not to mention personal pleasure, civil liberty and individual freedom which are not unfamiliar components of the addictions debate.

The close understanding and appreciation of the policy climate and the policy terrain mean that there are no simple answers to the question 'how do we prevent alcohol and tobacco problems?' However, this does not mean that nothing can be done. The mistake which is often, and understandably, made is to equate the need to avoid oversimplification with the feeling that single issues are unimportant. In fact, of course, single issues may be crucial. Single issues are what control, in reality, is all about. It is in relation to single issues that actual policy networks can be involved, mobilised and set priorities. It is in relation to single issues that the general population can be motivated, excited or, at least, interested. It is via single issues that the prevention of alcohol and tobacco problems moves up particular political agendas, and, as a consequence, leads to the readjustment of priorities and the redistribution of resources from production to health.

To facilitate this policy process, the inter-departmental Ministerial Group on Alcohol Misuse was established to review and develop the UK Government's strategy for combating alcohol-related problems (Home Office, 1987). It has been criticised by some for its concentration on a small number of high-profile issues: road safety, the use of alcohol at work, public disorder and young people. To the extent that this criticism is aimed at an assumed unwillingness by the Ministerial Group to address those issues which confront dominant trade interests, it may for that reason for some be justified. To criticise the group for taking on a small number of significant sets of problems and making policy proposals for their alleviation is unjustified. It is certainly banal to criticise any organisation for not doing everything. The members of the Ministerial Group have decided to address some high profile issues and mobilise cross-departmental action. However, given the extensive list of other major alcohol issues which all departments need to confront, the work of this Group is incomplete and needs to be complemented by health advocates raising new issues for its and other decisions makers' consideration.

This placing of the prevention debate within the routine business of social and political activity is necessary if progress is to be made toward the cultivation of better policies to control alcohol and tobacco problems. Within the policy world—as opposed to the world of apolitical exhortation—things do change and they can change rapidly and efficiently. Three current changes are particularly important.

First is the change in policy climate which was mentioned earlier. Here the movements for Health for All by the Year 2000 and for Healthy Public Policy are playing their part in trying to raise the issue of health higher up the political agenda. The aim is to make health less of an unintended consequence of other policy action and a residual category or lower order concern, and more of a defining characteristic of public policy.

The second change arises from the nature of the social policy process. Rather than pressing for a co-ordinated, supra-departmental, national policy—under which all action is geared to securing some well-defined objectives in a rational policy approach—the efficient policy demands that a desired national policy-in-action, rather than merely policy-on-paper, can only be cultivated through a process of what is often called 'partisan mutual adjustment' (Lindblom, 1965). As Larry Harrison and Philip Tether have succinctly described it:

> 'Agencies are 'partisan' in that they pursue their own interests but they are capable of 'mutual adjustment', in that they adapt to the decisions made by other agencies, or attempt to influence them through negotiation, bargaining and manipulation. The policy which emerges may not be the theoretical optimum, but it will be one over which agreement has been reached, and which therefore stands some chance of being implemented. [In Lindblom's analysis,] 'partisan mutual adjustment' is both descriptive and prescriptive in that it purports not only to describe what happens but to recommend it as a 'democratic' way of making policy.' (Harrison and Tether, 1987, p.82)

The policy task then for those seeking to alter alcohol, tobacco and other legal drug policy in what they consider to be the 'right' direction is to get involved in the policy cultivation process. This is clearly possible in the complexity of organisations which make up the policy terrain. It is particularly important to do so when the policy climate, as now, is conducive to change.

The third positive sign of change, and closely related to the second, is that there has been a growing emphasis on things other than *national* policy in relation to legal addictions. Obviously, national control policies are essential. But concentration on action at the national level to the exclusion of any serious consideration of anything else is mistaken. It implies, unhelpfully, that the only worthwhile response to contemporary health and social problems is global action by central government. Such a viewpoint diverts attention from the wealth of other—sectoral and local—prevention and control resources which are so often unrecognised and, therefore, untapped.

No local prevention policy package will, of course, be able to change directly such things as customs regulations, retailing law, the drink-driving law or the Chancellor of the Exchequer's taxation policies. Nevertheless, many effective and sensible measures can be taken at the local level without the backing of legislation, massive funding or central government commitment (Tether and Robinson, 1986; Robinson, Tether and Teller, 1989). What is required locally is the careful identification and cataloguing of resources (costs), together with specific intervention by interested people, at the right time, through appropriate organisations which will encourage, promote and co-ordinate minor, but important, changes in existing practices and procedures (benefits). The use of the cost-benefit framework is an essential component of the efficient policy process.

Those engaged in the identification, management and prevention of alcohol and tobacco problems in particular localities should not wait for national initiatives. They can create policy at the periphery where the problems and so many of the resources are located and where, moreover, developments serve as models for national policy makers. For good practice innovation at the local level today is often, as any policy analyst knows, the 'discovery' of tomorrow's central policy maker!

At the national level addictions policy is generally discussed and debated as though it exists in isolation, not merely from local activities but from the activities and interests of other nations. The internationality of the illicit addictions market is, of course, well recognised and increasing efforts are being made to develop both multinational agreements and programmes to deter and detect drug trafficking. The International Conference on Drug Abuse and Illicit Trafficking held in Vienna in 1987 called for active collaboration between intergovernmental organisations and member states. In the Australian National Campaign Against Drug Abuse (NCADA), which covers both legal and illegal drugs, one of the core principles of the Campaign is to control supply. The Campaign document particularly emphasises the fact that:

> 'drug abuse is a subject of growing significance in Australia's foreign relations, at the multinational, regional and bilateral level. (with Australia being)... an active, concerned and cooperative member of United Nations bodies dealing with drug control. ... Australia has been a member of the United Nations Commission on Narcotic Drugs continuously since 1973 and continues to be actively involved in United Nations initiatives to combat drug abuse and drug trafficking. The Australian Federal Police has been actively involved in regional operations and... will continue to pursue international drug law enforcement cooperation through participation in international liaison meetings and training. The Customs Service will pursue further opportunities for improving drug interception at the Customs barrier through the exchange of information and mutual assistance through Customs administrations.' (Department of Health, 1985, p.10)

The Australian NCADA addresses itself not just to supply reduction of illicit drugs through multinational activities of the kind just mentioned, but to demand reduction within its own boundaries. The interrelation between these two sets of control strategies is obvious and itself international. As George Shultz, the then American Secretary of State, acknowledged on his visit to Bolivia in 1988, there is no point in criticising that country for not reducing the production and exportation of cocaine if the United States, the main market, does nothing to reduce the demand for its importation. Such arguments are uncontentious in relation to illicit drugs.

But there are equally important international dimensions to the legal addictions debate which tend to be overlooked by those who call for and suggest possible components of national control policies. In particular, there are those who play down or do not acknowledge at all the implication of their own national actions for the development of problems in other countries. In the Australian NCADA document there is no mention of the increasing export and internationalisation of their alcohol trade. In relation to alcohol and tobacco no less than to illicit drugs 'no island is an island'. It is understandable and right for Australia to emphasise some of the early pointers to success in the NCADA. As the Minister of Health, Neil Blewett, modestly summed it up at the end of the 1987 Leonard Ball Oration: 'I am encouraged by some of the tentative indicators that we are on the right path' (Blewett, 1987, p.14). But a fully rounded national approach would also pay attention to those activities of its citizens and organisations which exacerbate the legal addiction problems of other countries. In short, the question to be addressed is 'how many problems are being exported with the products?'

The Australian NCADA provides the framework for such questions to be legitimately addressed because the Campaign document emphasises a comprehensive approach to drug use and drug problems since as it says 'it is inappropriate to focus exclusively on one type of drug or on one group of drug users' (Department of Health, 1985, p.3). This principle was also adopted by the WHO expert working group representing all WHO regions which in 1988 drew up the Consensus Statement *Towards Healthy Public Policies on Alcohol and Other Drugs* (WHO, 1988b) which raises cross-substance multinational questions within the context of the call to formulate national policies and programmes. WHO has already adopted as a target for 1995 the establishment of comprehensive national policies and programmes on alcohol and drugs in at least half the member states.

Another weakness of much discussion on the construction of those national policies is the assumption, usually implicit and, probably, unconsidered, that nations *can* control the aspects of their life which are focused on in the policy. During the 1970s and early 1980s in the United Kingdom there were many reports and recommendations from government departmental advisory committees, professional bodies and others which concluded that action needs to be taken to prevent the increase in alcohol and tobacco-related problems. Most of these reports called for the manipulation of taxes and the need for more and better information and education.

Now the good sense of these suggestions may well be undeniable. But rarely is there any discussion of whether such policy components, even if agreed by everyone in the country, could actually be implemented. For example, Larry Harrison and Christine Godfrey have spelled out in Chapter 3 the lack of control which the UK government might have over the advertising of alcohol within the European Community, while Melanie Powell in her Data Note in the *British Journal of Addiction* points out a similar national lack of control over excise duty levels:

> 'The European Commission has already tabled over 75 per cent of the 300 White Paper proposals on the internal market, including those required to achieve fiscal approximation. A report on the progress of Member States is due by 31 December 1988. There can be no doubt that substantial changes will occur in the taxation of alcohol and tobacco within the European Community. For countries like the UK which raise a larger proportion of revenues from excise, the Commission proposals will result in substantial reductions in the levels of excise duty charged on alcohol.' (Powell, 1988, p.971-972)

Even if such EC constraints on policy were absent, tax policies have effects on employment, prices and trade which a Chancellor may find more pressing than health issues. Policy cannot be and is not formulated in isolation, it is part of a complex whole which involves subtle trade-offs in economic, social and political means and ends.

CONCLUSION

The development of healthy public policies to control the use of tobacco and alcohol which, together, kill about 125,000 UK citizens prematurely each year, is a complex problem requiring the careful definition of attainable goals by the myriad of decision makers whose actions affect the markets for these products. The process of policy development is weak in the sense that its objectives are badly defined and many decision makers, health advocates, bureaucrats and producers, are ill-informed about the costs and benefits of the alternative means of achieving their goals. The process of identifying and ranking policy goals appears to be informed more by rhetoric rather than by scientific understanding.

The processes of identifying, evaluating and ranking policy issues and evolving policies amongst coalitions of public and private institutions concerned with furthering or obstructing changes in the use of alcohol and tobacco have been analysed throughout this volume and its companion (Maynard and Tether, 1989). This analysis demonstrates the complexities of the activities of the policy formation process and illuminates clearly the obstacles to specific prevention policies. Such policies, if based on a proper understanding of the policy networks and how decision makers in these networks make choices between competing goals and alternative means of achieving them, require careful integration of international, national and local activity to ensure that the attainable gains in health are achieved at the least cost in terms of the wealth of the producers and consumers of alcohol and tobacco.

References

Adelaide Recommendations, (1988), 'Report of the Second International Conference on Health Promotion', WHO/Australian Department of Community Services and Health.

Anderson, R., (1988), 'Excess mortality associated with alcohol consumption', *British Medical Journal*, 297, 824-27.

Blewett, N., (1987), *National campaign against drug abuse: assumption, arguments and aspirations,* the 19th Leonard Ball Oration, 11 March 1987. NCADA Monograph Series, 1, Australia Government Publishing Service.

Cahalan, D., (1987), *Understanding America's Drinking Problem: How to Combat the Hazards of Alcohol*, Jossey-Bass, London.

Declaration of Alma Ata, (1978), 'Report of the International Conference on Health Care', WHO/UNICEF, ICPHC/PRA/70.10.

Department of Health, (1985), *National Campaign Against Drug Abuse,* campaign document issued following the Special Premiers' Conference, Canberra, 2 April 1985, Australia Government Publishing Service, Canberra.

Harrison, L. and Tether, P., (1987), 'The coordination of UK policy on alcohol and tobacco: the significance of organisational networks', *Policy and Politics*, 2, 77-90.

Home Office, (1987), 'Home Secretary announces Ministerial Group on Alcohol Misuse', *News Release*, 18 September, Home Office.

Lindblom, C., (1965), *The Intelligence of Democracy*, Free Press, New York.

Mahler, H., (1977), 'Blueprint for health for all', WHO Chronicle 31, 491.

Maynard, A. and Tether, P. (eds.), (1989), *The Addiction Market: consumption, production and policy development*, Avebury/Gower, Aldershot.

'National health policy on alcohol', (1986), draft presented to the Ministerial Council on Drug Strategy, Canberra.

Ottawa Charter for Health Promotion, (1986), 'Report of the International Conference on Health Promotion', WHO/Health and Welfare Canada/Canadian Public Health Association.

Powell, M., (1988), 'Data Note 15, Alcohol and tobacco tax in the European Community', *British Journal of Addiction*, 83, 971-978.

Robinson, D., Tether, P. and Teller, J. (eds.), (1989), *Local Action on Alcohol Problems*, Routledge, London.

Royal College of Physicians, (1983), *Smoking or Health?*, Pitman, London.

Tether, P. and Harrison, L., (1988), *Alcohol Policies: Responsibilities and Relationships in British Government*, Addiction Research Centre Occasional Paper, Universities of Hull and York.

Tether, P. and Robinson, D., (1986), *Preventing Alcohol Problems: A Guide to Local Action*, Tavistock, London.

United Nations, (1978), *Marketing and distribution of tobacco,* Report No TD/B/C.1/205, United Nations, Geneva.

WHO, (1977), Resolution WHO 30.43, 'WHO official record'.

WHO, (1979), Resolution WHO 32.40, 'WHO official record'.

WHO, (1983), Resolution WHO 36.12, 'WHO official record'.

WHO, (1988a), 'Healthy public policy: issues and options', Conference working paper for the Second International Conference on Health Promotion, Adelaide.

WHO, (1988b), *Towards healthy public policies on alcohol and other drugs,* Consensus Statement proposed by a WHO Expert Working Group, Sydney-Canberra 24-31 March 1988.

Williams, A., (1987), 'Screening for risk of CHD: is it a wise use of resources?', in Oliver, M., Ashley-Miller, M. and Wood, D. (eds.), *Screening for Risk of Coronary Heart Disease,* J. Wiley & Sons Ltd, Chichester.

Contents of Volume 1:

The Addiction Market: consumption, production and policy development

Addiction Research Centre bibliography

Alaszewski, A. and Harrison, L., (1989), 'Collaboration and coordination between welfare agencies', *British Journal of Social Work*, (forthcoming).

Anderson, P., Bennison, J., Orford, J., Spratley, T., Tether, P., Tomson, J. and Wilson, T., (1986), *Alcohol: A Balanced View*, Report from General Practice No. 24, Royal College of General Practitioners, London.

Baggott, R., (1986), 'By voluntary agreement: the politics of instrument selection', *Public Administration*, 64, 51–68.

Baggott, R., (1986), 'Alcohol, politics and social policy', *Journal of Social Policy*, 15, 467–488.

Baggott, R., (1986), *The Politics of Alcohol: Two Periods Compared*, Occasional Paper No. 8, Institute of Alcohol Studies, London.

Baggott, R., (1987), 'Government Industry Relations in Britain: the regulation of the tobacco industry', *Policy and Politics*, 15, 3, 137–146.

Baggott, R., (1987), *Licensing Law Reform: Social Welfare or Public Thirst*, Occasional Paper No. 12, Institute for Alcohol Studies, London.

Baggott, R., (1987), *The Politics of Public Health: Alcohol, Politics and Social Policy*, Ph.D. Thesis, University of Hull.

Baggott, R., (1988), 'Drinking and driving: the politics of social regulation', *Teaching Politics*, 17, 66–85.

Baggott, R., (1988), *Health v Wealth: The Politics of Smoking in Norway and the UK*, Papers on Government and Politics No. 57, University of Strathclyde, Glasgow.

Baggott, R., (1988), 'Licensing law reform and the return of the drink question', *Parliamentary Affairs*.

Baggott, R., (1989), 'Alcohol and tobacco: the politics of prevention', in Maynard, A. and Tether, P. (eds.), *The Addiction Market: consumption, production and policy development*, Avebury/Gower, Aldershot.

Baggott, R., (1989), 'The politics of the market', in Robinson, D., Maynard, A. and Chester, R. (eds.), *Controlling Legal Addictions*, Macmillan, London.

189

Baggott, R. and Harrison, L., (1986), 'The politics of self regulation: the case of advertising control', *Policy and Politics*, 14, 143–159.

Booth, M., Hardman, G. and Hartley, K., (1986), 'Data Note 6, The UK alcohol and tobacco industries', *British Journal of Addiction*, 81, 825–830.

Booth, M., Hardman, G. and Hartley, K., (1988), 'Data Note 14, Mergers in the UK alcohol and tobacco industries', *British Journal of Addiction*, 83, 707–714.

Booth, M., Hartley, K. and Powell, M., (1989), 'Industry and employment policy: department and group relations', in Maynard, A. and Tether P. (eds.), *The Addiction market: consumption, production and policy development*, Avebury/Gower, Aldershot.

Booth, M. and Weir, R., (1989), 'Prevention and policy in the Scotch whisky industry', in Maynard, A. and Tether, P., (eds.), *The Addiction Market: consumption, production and policy development*, Avebury/Gower, Aldershot.

Godfrey, C., (1986), Factors Influencing the Consumption of Alcohol and Tobacco—A Review of Demand Models, Discussion Paper 17, Centre for Health Economics, University of York.

Godfrey, C., (1986), 'Government policy, advertising and tobacco consumption in the UK: a critical review of the literature', *British Journal of Addiction*, 81, 339–346.

Godfrey, C., (1988), 'Licensing and the demand for alcohol', *Applied Economics*, 20, 1541–1558.

Godfrey, C., (1989), 'Modelling demand', in Maynard, A. and Tether, P. (eds.), *The Addiction Market: consumption, production and policy development*, Avebury/Gower, Aldershot.

Godfrey, C., (1989), 'Evaluating alternative advertising policies', in *Alcohol Advertising: Who Benefits? Why Ban?*, Action and Alcohol Abuse, London.

Godfrey, C., (1989), 'Price regulation', in Robinson, D., Maynard, A. and Chester, R. (eds.), *Controlling Legal Addictions*, Macmillan, London.

Godfrey, C., (1989), 'Factors influencing the consumption of alcohol: the use and abuse of economic models', *British Journal of Addiction*, (forthcoming).

Godfrey, C. and Hardman, G., (1987), 'Data note 11, Employment in the UK alcohol and tobacco industries', *British Journal of Addiction*, 82, 1157–1167.

Godfrey, C., Hardman, G. and Maynard, A., (1986), 'Data Note 2, Measuring UK alcohol consumption', *British Journal of Addiction*, 81, 287–293.

Godfrey, C., Hardman, G. and Powell, M., (1986), 'Data Note 1, Alcohol, tobacco and taxation', *British Journal of Addiction*, 81, 143–149.

Godfrey, C. and Harrison, L., (1989), 'Alternative tax policies', in Maynard, A. and Tether, P. (eds.), *The Addiction Market: consumption, production and policy development*, Avebury/Gower, Aldershot.

Godfrey, C. and Hartley, K., (1988), 'Data Note 16, Employment and prevention policy', *British Journal of Addiction*, 83, 1335–1342.

Godfrey, C. and Hartley, K., (1989), 'Employment', in Maynard, A. and Tether, P. (eds.), *The Addiction Market: consumption, production and policy development*, Avebury/Gower, Aldershot.

Godfrey, C. and Maynard, A., (1988), 'Economic aspects of tobacco use and taxation policy', *British Medical Journal*, 297, 339–343.

Godfrey, C. and Maynard, A., (1988), 'An economic theory of alcohol consumption and abuse', in Chaudron, D. and Wilkinson, A. (eds.), *Theories of Alcoholism*, Addiction Research Foundation, Toronto.

Godfrey, C. and Powell, M., (1986), 'Alcohol and tobacco taxation: barriers to a public health perspective', *Quarterly Journal of Social Affairs*, 1, 329–252.

Godfrey, C. and Powell, M., (1987), Budget Strategies for Alcohol and Tobacco in 1987 and Beyond, Discussion Paper 22, Centre for Health Economics, University of York.

Godfrey, C. and Powell, M., (1987), 'Making sense of the social cost studies of alcohol, drugs and tobacco', in *The Cost of Alcohol, Drugs and Tobacco to Society*, 31–52, Institute for Preventive and Social Psychiatry, Erasmus University, Rotterdam.

Godfrey, C. and Powell, M., (1989), 'The relationship between Government policy and individual choice in the decision to consume hazardous goods', in Baldwin, S., Godfrey, C. and Propper, C. (eds.), *Quality of Life: Policy and Perspectives*, Routledge, London.

Godfrey, C. and Robinson, D. (eds.), (1989), *Manipulating Consumption: information, law and voluntary controls*, Avebury/Gower, Aldershot.

Hardman, G. and Maynard, A., (1989), 'Consumption and taxation', in Maynard, A. and Tether, P. (eds.), *The Addiction Market: consumption, production and policy development*, Avebury/Gower, Aldershot.

Harrison, L., (1985), 'Light the blue touch-paper: the cigarette as a fire hazard', *Radical Community Medicine*, 27–28.

Harrison, L., (1986), 'Is a coordinated prevention policy really feasible?', *Alcohol and Alcoholism*, 21, 5–6.

Harrison, L., (1986), 'Tobacco battered and the pipes shattered; a note on the fate of the first British campaign against tobacco smoking', *British Journal of Addiction*, 81, 553–558.

Harrison, L., (1987), 'Data Note 7, Drinking and driving in Great Britain', *British Journal of Addiction*, 82, 203–208.

Harrison, L., (1987), 'Drinking and driving in Northern Ireland', *British Journal of Addiction*, 82, 210.

Harrison, L., (1988), 'Alcohol statistics: time to sort out the muddle', *Alliance News*, 14–16.

Harrison, L., (1988), 'The deadly habit that Governments can't give up', *The Listener*, 21 January, 15.

Harrison, L., (1989), 'Research perspectives, 2', in Steele, D. (ed.), *Alcohol Advertising: Who Benefits Why Ban?*, Action on Alcohol Abuse, London.

Harrison, L., (1989), 'The information component', in Robinson, D., Maynard, A., and Chester, R. (eds.), *Controlling Legal Addictions*, Macmillan, London.

Harrison, L. and Godfrey, C., (1989), 'Alcohol advertising', in Godfrey, C. and Robinson, D. (eds.), *Manipulating Consumption: information, law and voluntary controls*, Avebury/Gower, Aldershot.

Harrison, L. and Godfrey, C., (1989), 'Alcohol advertising controls in the 1990s', *International Journal of Advertising*, (forthcoming).

Harrison, L. and Tether, P., (1987), 'Coordinating the UK's policy on alcohol and tobacco: the significance of organisational networks', *Policy and Politics*, 15, 77–90.

Harrison, L. and Tether, P., (1988), 'Data Note 13, Alcohol policy and the British Government bureaucracy', *British Journal of Addiction*, 83, 451–460.

Harrison, L. and Tether, P., (1989), 'Tax policy: structure and process', in Maynard, A. and Tether, P. (eds.), *The Addiction Market: consumption, production and policy development*, Avebury/Gower, Aldershot.

Harrison, L. and Tether, P., (1989), 'Information and voluntary agreements: the policy networks', in Godfrey, C. and Robinson, D. (eds.), *Manipulating Consumption: information, law and voluntary controls*, Avebury/Gower, Aldershot.

Harrison, L., Tether, P. and Baggott, R., (1989), 'Regulation and voluntary agreements', in Godfrey, C. and Robinson, D. (eds.), *Manipulating Consumption: information, law and voluntary controls*, Avebury/Gower, Aldershot.

Hartley, K., (1985), 'Exogenous factors in economic theory: neoclassical economics', *Social Science Information*, 24, 457–483.

Hartley, K., (1985), 'Bureaucracy and power without responsibility', *Economic Affairs*, 6, 16–18.

Hartley, K., (1989), 'Industry, employment and prevention policy', in Robinson, D., Maynard, A. and Chester, R. (eds.), *Controlling Legal Addictions*, Macmillan, London.

Hartley, K., (1989), 'Alcohol, tobacco and public policy: the contribution of economics', *British Journal of Addiction*, (forthcoming).

Jones, A., (1986), First Hurdle Dominance: Theoretical Foundations for an Empirical Investigation of Cigarette Consumption, Discussion Paper 117, Department of Economics, University of York.

Jones, A., (1987), *A Theoretical and Empirical Investigation of the Demand for Addictive Goods*, D.Phil Thesis, University of York.

Jones, A., (1987), A Double-Hurdle Model of Cigarette Consumption, Discussion Paper 128, Department of Economics, University of York.

Jones, A., (1989), 'The UK demand for cigarettes 1954–1986, a double-hurdle approach', *Journal of Health Economics*, (forthcoming).

Jones, A. and Posnett, J., (1988), 'The revenue and welfare effects of cigarette taxes', *Applied Economics*, 20, 1223–1232.

Keeley Robinson, Y. and Baggott, R., (1985), 'Health education and the prevention of alcohol-related problems', *Health Education Journal*, 44, 174–177.

Leedham, W., (1987), 'Data Note 10, Alcohol, tobacco and public opinion', *British Journal of Addiction*, 82, 935–940.

Leedham, W. and Godfrey, C., (1989), 'Tax policy and budget decisions', in Maynard, A. and Tether, P. (eds.), *The Addiction Market: consumption, production and policy development*, Avebury/Gower, Aldershot.

Maynard, A., (1983), 'Modelling alcohol consumption and abuse', in Grant, M., Plant, M. and Williams, A. (eds.), *Economics and Alcohol*, Croom Helm, London.

Maynard, A., (1984), 'The social costs of alcohol use', in *Alcohol: Preventing the Harm*, Conference proceedings published by the Institute of Alcohol Studies, 232–242.

Maynard, A., (1985), 'The role of economic measures in preventing drinking problems', in Heather, N., Robertson, I. and Davies, P. (eds.), *The Misuse of Alcohol*, Croom Helm, London.

Maynard, A., (1985), 'Alcohol: preventing the harm', *Alliance News*, 3693, 3–4.

Maynard, A., (1985), 'Alcohol use: costs and benefits', *Alcohol Concern*, 11–12.

Maynard, A., (1986), 'Economic aspects of addiction policy', *Health Promotion Journal*, 1, 61–71.

Maynard, A., (1987), 'A economia das toxico-dependencias', in Correlade Campos, A. and Pereira, J.A. (eds.), *Sociedade, Sande e Economia*, Escola Nacional De Saude Publica, Lisbon.

Maynard, A., (1989), 'Price as a determinant of alcohol consumption', *Australian Drug and Alcohol Review*, (forthcoming).

Maynard, A., (1989), 'The costs of addiction and the costs of control', in Robinson, D., Maynard, A. and Chester, R. (eds.), *Controlling Legal Addictions*, Macmillan, London.

Maynard, A., Hardman, G. and Whelan, A., (1987), 'Data Note 9, Measuring the social costs of addictive substances', *British Journal of Addiction/, 82, 701–706*.

Maynard, A. and Jones, A., (1987), *Economic Aspects of Addiction Control Policies*, Centre for Health Economics and Addiction Research Centre, University of York.

Maynard, A. and O'Brien, B., (1982), 'Harmonisation policies in the European Community and alcohol abuse', *British Journal of Addiction*, 77, 235–244.

Maynard, A. and Powell, M., (1985), 'Addiction control policies, or there's no such thing as a free lunch', *British Journal of Addiction*, 80, 265–267.

Maynard, A. and Robinson, D., (1989), 'Preventing alcohol and tobacco problems', in Godfrey, C. and Robinson, D. (eds.), *Manipulating Consumption: information, law and voluntary controls*, Avebury/Gower, Aldershot.

Maynard, A. and Tether, P. (eds.), (1989), *The Addiction Market: consumption, production and policy development*, Avebury/Gower, Aldershot.

McDonnell, R. and Maynard, A., (1985), 'The costs of alcohol misuse', *British Journal of Addiction*, 80, 27–35.

McDonnell, R. and Maynard, A., (1985), 'Counting the costs of alcohol: gaps in epidemiological knowledge', *Community Medicine*, 7, 4–17.

McDonnell, R. and Maynard, A., (1985), 'Estimation of life years lost from alcohol-related premature death', *Alcohol and Alcoholism*, 20, 435–443.

Powell, M., (1987), 'Data Note 8, Alcohol data in the European Community', *British Journal of Addiction*, 82, 559–566.

Powell, M., (1988), 'Data Note 15, Alcohol and tobacco tax in the European Community', *British Journal of Addiction*, 83, 971–978.

Powell, M., (1988), 'Licence reform: less regulation, more individual restraint?', *Contemporary Review*, 253 (1474), 243–247.

Powell, M., (1989), 'UK opposition to tobacco tax harmonisation: the hidden agenda', *Contemporary Review*, 254 (1477), 77–82.

Powell, M., (1989), 'Behind the smoke screen: a data analysis of the tobacco industry', *Business Studies*, (forthcoming).

Powell, M., (1989), *Economic Aspects of Alcohol Policy: Prevention or Profits*, Routledge, (forthcoming).

Powell, M., (1989), 'Tax harmonisation in the EC', in Robinson, D., Maynard, A. and Chester, R. (eds.), *Controlling Legal Addictions*, Macmillan, London.

Powell, M., (1989), 'The health policy implications of international trade in alcohol and tobacco', *British Journal of Addiction*, (forthcoming).

Robinson, D., (1983), 'SSRC Addiction Research Centre', *British Journal of Addiction*, 78, 227–229.

Robinson, D., (1983), 'The growth of Alcoholics Anonymous', *Alcohol and Alcoholism*, 18, 167–172.

Robinson, D., (1985), 'The WHO three-centre study: a good first step', *British Journal of Addiction*, 80, 137.

Robinson, D., (1986), 'Data for informed debate', *British Journal of Addiction*, 81, 6.

Robinson, D., (1986), 'Mutual aid in the change process', in Heather, B. and Miller, P. (eds.), *Treating Addictive Behaviours*, Plenum, New York.

Robinson, D., (1986), 'Alcohol, education and action: shifting emphases', *Health Education Research: Theory and Practice*, 1, 325– 331.

Robinson, D., (1987), *Preventing Alcohol Problems*, the first Aquarius lecture, Aquarius, Birmingham.

Robinson, D., (1988), 'Prevention policy: alcohol and tobacco', *ESRC Newsletter*, 62, 12–14.

Robinson, D., (1989), 'Controlling legal addictions: taking advantage of what's there', in Robinson, D., Maynard, A. and Chester, R. (eds.), *Controlling Legal Addictions*, Macmillan, London.

Robinson, D. and Maynard, A., (1987), 'Reports from research centres – 5, Addiction Research Centre: Hull-York, UK', *British Journal of Addiction*, 82, 1185–1190.

Robinson, D. and Maynard, A., (1989), *Alcohol: Preventing a Legal Addiction*, ESRC Briefing, (forthcoming).

Robinson, D., Maynard, A. and Chester, R.L.C. (eds.), (1989), *Controlling Legal Addictions*, Macmillan, London.

Robinson, D. and Maynard, A., (1989), 'Controlling legal addictions', *British Journal of Addiction*, (forthcoming).

Robinson, D. and Tether, P., (1983), 'The environment debate', in Grant, M. and Ritson, B. (eds.), *Alcohol: the Prevention Debate*, Croom Helm, London.

Robinson, D. and Tether, P., (1985), 'Prevention: potential at the local level', *Alcohol and Alcoholism*, 20, 31–33.

Robinson, D. and Tether, P., (1987), 'Alcohol problems: (i) prevention at the local level', *Health Trends*, 19, 19–22.

Robinson, D. and Tether, P., (1989), *Preventing Alcohol Problems: Local Prevention Activity and the Compilation of 'Guides to Local Action'*, World Health Organisation, Geneva, (forthcoming).

Robinson, D., Tether, P. and Teller, J. (eds.), (1989), *Local Action on Alcohol Problems*, Routledge, London, (forthcoming).

Tether, P., (1985), *Preventing Alcohol-Related Accidents: A Guide to Local Action*, Occasional Paper No. 6, Institute of Alcohol Studies, London.

Tether, P., (1985), 'A lethal cocktail: alcohol and water', *Alcohol Concern*, 1, 13–14.

Tether, P., (1986), 'Cutting the risks of alcohol at sea', *Alcohol Concern*, 2, 6–8.

Tether, P., (1987), 'Preventing alcohol-related problems: the local dimension', in Stockwell, T. and Clement, S. (eds.), *Helping the Problem Drinker*, Croom Helm, London.

Tether, P., (1989), 'Legal controls and voluntary agreements', in Robinson, D., Maynard, A. and Chester, R. (eds.), *Controlling Legal Addictions*, Macmillan, London.

Tether, P. and Godfrey, C., (1989), 'Tobacco advertising', in Godfrey, C. and Robinson, D. (eds.), *Manipulating Consumption: information, law and voluntary controls*, Avebury/Gower, Aldershot.

Tether, P. and Godfrey, C., (1989), 'Liquor licensing', in Godfrey, C. and Robinson, D. (eds.), *Manipulating Consumption: information, law and voluntary controls*, Avebury/Gower, Aldershot.

Tether, P. and Godfrey, C., (1989), 'Drinking and driving', in Godfrey, C. and Robinson, D. (eds.), *Manipulating Consumption: information, law and voluntary controls*, Avebury/Gower, Aldershot.

Tether, P. and Harrison, L., (1986), 'Data Note 3, Alcohol-related fires and drowning', *British Journal of Addiction*, 81, 425–431.

Tether, P. and Harrison, L., (1988), *Alcohol Policies: Responsibilities and Relationship in British Government*, Addiction Research Centre, Universities of Hull and York.

Tether, P. and Harrison, L., (1989), 'Industry and employment policy: department and group relations', in Maynard, A. and Tether, P. (eds.), *The Addiction Market: consumption, production and policy development*, Avebury/Gower, Aldershot.

Tether, P., Leedham, W. and Harrison, L., (1989), 'Legislation: the policy networks', in Godfrey, C. and Robinson, D. (eds.), *Manipulating Consumption: information, law and voluntary controls*, Avebury/Gower, Aldershot.

Tether, P. and Robinson, D., (1985), 'Alcohol and work: 'policies' are not enough', *Alcohol and Alcoholism*, 20, 1–3.

Tether, P. and Robinson, D., (1986), *Preventing Alcohol Problems: A Guide to Local Action*, Tavistock Publications, London.

Tether, P. and Robinson, D., (1988), 'Alcohol problems: (ii) alcohol and work', *Health Trends*, 20, 24–26.

Tether, P., Robinson, D. and Wicks, M., (1984), 'Liquor licensing: its role in a prevention strategy', *Alcohol and Alcoholism*, 19, 272– 79.

Wagstaff, A. and Maynard, A., (1986), 'Data Note 5, The consumption of illicit drugs in the UK', *British Journal of Addiction*, 81, 691– 696.

Wagstaff, A. and Maynard, A., (1988), *Economic Aspects of the Illicit Drug Market and Drug Enforcement Policies in the United Kingdom*, Home Office Research Study No. 95, HMSO, London.

Weir, R., (1984), 'Distilling and agriculture 1870–1939', *The Agricultural History Review*, 32, 20–33.

Weir, R., (1984), 'Obsessed with moderation: the drink trades and the drink question', *British Journal of Addiction*, 79, 93–107.

Weir, R., (1988), 'Alcohol controls and Scotch whisky exports 1900– 1939', *British Journal of Addiction*, 83, 1289–1297.

Index

197

British Tourist Authority 105, 107, 108
broadcasting 34
Broadcasting Act (1981) 32, 46, 77
Broadcasting Authority 32, 33
Broadcasting in the '90s 48
Budweiser 17
Bureau Européen des Unions de
    Consommateurs 56
businesses tobacco-related 170

CAA see Civil Aviation Authority
CAMRA see Campaign for Real Ale
CAP Committee see Code of
    Advertising Practice Committee
CPU see Crime Prevention Unit
Cabinet 81, 142
Cabinet Office 10
Cable and Broadcasting Act (1984) 11,
    32
Cable Authority 11, 32, 48
—Code 46, 51–52, 55, 60, 76
Cable Copy Panel 52
Cable Television Act (1984) 51
Cable Television Authority 51
Campaign for Real Ale (CAMRA) 106,
    129
Canada 65
Cancer Research Campaign 37
carcinogens 83
Castle, Barbara 142
Castlemaine 16
Casualty Surgeons' Association 112
caterers 106
Ceefax 49
Celanese Corporation 83
Central Council for Physical Recreation
    57
Chancellor of the Exchequer 182, 184
'Cheshire Blitz' 144
Chest, Heart and Stroke Association 37
Chief Constable 105, 114, 148, 150, 178
Chief Scientists Office 29
children
—non-smokers 92
—smoking habits 89
—smokers 92
Children and Young Persons Act (1969)
    8
cider see alcoholic drinks

'Cigarette Code' 80, 82, 86, 87
cigarettes 14, 16, 170
—brands 92; consumption 89, 91;
    expenditure on 90; filter tip 14; low
    tar 14; packaging 84, 171; price 90,
    96; sales 90; tar content 26; tobacco
    content 14
cigarillos 82
cigars 170
Cinema Advertising Association 36, 37
circulars 10
—departmental 25
city centre disorder 102
City of London 12
civil liberties 141, 151, 154, 180
civil servants 40, 145
Civil Aviation Authority (CAA) 109,
    110, 112
—Air Operators Certificate 110
—Medical Department 111
Clayson report 131
Clerk to the (Licensing) Justices 105
clubs 117, 121, 122–128 passim,131
Code of Advertising Practice Committee
    (CAP Committee) 52, 53, 80, 87
Code of Advertising Practice 57, 79
Code of Advertising Standards and
    Practice 47
codes of conduct 19, 22, 25, 34, 44, 46,
    78
codes of practice 4, 7, 75, 87, 97
—ethical codes 26
—governing alcohol advertising 33
—self-regulatory 1, 2, 3, 7, 12, 32, 55
commercial organisations 25
Communication, Advertising and
    Marketing Education Foundation 39
companies
—alcohol 34
—retail 128
—tobacco 10, 14, 34, 57, 75, 79, 81, 83,
    85, 86, 87, 88, 89, 94, 95, 96, 97, 170
competition 13, 14–17, 22, 33, 69, 70,
    96, 98, 106, 124–130, 135
—policy 106
—overseas 14
—price 69, 70
complaints see public complaints
Conservative Party 12, 141

—Secretary of State 28
Department of Employment 103, 130, 179
Department of Energy 103
Department of Health and Social Security (DHSS) xiii, 10, 27, 28, 29–30, 32, 33, 34, 36, 37, 38, 77, 81, 97, 103, 107, 111, 112, 114, 179
—Children, Maternity and Prevention Division 29
—Secretary of State 81
—Under Secretary of State 89
Department of Trade and Industry (DTI) 20, 28, 33, 37, 41, 60, 103, 105, 106, 107, 108, 130, 179
—Consumer Affairs Division 33
—Consumer Market Division 33
—Enterprise and Deregulation Unit (EDU) 103, 105, 106
—General Policy Division 106
—Minister of State for Consumer Affairs 40
—Secretary of State for Consumer Affairs 40
—Secretary of State for Trade and Industry 33
—Working Party 40
Department of Transport (DoT) 3, 5, 28, 31, 34, 35, 36, 103, 109–113 passim, 139, 148, 176, 179
—Accident Investigation Branch 176
—Aircraft Accident Investigation Branch 109, 111, 112; Accident Inspectors 111
—Civil Aviation Policy Directorate 109, 110, 176
—Driver and Vehicle Licensing Centre (DVLC) 109, 147, 148; Medical Advisory Branch 109–110, 145
—Highway Code 113
—Marine and Ports Directorate 109, 111, 176, 177; Occupational Health and Safety Section 176, 177
—Minister of Transport 156
—Railway Inspectorate 111, 112, 113; Chief Inspections Officer 111
—Railways Directorate 109, 176
—Road and Vehicle Safety Directorate 31, 109, 111, 113, 176

—Road Safety Division 111, 112, 113
—Secretary of State 111, 146, 147, 149, 150
Department of the Environment (DoE) 28, 34, 103, 105, 106
—Senior Management Support Unit 105
—Small Firms and Tourism Division 103, 105
—Sport and Recreation Division 34
Departmental Committee (of Enquiry) 112, 143
departmental working parties 40
deregulation 12
—economic 130
—legislative 130
Direct Broadcasting Satellites (DBS) 58
Direct Mail Services Standards Board 53
The Director 40
Director General of Fair Trading 11, 40, 52, 55, 60, 80
disease
—smoking-related 171
distillers 14–15, 16, 57
distilling
—industry 127
distribution xv, 174
distribution networks 94
drink-driving 101, 117, 151
—advertising campaigns 34, 113, 154
—and the young 155, 156, 157
—behaviour 161; convictions 131, 147, 152
—debates 143, 162; education 112
—interests 111; issues 112, 114, 150
—policy 2, 110, 139, 140, 145–147, 150–161
—publicity 35
—statistics 157
drinkers
—beer 160
—heavy 132
—problem 141, 143, 147, 148, 162
drinking 18, 125, 153, 157
—and driving xiv, 1–5 passim, 26, 35, 44, 46, 101, 109–115, 139–165, 175, 178
—behaviour 125; consequences of 26
—habits 118, 133
—in television programmes 33

Shipping
GGT *see* Gammaglutamyl Transferase
  levels
Gallaghers 83, 90
Gammaglutamyl Transferase levels
  (GGT) 145, 147
General Council of British Shipping
  (GCBS) 177
Germany 59
gin *see* alcoholic drinks
Gin Act (1736) 116
Gin Rectifiers and Distillers Association
  39
Government 2, 22, 38, 45, 69, 70, 71,
  75, 78, 81, 87, 104, 108, 124, 130,
  136, 169, 178
—agencies 22
—British 4, 10, 11, 12, 27, 34, 35, 38,
  57, 59, 60, 94, 97, 125, 134, 135,
  140, 144, 147, 153, 184
—Conservative 8, 12, 108, 130, 145
—departments 3, 25, 28–34, 103, 166,
  178
—interests 101; intervention 26
—Labour 7, 8, 10, 40, 81; organisations
  25
—policies 7, 8, 19, 40, 89, 96, 106, 154
Grand Metropolitan 17
Guild of Experienced Motorists 179
Guinness
—DCL 15

HEA *see* Health Education Authority
HMI *see* Her Majesty's Inspectorate
HM Customs and Excise xiii, 27, 84
HM Treasury 27, 103
HRO *see* High Risk Offender
HSE *see* Health and Safety Executive
Hampshire Probation Service 148, 150
harm
—in relation to alcohol consumption 45,
  118, 130, 134, 159
—in relation to smoking 88
health 69, 124–134, 169, 175, 181
—and smoking 171; arguments
  131–134; behaviour 67; benefits 97;
  campaigns 2, 35; campaigners 34;
  care 167, 168; consequences 85;
  damage to 172; departments 35, 84,

108; education 26, 27, 30, 35, 36, 44,
  45, 57, 90; effects 89, 93; information
  25, 41, 92, 93; issues 35, 95, 184;
  objectives 70; organisations 37;
  policies 28, 60, 70, 169; promotion
  30, 34, 41, 42, 168
—risks 92, 93, 171
—warnings 10, 14, 26, 32, 34, 35, 77,
  81–82, 87, 88, 93, 96, 97, 171
Health and Safety Executive (HSE) 103,
  113, 179
—Railway Institute Advisory
  Committee 113
—Chief Inspecting Officer of Railways
  113
Health Education Advisory Committee
  for Wales 30
Health Education Authority (Council)
  xiii, 3, 25–37 *passim*
Health for All by the Year 2000 172, 181
health-related professions 19
Health Promotion Research Trust xiii
healthy public policy 5, 167–172, 181
Her Majesty's Inspectorate (HMI) 28
High Risk Offender (HRO) procedure
  110, 112, 148
High Risk Offenders 144, 145, 147–148,
  150, 154
Hogarth, W. 117
Home Affairs Backbench Committee 146
Home Office xiii, 3, 5, 28, 32–33, 37,
  102–113 *passim*, 131, 135, 140, 143,
  147, 149, 153
—Broadcasting Department 32
—Constitutional Department 104, 105
—FS Division 111, 113
—Home Secretary 11, 33, 78
—Liquor Licensing Section 102, 103,
  105
—Permanent Under Secretary 103
—Police Department 103, 113, 114
—Police Training Division 113, 114
—Road Traffic Division 113, 114
—Police Dependents Trust 113, 114
—Research and Planning Unit 102
—Secretary of State for Home Affairs
  46, 150
Home Safety Committees 179
hotels 131

House of Commons 10, 142
House of Commons Select Committee
on Transport 113
House of Lords Select Committees xiii
Houses of Parliament 113

IBA *see* Independent Broadcasting
Authority
ICAP *see* International Code of
Advertising Practice
ISCSH *see* Independent Scientific
Committee on Smoking and Health
ITCA *see* Independent Television
Association
Imperial Cancer Research Foundation 37
Imperial Chemical Industries 83
Imperial Tobacco 83, 90, 170
importation 174
imports
income 62, 89, 122, 159
—changes 132
—levels 162
Incorporated Society of British
Advertisers 37
Independent Broadcasting Association
(IBA) 32, 39, 47, 48, 51, 52, 54, 55,
59, 60, 87
—Advertising Control Division 47
—Code of Advertising Standards and
Practice 11, 46–48, 49, 55, 76, 77–78
Independent Scientific Committee on
Smoking and Health (ISCSH) 77,
82–85
Independent Television Association 15,
19, 39, 78
—Copy Clearance Secretariat 47
—Copy Committee 39
—*Notes of Guidance* to advertisers 47,
48
Independent Television Authority 46
—companies 87
Independent Television Commission 11,
48
industry 9, 45, 136
—spirits 70
information xiv, 5, 19, 25–43, 67, 70,
71, 154, 155, 158, 166
—campaigns 1
—market 26, 27

—policy 2, 3, 25, 27, 32, 34, 41, 42, 45,
92, 156, 162
—technology 41, 48, 71
injury on the roads 143, 146
Institute for Alcohol Studies xiii
Institute of Practitioners in Advertising
37
Institution of Highway Engineers 179
insurance
—accidental death 153
—companies 179
—policies 150, 154
Inter-Departmental Group on Crime
Prevention 102
Inter-Departmental Advisory Committee
on Road Safety 111, 113
interest groups 106, 124
see also lobbies, pressure groups
International Advertising Association 38
International Chamber of Commerce 79
International code of Advertising
Practice (ICAP) 58, 79
International Code of Ethics for
Advertising Wines and Spirits 58
International Conference on Primary
Health Care 167
International Conference on Drug Abuse
and Illicit Trafficking 182
International Union against Cancer 37
Intoxicating Liquor (Sale to Children)
Act (1901) 119
Intoxicating Liquor (Sale to Persons
under 18) Act (1923) 119
Ireland 59
Italy 58

Joseph, Sir Keith 44, 81, 82
Justices
—Licensing 107, 117, 119, 120, 121,
125, 129, 130, 150
—Of the Peace 116
Justices' Clerks' Society 104, 108, 146

Labelling Code 82, 84, 87
Laboratory of the Government Chemist
82, 84
Labour Party 12, 142
lager *see* alcoholic drinks
law(s) 1, 22, 166, 174

205

—and order 175; changes in 3, 158; drink-driving 7, 113, 114, 178, 181–182; enforcement 8, 21, 102, 109, 113; implementation of 152; licensing 4, 7, 14, 103, 107, 116–120, 124, 127, 128, 129, 135, 140, 144; minimum drinking age 152, 157, 158; on alcohol sales to minors 1; on tobacco sales to minors 1, 82; retailing 181; Sunday Trading 107

Leeds Polytechnic
—Department of Health Education xiii

legal limit 139, 141, 142, 143, 144, 146, 147, 150

legal system
—England and Wales 9
—Northern Ireland 9
—Scotland 9

legislation 1–5 *passim*, 7, 9, 12, 20, 21, 66, 81, 89, 97, 101–115, 124, 129, 139, 166, 172, 174
—change in 162
—drink-driving 3, 9, 109, 113, 146, 149, 151, 152, 161; enforcement of 9; European 32, 38; government 8; on labelling of drinks containers 31; primary 8–9, 21, 25; restrictive trading practices 106; secondary 9, 25; sentencing patterns 9

legislative change 5, 115
legislative policies 93–94
legislative reform 7
legitimacy 18–20
Leonard Ball Oration 183
liberalisation of licensing controls 118, 129, 131
Lib/Lab Coalition 145
licensees (licence holders) 120, 150–151, 156
licensed premises 62, 104, 119, 121, 122, 123, 124, 135
see also public houses
licensed trade 127, 141
licences 121–125 *passim*, 131
—combined 118
—liquor 119
—residential 118, 119
—restaurant 118, 119
licensing 63, 127

—debate on 124
—elasticities 123
—hours 5, 103, 124–134
—liquor xiv, 1, 2, 3, 4, 9, 101, 102–109, 109, 116–138, 178
—policy 3, 118, 120–124, 134, 135, 162
—reform of law 102, 107, 108, 124–134, 136
Licensing Act (1872) 119
Licensing Act (1921) 117
Licensing Act (1961) 118, 119, 125
Licensing Act (1964) 119
Licensing Act (1988) 104, 118
Licensing (Restaurant Meals) Act 134
Licensing (Scotland) Act (1976) 131
Liquor Control Board 117
liver cirrhosis 133
Lloyd George, David 117
lobbies 89
—advertising 95; anti-advertising 36; anti-smoking 37; health 32, 33, 37, 41, 42, 61, 83, 89, 124; industrial 97; prevention 3; trade 37, 61, 124, 129, *see also* interest groups, pressure groups
lobbying 36, 40, 68
Lord Hunter 82
Lord Thomson of Monifieth 39, 40
Lord Young 193

MA *see* Magistrates' Association
MADD *see* Mothers Against Drunken Drivers
MAFF *see* Ministry of Agriculture, Fisheries and Food
MCAP *see* Medical Committee on Accident Prevention
MMC *see* Monopolies and Mergers Commission
MMWR *see* Morbidity and Mortality Weekly Report Survey
MPs *see* politicians
Magistrates' Association (MA) 104, 108, 143
—Legal Committee 104
—Licensing Committee 104
Mahler, Dr. 168
Malawi 171
Manitoba. Ban on beer advertising 66
market shares 16

marketing 70, 72
Marketing Board 15
market(s) 13, 14
—beer 125
—British 15, 16, 17, 96
—domestic 16
—forces 171
—German 14
—international 171
—off–licence 70
—on–licence 70
—pressures 15
media 2, 19, 75, 175
Medical Committee on Accident
    Prevention (MCAP) 112, 144, 148
—Transport Committee 112
—Alcohol Committee 112
medical interest 143
medical practices 133
medical profession 11, 47, 179
Medicines Act (1968) 11
Merchant Navy 109, 176
mergers and take-overs 106
minimum drinking age 156–158, 160
Minister for Agriculture *see* Ministry of
    Agriculture, Fisheries and Food
Minister for Consumer Protection 80
Minister for Sport 87
Ministerial Group on Alcohol Misuse
    33, 34, 42, 102, 106, 151, 180
Ministry of Agriculture, Fisheries and
    Food (MAFF)
—Alcoholic Drinks Division 20, 31, 32
—Standards Division 32
Ministry of Defence 28, 30–31, 34
Ministry of Health 81
Ministry of Transport 140, 143
—Secretary of State for Transport 142
Misleading Advertisements Regulations
    1987 52
models 67
—demand 61, 64, 65, 123
monopolies 106
Monopolies and Mergers Commission
    (MMC) 16, 106, 125
—Monopolies Commission report
    (1969) 124
Morbidity and Mortality Weekly Report
    (MMWR)

—Survey 156
MORI 56
mortality xv
—alcohol-related 67
—liver cirrhosis 131, 132
Mothers Against Drunken Drivers
    (MADD) 156
motoring organisations 141
multi-organisational networks 27

NACRO *see* National Association for
    the Care and Resettlement of
    Offenders
NALHM *see* National Association of
    Licensed House Managers
NCADA *see* Australia
NEDO *see* National Economic
    Development Office
NHS *see* National Health Service
NULV *see* National Union of Licensed
    Victuallers
Nabarro, Sir Gerald 81
narcotics market 172
National Association for the Care and
    Resettlement of Offenders (NACRO)
    104
National Association of Licensed House
    Managers (NALHM) 106
National Association of Victim Support
    Schemes 104
National Chamber of Trade 35
National Consumer Council 37
National Council on Alcoholism 146
National Economic Development Office
    (NEDO) 108
—Brewing Sector Working Party 107
National Health Policy on Alcohol in
    Australia 173
National Health Service 10, 36
—Health Authority 29
National Maritime Board 177
National Society of Non-Smokers 36, 37
National Union of Licensed Victuallers
    (NULV) 106, 107, 141
The Netherlands 58
networks *see* multi-organisational
    networks, organisational networks,
    policy networks
New Smoking Material 83

207

210

212